THE TRADER'S PENDULUM

The 10 Habits of Highly Successful Traders

Jody Samuels

WILEY

The Wiley Trading series features books by traders who have survived the market's ever-changing temperament and have prospered—some by reinventing systems, others by getting back to basics. Whether a novice trader, professional, or somewhere in-between, these books will provide the advice and strategies needed to prosper today and well into the future. For more on this series, visit our website at www.WileyTrading.com.

Founded in 1807, John Wiley & Sons is the oldest independent publishing company in the United States. With offices in North America, Europe, Australia, and Asia, Wiley is globally committed to developing and marketing print and electronic products and services for our customers' professional and personal knowledge and understanding.

Published by John Wiley & Sons, Inc., Hoboken, New Jersey.
Published simultaneously in Canada.

For general information on our other products and services or for technical support, please contact our Customer Care Department within the United States at (800) 762-2974, outside the United States at (317) 572-3993 or fax (317) 572-4002.

Wiley publishes in a variety of print and electronic formats and by print-on-demand. Some material included with standard print versions of this book may not be included in e-books or in print-on-demand. If this book refers to media such as a CD or DVD that is not included in the version you purchased, you may download this material at http://booksupport.wiley.com. For more information about Wiley products, visit www.wiley.com.

Library of Congress Cataloging-in-Publication Data:
Samuels, Jody, 1957–
 The trader's pendulum + website : the 10 habits of highly successful traders / Jody Samuels.
  pages cm. – (The Wiley trading series)
 Includes bibliographical references and index.
 ISBN 978-1-118-99557-0 (paper/website) – ISBN 978-1-118-99644-7 (ePDF) –
ISBN 978-1-118-99658-4 (ePub) 1. Investments. 2. Investment analysis. 3. Speculation. I. Title.
 HG4521.S3314 2015
 332.64--dc23

                                                          2015017700

Cover Design: Wiley
Cover Images: Newton's cradle © iStock.com/gl0ck;
Foucault pendulum © iStock.com/M_MUC1968

Printed in the United States of America

10 9 8 7 6 5 4 3 2 1

This book is dedicated to my loving family: my husband, Malcolm, and daughters, Jackie and Rebecca

CONTENTS

v

The Trader's Pendulum – The Ten Habits of Highly Successful Traders is an honest, educational and most importantly, an enjoyable book to read. Jody Samuels' style makes concepts understandable. She writes as she speaks: with simplicity and clarity; this comes from her many years of experience turning willing traders into consummate professionals.

I love reading books. The ones that have left a lasting impression on me have one thing in common: They grabbed me in the first chapter and held me to the final word. *The Trader's Pendulum – The Ten Habits of Highly Successful Traders* has done just that. That is why I strongly recommend this book for the complete novice; not only is it an enjoyable read, but it is written from an understanding of your perspective.

The veteran trader should also read this book. You will find yourself enlightened by Jody's depth of understanding in specific areas. It will allow you to open your mind and stretch that little bit further. I know the commitment to being the best trader you can be comes with the understanding that learning never stops.

Understanding that "engaging in a coach is an investment not an expense" is so meaningful to me because Jody stopped my journey from heading in the wrong direction.

I have been fortunate enough to be one of Jody's coaching clients. I worked one-on-one with Jody as she showed me how to pave the way to my dream of becoming a full-time, million-dollar currency trader.

As a child, I always knew I wanted to be self-employed, free of having a boss. I wanted to make good money based on my decisions, and I wanted freedom to travel and explore while I spent the money I made helping out where I could. Even as a child I always dreamt big.

I spent years thinking, reading, and growing to better understand what I was looking for and how it could be most effectively expressed. My belief was if I knew exactly what I wanted, then planning the path to attain it would be more obvious.

My search for understanding allowed me to find three little words that were simple, but extremely powerful.

Autonomy, Purpose, and Mastery

Autonomy: I wanted my decisions to have a positive impact on outcomes. I wanted to be accountable for how I thought and the actions I took. I didn't want to belong to a corporate structure where progress wasn't always based on merit.

Purpose: I wanted to know that with financial independence I could contribute to something bigger than myself to help make our world a safer, happier, and cleaner place to live. That is truly empowering.

Mastery: In our core we all want to master something. I believe this is why so many hours are dedicated to playing a musical instrument, learning to cook complex recipes, or improving our golf game. Mastering anything is frustrating and difficult, but it gives our souls absolute pleasure as we improve at our chosen task.

Eventually, I knew what I wanted, but I was unsure as to the vehicle required to take me there. The day I placed my first trade I knew I had found my answer. I found something I loved to do and solved the question of how to find autonomy, purpose, and mastery all rolled into one.

Trading became my passion. I could sit at home and make money. I could take holidays and still make money. My friends were envious. For me, trading is the perfect job, but with any job it takes time, patience, and experience to become proficient. During my struggles, I met Jody Samuels.

Many times, I stumbled, but Jody never gave up. When I doubted myself and was confused and frustrated, Jody held strong. When I lost sight of the bigger picture, Jody did not. Jody brings understanding and compassion to her work.

While reading *The Trader's Pendulum – The Ten Habits of Highly Successful Traders*, I found myself enjoying the compare and contrast theme as the pendulum swings. There were different moments when I laughed because I knew the central characters well enough to say I have met them because at any stage they were me. With Jody's help, I now trade in the middle of the pendulum.

For many years, Jody traded successfully in the highest echelons of the banking industry before transitioning into a highly acclaimed, internationally recognized Trading Coach. When you combine all her experience, understanding, and commitment to seeing others succeed, you can understand why *The Trader's Pendulum – The Ten Habits of Highly Successful Traders* is an absolute must-read for you.

Now you are holding this book, and you are confronted with a choice:

Either you do nothing, or you take the first step in changing your life forever. A step toward your own personal freedom and a lifestyle envied by your friends and family.

I wish you good luck and happiness with your decision.

Kel Talty
Professional Currency Trader
Queensland, Australia

ACKNOWLEDGEMENTS

For me, writing *The Trader's Pendulum* is really putting a story about my trading business down on paper. In 2008 when I decided to create a coaching program for traders based on my market experience, I started with an outline that I wrote called the 10 Habits of Successful Traders. I thought about the 10 Habits a trader needs to develop in order to run a successful trading business as an entrepreneur. I also thought a lot about traders chasing the latest and greatest black boxes and automated trading systems and the promises from gurus who claim you can have overnight trading success.

And so the *Technical Trader's Trap*, which you will read about in this book, was born.

I also felt at the time that there would be nothing that a trader could experience that I haven't experienced myself during my 30 year trading career, beginning as an institutional trader with a major investment bank. That's another way of saying that I thought I couldn't learn much more about trading - but I could never have been more wrong about that!

For the seven years leading up to writing this book, I have had the opportunity to work with and coach many traders. This has been nothing short of a gift. When I think back over the years, the word that keeps popping up is "gratitude". Gratitude for meeting wonderful and insightful people, gratitude for connecting with dedicated, knowledgeable and serious traders and gratitude for realizing that my students have been the greatest teachers in my recent trading career.

On this note, to all of my students from whom I have learned so much, may you continue to have trading success and reach your full potential. And may I continue to show my gratitude to you daily.

I would also like to thank my FX Trader's EDGE team, all of whom are great mentors in our trading community, and whose dedication and expertise have allowed me the freedom to spend the time on this endeavor. Juan Maldonado, thank you for your utmost commitment to making sure the business ran smoothly and for being one of the best Elliott Wave strategists in the industry. Neil Bradford, thank you for contributing top notch mentoring and trading tools for our trading community and for reviewing a few chapters in the book brilliantly. Vince Vacarella, thank you for your round-the-clock attention to the markets to make sure our traders are clued into the trading opportunities. Thank you to Andre Porco, Tim Stuyts, Fernando Luna, Alex Kaziyev, Robert Mis and John Thomas for your important contribution to FX Trader's EDGE and the Elliott Wave Desk.

I would be remiss if I didn't remember my original FX Trader's EDGE team, all of whom played an important role in the early stages of the development of FX Trader's EDGE: Mick Lewis, Tanya Harrison, Michael Syvertsen, Neil Bradford and Randy Dodgen – thank you!

These acknowledgements wouldn't be complete without thanking my parents. Dad, you were always so proud of my accomplishments, and it is from you that I learned the importance of balance in my life. When I think of being balanced on the continuum between fear and greed, I think of you. Mom, you always had such good trading instincts even though you never traded. In my early days I can remember asking you if I should go short, long, hold, or close and you always gave me your assessment of the situation which ended up being correct most of the time!

Finally, thank you again to my wonderful family, to whom this book is dedicated.

ACKNOWLEDGEMENTS

Jody Samuels is one of North America's leading coaches for successful traders, and the creator of The FX Trader's EDGE Coaching Program modelled after the "10 Habits of Successful Traders". She works with members of her program in group and private coaching sessions and is passionate about teaching individuals how to trade the market cycles and use entrepreneurial skills and habits to effectively manage their business.

Jody's educational background includes Bachelor of Science in Economics from The Wharton School, University of PA, followed by an MBA at NYU Stern School of Business. Jody's trading expertise spans the financial, currency and commodity markets, as a former trading professional for US global investment bank JP Morgan, a sales professional for an energy company and now CEO of FX Trader's EDGE, an Elliott-wave based education and coaching company for traders.

Jody soon realized from her institutional trading experience, that new and seasoned traders lacked the guidance to graduate from the *Technical Trader's Trap* to becoming an Entrepreneurial Trader. Jody wrote *The Trader's Pendulum: The 10 Habits of Highly Successful Traders* based on her 30-year trading and coaching experience to help traders transition to managing their trading accounts as a business.

She has moderated a daily online trading room, been interviewed on Bloomberg Television, and is a sought after speaker at the *Toronto Money Show* and the NY and Las Vegas *Traders EXPOs*. Her most recent and very exciting speaking debut occurred in Shanghai this year. She has authored articles published in *Stocks and Commodities Magazine* and has been interviewed by the *Money Show*, and by *FX Street* for the *Women in Forex* article which appeared in FX Trader Magazine.

It's 5:50 a.m. on a typical weekday. Before everyone else in his family has woken up—in fact, before most of the population of the city are awake—Charles Thompson is already out of his pajamas and has his coffee brewing. For the past 15 years, Charles's habit has been to start his day before dawn. He believes that starting his daily race before everyone else does will give him a winning edge.

By 6:10 a.m., Charles begins his meditation sitting in his study. Admittedly, he has to fight the drowsiness, but he does it anyway. He added this habit to his morning routine less than half a year ago, and he is improving day-by-day. The meditation practice is more than a mind training that clears his mind, but also a discipline of focus and determination. These are important to both his life and his work. So he shows up on his meditation mat every single morning.

Twenty minutes later, as he stands up from his meditation mat, he does a brief stretching exercise. He feels his blood rushing to every cell in his body, and is fully refreshed and awake. He puts on his training shoes and gets out of his house for a 30-minute jog in the neighborhood park. If it rains or snows, Charles will opt for running on the treadmill in his home gym, but he prefers running in the park, for the jolt of fresh and frosty morning air.

Back home over breakfast after a hot shower, Charles launches the newsfeed application on his iPad to read about the major events that have happened overnight around the world. He makes a note of anything that he thinks he should pay attention to. Reading the news is his effort to connect with the world at large. Besides, his job requires him to keep abreast of the major daily events that may have an effect on the global markets.

By 7:30 a.m. Charles is at work in his home office. Although he does not have a boss to report to and no one will know if he slacks off, it is his habit to show up punctually at his desk by 7:30 a.m. He reviews the notes that he made and starts planning his trading day. Every morning he follows a set of well-defined steps. From 8:00 a.m. to noon, he gives his undivided attention to trading. Nobody is allowed to disturb Charles until lunchtime.

That is how Charles has begun his typical morning for the past 15 years. Charles is a trader—a highly successful one. He is enjoying the freedom, monetary rewards, and a rejuvenating sense of satisfaction from his career. He credits his success to the morning routine that prepares him both physically and mentally for a long day at work. He also thinks that keeping to a strict routine has given him discipline and determination, both being important ingredients for success in trading.

But this is only part of the reason why he is successful.

■ A Trader's Work Begins before He Starts to Trade

Every morning, Charles switches on his "work mode" during breakfast.

At the dining table, as he is reading the news, he is scanning for interesting events that happened overnight. Particularly, he will look for clues that might impact the currency, commodity, and stock markets, the business world, and the global economy.

At this point, he is merely gathering information, because Charles still wants to enjoy his breakfast. But he makes mental notes for further investigation for when he starts working later. Charles knows that news can impact global markets, and he wants to make sure he takes into consideration the potential event risks, as well as the emotional and psychological responses of investors in the markets, when he plans out his trading strategy for the day.

Being an independent trader with no manager or boss to report to, Charles knows that he has to be accountable for his trading. Every morning, he will define a set of *practical* financial goals that he wants to achieve out of the day's work. How does he know whether these goals are practical? He doesn't have a *scientific way* to determine this, but he does it based on a number of factors, including the past performance of the trades, the recent market performance, a gauge of his own capability—and, of course, the breakdown of his long-term (monthly and yearly) earning targets.

But these goals are merely a dream without proper executable steps to achieve them. Charles knows this well. He has the habit of planning out clear trading rules before he starts trading and stalking the markets for his high probability trade setups. For Charles, trading is a survival game that requires him to constantly keep his eyes on the destination, and to be clear of the route and strategy to get there. In addition, he is cautious about following his rules and checking the price action before he enters a trade. All these habits have helped him to survive in the game—and the ultimate goal of the game is to survive as long as possible.

Charles understands that it is useless to have a fantastic strategy and plan sketched out if he doesn't follow them. As part of the morning routine, right after he logs into the trading platform and before he executes the first transaction, he will do something unorthodox: He will stand up straight, gather his strength, and with his fists clenched, chant this *mantra* three times to himself:

"I have planned my trade, and now I will trade my plan.

When it's time to strike, I will strike.

I shall not overanalyze, I shall not procrastinate, and I shall not hesitate."

He adopted this habit when he started his trading career at a relatively young and energetic age, and still keeps doing it. Somehow his little ritual gives him a jolt of motivation to start trading.

Silly? Maybe. But it works for Charles, and he regards this to be one of the habits that are responsible for his success. The habit to "plan his trade and trade his plan" has helped to keep his emotions at bay when he trades, and allows him to make logical trading decisions. What's important to him as a professional trader is to win the game, whatever it takes, even if it's a silly ritual like repeating a mantra.

■ The End of Trading Isn't the End of His Day

It's 4 o'clock in the afternoon, the stock markets are closing, and Charles is getting ready to wrap up his trading activity.

But a professional trader's day never ends right at the point when he ends his trading session. Charles will take a 15-minute break, do some simple stretches, grab a cup of freshly brewed coffee, and begin another important task while his memory of today's trading is still fresh.

Because Charles is a committed trader, he seeks daily improvement in his trading—no matter how big or small it might be. He uses a trading journal to aid him with that. He will record his trades, the results, and his observations, and review them one by one against the plan, strategy, and goals that he defined earlier in the day.

As an effort to reflect on his daily performance, he will fill up a trading blotter. In the process, he asks himself some of the following questions:

Was I in a good frame of mind today? Was I "in the zone"? Did my personal life affect my trading?

Did feelings of perfectionism and overconfidence creep in?

Did I plan my trades well? Or was the plan based on speculation or unproven tips from other traders?

Did I trade my plan? Did I trade impulsively? Did ego take over my logical analysis? Overall, was I satisfied with the results of today's work?

By answering these questions, he learns his lessons from what he has not done right, and commits to not repeat the same mistakes again. But it's not only the mistakes that he wants to discover. He also wants to be reminded of the right decisions that he has made, so that he can apply the same actions when similar situations arise.

When nothing spectacular happens during the day, the review can be done within 30 minutes; but when major events take place, Charles might work past dinnertime to get his review done. To him, every experience is an important lesson. He wants to make sure he does not do a sloppy job in his review, and miss any of the lessons. Only after Charles is satisfied that he has learned all he should from today's trading will he call it a day.

This habit of self-coaching and accountability has played a major role in helping Charles to reach his level of success today—along with many other hallmark traders' habits.

◼ What Can We Learn from This Successful Trader?

As you read about the morning routine of Charles, I am sure one keyword that repeatedly appears in the passage has caught your attention: *Habit*.

The Merriam-Webster Dictionary defines *habit* as "a usual way of behaving; something that a person does often in a regular and repeated way." Force of habit makes us brush our teeth in the morning; it is what makes us crave food at around the same time every day; it is what sends us to bed before the clock strikes midnight.

If these seem too trivial, what about the habit we developed to exercise three times a week so we keep in shape? What about the one that makes a worker arrive at the office on time to avoid reprimand from his supervisor, and finish his work at 5 p.m. so that he can enjoy some life after work? What about the habit that prompts a business owner to review the accounts and take note of irregularities every evening?

On a negative note, habits are not always good. Overeating is one of the main causes of obesity; people who are mindless when walking (e.g., busy checking for Facebook or Twitter updates) could become victims of road accidents; those who habitually give up at the first encounter of failure are less likely to succeed in life.

We are creatures of habit, and our habits shape who we are. I have shown you how Charles allows his good habits to guide him in his trading. But what you have seen is only what he does in one day—what you haven't seen are the habits that he has formed over 15 years, which dictate how he deals with this trading business as a whole and which keep him in good mental and physical shape for peak performance.

Charles is not the only one who conscientiously forms and maintains habits. All of the highly successful traders do. In my years of association with the high flyers in this industry, I have seen over and over again that they are relentless in cultivating positive habits that will bring them success, and doing away with the negative ones that are in their way.

Here are the important questions for you to ask as a trader: What are the habits that successful traders have in common? What can I learn from these habits? And how do I model them for my own success?

You will find the answers in this book. But before we move on, let's take a look at the common pitfalls that most traders, including the experienced ones, fall into.

PART I

Introduction

All traders ride on a pendulum every day. Unsuccessful traders ride the pendulum back and forth with no real idea of the pendulum's swing. Successful traders recognize that the pendulum swings and ride it mindfully; as a result, they make better decisions and better trades.

The Futile Search for the "Perfect System"

When Peter, one of the clients that I coach, showed me how well versed he had become with his trading skills, I was impressed. Although he was a part-time trader (aspiring to turn trading into his full-time profession), he had gone through the grind to learn about price action, Fibonacci, support and resistance areas, chart patterns, moving averages, and other technical indicators.

Looking at how he understood price action and maneuvered these technical tools, I saw how good he was at reading his charts. His skills were on par with most professional traders; maybe better. Especially considering how busy he was with his day job, I knew he must have burnt the midnight oil on his evenings and weekends to learn them.

However, I could not help frowning a little when he asked me, "What techniques am I still lacking? Do you have a better strategy for me?"

These are typical questions asked by traders. It showed that Peter did not understand what he needed to do to succeed. Or perhaps he was just misguided.

From my experience, most traders are like Peter. They think trading is all about mastering as many technical skills as possible to apply them to analyze chart price data and make intelligent buy/sell decisions, so they will continuously bring in heaps and heaps of money day after day.

To them, the key to winning big in trading is landing a powerful technique or strategy that is guaranteed to work. That's why they spare no effort to find tips to improve their technical skills even though they may have all they need to do well. They are keen in trying "hot off the press" software and jumping from one website to another to look for the next life-changing piece of advice.

In short, they keep looking, looking, looking, in hope to find that "perfect system" that will *transform* their trading into a business success.

Unfortunately, this is never going to happen. The search for a fail-safe system in trading will lead them nowhere, because the Holy Grail simply does not exist. Worse, it will trap them in the *Technical Trader's Trap* (more about this in the following chapters), limit their potential to achieve greater outcomes from their trading career, and even cause them to lose their hard-earned money.

■ The Real Transformation Starts within the Trader

As a professional trader and educator for the past 30 years, I have had the opportunity to closely observe the top performers in the industry. What I've noticed is that although most of them have expert technical skills, technical knowledge alone does not make them high flyers. Learning entrepreneurial skills and cultivating the right habits does.

These successful traders are *Entrepreneurial Traders* who treat trading as a serious business, and embrace an entrepreneurial style in running and managing their trading business. Entrepreneurial Traders set goals, plan for their business, constantly review their plans, execute them, and improve themselves. Success can be expected.

On the other hand, average traders are *"technical junkies"* who trap themselves in the *Technical Trader's Trap*, obsessed with feeding on new technical knowledge or trying out new trading systems, at the expense of making a consistent income. How can they move their trading into the passing lane of the highway of success? They don't know or they think they can get there by gathering more information.

I have a plan that will help Peter transform himself from a "technical junkie" into an Entrepreneurial Trader. My plan has helped many traders that

I have coached with their transformation process, and I am confident that it will help Peter, too.

Most importantly, it will also help *YOU*.

How to Benefit from This Book

The central focus of this book is based on my model of the 10 Habits of Successful Traders. In the following chapters, you will discover the following:

- *What the 10 common habits of successful traders are.* The simplest way to succeed in trading is to learn from the best and model their habits. This book shows you what successful traders are doing, what you're not doing, and what you can learn from their habits.

- *Why you should practice the 10 common habits.* You will find out the benefits of cultivating these habits and how they have helped the top performers to gain financial success, a great sense of achievement, and a well-balanced life.

- *How to replace your negative habits with positive habits.* When you examine the positive habits of successful traders, you might discover your own negative habits that prevent trading success. Find out how you can replace the negative habits with the positive ones.

The Pendulum Scenarios

In Chapter 1, I will introduce you to two traders, Stacey and Fred. You will see how they adopt the typical habits and characteristics of an Entrepreneurial Trader and a "technical junkie." You'll see how they treat their trading businesses differently, and how their mentalities and behaviors affect their trading results.

The stories of Stacey and Fred do not end in Chapter 1. In between each chapter of the book are 26 case studies that I call the Pendulum Scenarios. In these "addendum" to the chapters, we will examine the emotional-psychological roller-coaster ride that the two traders go through and how these challenges expose their strengths and weaknesses. It might surprise you, but there are strengths in Fred you can learn from and weaknesses in Stacey you can learn to avoid.

Although we are using two fictional traders as the protagonists of these case studies, these are not contrived examples; instead, they are real situations that happened in real trading scenarios that I have experienced with my students.

Here are the Pendulum Scenarios that Fred and Stacey deal with every day in their trading:

- Fear vs. Greed
- Get Rich Quick or Go Broke Quick
- Realistic vs. Unrealistic Trader
- Clarity vs. Muddled Thinking
- Forgiving vs. Angry Trader
- Courage vs. Conformity
- Taking Action vs. Feeling Remorse
- Enthusiastic vs. Apathetic Trader
- Foresight vs. Hindsight
- The Lucky vs. Unlucky Trader
- Calm vs. Nervous Trader
- Self-Doubting vs. Overconfidence
- Cautious vs. Reckless Trading

- Optimistic vs. Pessimistic Trader
- Flexible vs. Stubborn Trader
- Accepting vs. Willful
- Pragmatic vs. Idealistic Trader
- Pulling the Trigger vs. Having Regrets
- Conservative vs. Impulsive Trader
- Organized vs. Disorganized Trader
- Proactive vs. Reactive Trader
- I Can vs. I Can't
- Patient vs. Impatient Trader
- Relaxed vs. Stressed Trader
- Clear-headed vs. Sorrowful Trader
- Good Mood vs. Bad Mood Trading

The scenarios above are based on these key pendulum factors.

The Pendulum Factors

The *pendulum factors* represent duality situations arising from trading the markets. On one end of the pendulum swing there is a condition, and on the other end there is another (often opposing) condition. Ideally, you, as a trader, want to remain or get back to the neutral position because staying at either end can be unproductive.

The pendulum swings are typically caused by the constant flux of the market. You can do nothing about the swings of a pendulum, but you need to learn how to ride them as all successful traders do. The lack of skills to weather the swings is what makes trading an emotional-psychological roller-coaster ride for traders.

Pendulum factors have three aspects:

1. Market Pendulum

Skillful traders know when to enter and exit a trade. They have learned how to recognize the pendulum swings in the market and not to enter trend trades after extreme and exhaustive moves. They readily understand the market cycles and will only enter after the corrections.

2. Financial Pendulum

Making money from trading is not a one-way street. On one end of the pendulum swing there are times when you make money, and on the other end are times when you lose money. Both winning and losing money are part and parcel of trading. It is how you manage the equity in your account and take appropriate actions through habits that will determine your success (or failure).

3. Emotional Pendulum

The emotional pendulum is best described with the fear and greed continuum. On one end of the pendulum swing, you have the desire to earn more money from your trades and might be driven by greed to take larger positions irresponsibly; on the other end, you are in fear of losing money, and fear might hold your actions back. Learning how to balance between these two factors is the focus of the Pendulum Scenarios in this book.

■ Complementary Resources

Complementary to this book are several materials available on the accompanying website, including the Trader's Business Plan, Trader's Scorecard, Simple Trading System Template, Trading Blotter, and the "10 Habits" videos. Flip to the "Resources" page to find out how you can download them.

The discussion in this book is completed with detailed technical descriptions of an array of tools straight out of the Trader's Analysis Toolbox, which I call the *building blocks* for building strategies and trade plans. These are the essential tools that will help you to gain insights into the markets and make better trading decisions. Find out about them in PART V, The Trader's Tools.

■ The Trader's Scorecard

The best way for you to take advantage of this book is to go online and complete *The FX Trader's EDGE™ Scorecard* presented in Table I.1. Then, after you finish reading the book and implement some of the 10 habits, you will be asked to take the test again. By comparing your results before and after working through the ideas in this book, you can gauge how much you have progressed as a trader.

TABLE I.1	The Trader's Scorecard										
I do not have a clear vision of my future.	1	2	3	4	5	6	7	8	9	10	I have a clear, well-defined vision of my future.
I do not have clear goals for my trading business.	1	2	3	4	5	6	7	8	9	10	I have clear goals for my trading business.
I am not operating my trading as a business.	1	2	3	4	5	6	7	8	9	10	I am operating my trading as a business.
I do not have a business plan to achieve my trading objectives.	1	2	3	4	5	6	7	8	9	10	I have a business plan to achieve my trading objectives.
I do not have well-defined trading strategies.	1	2	3	4	5	6	7	8	9	10	I have well-defined trading strategies.
I am not making as much money as I would like as a trader.	1	2	3	4	5	6	7	8	9	10	I am making a lot of money as a trader.
I am trying to do everything myself.	1	2	3	4	5	6	7	8	9	10	I have a coach and a support group helping me achieve my goals.
I react emotionally to the markets.	1	2	3	4	5	6	7	8	9	10	I have a disciplined and committed approach to trading.
I tie my self-esteem to the success and failure of my trades.	1	2	3	4	5	6	7	8	9	10	I am detached from my wins and losses in the markets.
I do not feel I am achieving my full potential as a trader.	1	2	3	4	5	6	7	8	9	10	I feel I am achieving my full potential as a trader.
ADD COLUMN TOTALS											YOUR SCORE _____

So now, complete the Trader's Scorecard to gain a clear understanding of your current situation. Rate your reactions to each pair of phrases. Decide where you lie on the scale from 1 to 10. Add up your total from each column.

Visit www.wiley.com/go/traderspendulum (see About the Companion website) to complete the Trader's Scorecard online. (Or, go directly to the interactive site now: http://fxtradersedge.com/scorecard/)

It is my sincere hope that what you learn from these *10 Habits of Successful Traders* and the Pendulum Scenarios will give you an edge in trading and move you over to the right side of the scorecard as you progress as an Entrepreneurial Trader.

CHAPTER 1

The Successful Trader versus the Average Trader

F red Boros, a man in his early thirties, had reached his breaking point. He pushed away from his desk, stood up, and switched off his computer screen. It had happened again. Things just weren't working out as he had hoped. He began to pace back and forth in his office.

Fred had been trading stocks for over a year and had envisioned that by this time, he would have been successful enough to move out of his cramped apartment and up the financial ladder. Previously, Fred had worked as an engineer with a large defense contractor, a job that paid him well but required long, unfulfilling hours. He had wanted a fuller life outside the cubicle prison. But it didn't seem to be working out.

■ The Conversation that Changed Fred's Life

One evening, two years earlier at his neighborhood health club, Fred had the conversation that changed the course of his life.

While waiting for a pick-up game of racquetball, Fred started talking with an ex-work associate. The man told him how he had escaped from the corporate world and became a self-employed day trader. He was full of excitement about his new life, and had spun such a wonderful story that Fred was excited to know how he, too, could be free and financially stable.

Fred became obsessed with learning to trade. He invested his time and money attending seminars, read every book he could get his hands on, and paid expensive membership fees to join online forums where he could exchange notes with fellow traders.

Always a top-notch student, Fred learned quickly and began to trade actively in his paper trading account. He still held his day job, but found himself spending more and more time monitoring and analyzing his paper trades. Within several months, he was stuck to his computer screen like a teenager to a game console. He fell behind with his engineer work projects and found himself putting in extra hours just to keep up with his work responsibilities.

One day, fate stepped in.

To weather a major financial hit, his company had to tighten budgets and cut back on human resources. They let Fred go. Although he was shocked by the news, he was strangely not upset. On the contrary, he felt a sense of relief and an inexplicable surge of excitement.

He took this as a "sign" to pursue his dream. He thought that he was being guided toward a new future. He felt what lay in front of him was a worthier journey with a more enjoyable lifestyle, where he would have more control over his life, more freedom of time and, of course, a fuller bank account.

◼ When Reality Kicked in: Paper Trading versus "Real" Trading

Fred took a portion of his savings and moved it into his active trading account. He felt a bit nervous trading with real money rather than just making trial trades. This uneasy feeling heightened when he quickly found out that the system that he had developed during his period of successful paper trading didn't seem to work as well with "real" money.

When he was making paper trades, he never hesitated to enter into a trade when he felt it looked right. Most of the time, he made successful trades. The win/loss ratio in his paper trading had been consistently above 75 percent. But after a few losses from real trades, he found himself losing confidence in the system he had set up from paper trading. He tried to make adjustments as he continued, but his win/loss ratio fell through the floor. Days went by with no net profits and Fred began to panic. Despite this, he traded every day, because as a day trader he needed to do this in hopes that his small profitable trades could accumulate over time.

Even more discouraging, Fred found himself glued to his computer as much as he used to be at his engineering job. He wasn't used to feeling like a loser. But Fred had to admit that it wasn't fun anymore. He once again felt trapped in a routine that sucked joy out of his life.

But he wasn't ready to give up. Not yet. He was determined to make his trading a success.

The Path Forward

Fred believed that he was an intelligent person who could do well in any intellectual activity. Never in his wildest dreams did he realize how challenging stock trading could be, and how difficult it is to earn a living by trading full time. Because there seemed to be a distance between where he was and where he wanted to be, Fred decided to seek more training, to learn more techniques, and pick up more advanced systems to bridge the gap.

He asked himself:

How will I get the know-how to succeed?

What's the secret to making it big?

Can I create my own winning strategy?

Fred jumped from one website to another looking for advice, spent money and time on trading courses, and subscribed to expensive software. Would this improve his situation? He was hopeful.

The Struggle of a Young Family

Stacey Braverman and her husband, Brad, had always wanted a family. They began to put a plan together to adjust their lifestyle to welcome a baby, and at the same time make ends meet. They agreed that Stacey should stay at home to take care of the baby for at least the first three years. They wanted to make sure the baby got the full care and attention from his parents, was taught well, and grew up to be happy and healthy.

But this decision meant that a major sacrifice had to be made.

Stacey would have to give up her high-paying job as a sales representative. For years, she had been one of her company's top producers, generating remarkable profits for the company and earning huge paychecks. Her sales commissions contributed the major part of her family's income.

It was beyond Brad's capability to shoulder the family's finances alone. They needed an extra income source. The only option was for Stacey to work part-time to supplement his income.

■ A Perfect Plan Found?

After careful consideration, they found a plan to address both concerns: Stacey would learn to become a forex trader. They knew they wanted something that allowed Stacey the freedom to work from home, on her own time, and they had heard about the high potential returns of forex trading. At the same time, they were fully aware of the high risks, so they had put aside a cushion of cash to weather the loss if things did not turn out well. Stacey knew she had a knack for business, mathematics, and logical analysis, and could easily imagine how she could use all these in trading. Forex trading seemed to be the perfect fit.

Stacey planned to dedicate most of her time at home to take care of the baby and trade for three hours every day. This way, she could plan her working hours around her life and the parenting plan, and have the luxury of a flexible schedule.

During her pregnancy, she started training herself in trading, received coaching from an experienced forex mentor, and tested her skills with a demo trading account. Within a couple months, she had established a trading system that fit her personality and preference, and so she took the leap of faith and started trading with hard cash.

Seven months later, their baby, Brad Jr., arrived. Soon after her maternity leave was over, Stacey quit her job and, according to their plan, started to trade forex at home while enjoying her new role as a mother. What astounded her was the fact that over time, she actually found herself making more money trading at home for three hours a day than when she worked a full-time job!

She was overjoyed, but cautious at the same time. She learned from her training that "each trade is a new trade," and she held no illusions that there are any guarantees of success in trading. She understood that trading was much more than making a best guess on where a currency pair movement was heading, but rather, a deliberate study of the market fundamentals, cycles, and price action and skillful application of the trader's psychology. She was cautious, all of the time.

■ A Typical Afternoon of a Trader

One day, as Stacey was feeding Brad Jr. and watching *Bloomberg Financial News*, she glanced over at her laptop computer. She noticed that her last trade was stopped out for a slight loss. She opened up her trading journal and clicked on a worksheet where she tracked her trades. She took a screenshot of the well-documented chart and pasted it on the worksheet, and then analyzed the trade.

Stacey posted the losing trade and the $120 loss into another spreadsheet called "the P&L and Win/Loss Ratio." She looked at the running P&L column and then at the Win/Loss column. This told her that she was holding around her 68 percent trade wins and her profits were slightly behind this month's goal.

After putting Brad Jr. down for his nap, she went over the trade again to examine in detail what had happened. From previous experience, she learned that she was guilty of not being patient enough to wait for confirmation before entering a position. She was not upset about this, because she knew that all she had to do was to remind herself more often to execute her trades with patience.

At the end of her day, after reviewing her trading activities, she logged on to her trading coach's website and entered the chat room. She posted the screenshot of the chart of her losing trade and asked her fellow traders: "Do you think this was a viable trade according to this setup?" She got up and went about some of her household chores and periodically checked to see if there was any response to her question. As expected, she received the valuable feedback she was looking for.

Stacey paid a sizable fee for the guidance from a veteran coach, and used his website to network with fellow traders, exchange ideas and tips with them, and receive support and motivation when she needed it. She knew the hefty sum that she had been paying for all this was a sensible investment.

■ Trader by Chance

From the start, Fred had entered into stock trading by a chance encounter with his ex-colleague at the local health club. It was the wonderful outlook of the life of a day trader that lured him into the day-trading sphere. No detailed forethoughts and contingency plan were made before he made the leap:

- He did not plan his trading education.

- He was blinded by the potential rewards of a successful trading career but did not consider the risks.

- His decision to trade was reactive (to his job loss) and not aligned with his skills or personality.

In essence, he entered this career for the sheer reason that he was convinced by the story that his ex-colleague had spun.

Fred had also not tested his system thoroughly before he relied on it for income. He had traded it with his paper trading account, but did not start small in trading real cash to gain confidence, so he did not know what to expect when the technical and psychological complications of trading live cropped up.

Worse, he allowed his emotions to get the better of him when he traded. A few losses in the beginning aroused his doubt about his system (although it had a win/loss ratio of 75 percent in paper trading). There might indeed be some flaws in the system, but he was not experienced enough to effectively detect and then fix them, because he did not have any strategy to track his trades and find out where the "leakage" was.

He thought he was lacking some secret trading techniques or a more robust trading system, so he devoted more time, money, and effort to finding them. Fred was setting himself up to fail.

■ Trader by Plan

By contrast, Stacey had planned appropriately before she launched her trading career. She planned her training and received coaching to prepare herself mentally and technically to become a trader. She knew the schedule for leaving her job and planned the steps leading to that.

She started small, failed a lot, and failed fast to verify her trading system before developing a robust one that she could fully rely on. But things still went wrong even with these experiments. When it happened, she did not react emotionally. She calmly tracked her trades and analyzed her failures. To her, every failure was a lesson to learn, and one step closer to success.

But she did not do this alone. She used her coach and fellow traders for feedback and improved her results through experience and learning.

■ Dedicated Trader ... or Slacker?

When Fred worked for the engineering firm, he was a dedicated and responsible worker. He would turn up at his office on time every day, never missed a project deadline, and made sure he delivered quality work, even if it meant he had to work extra hours. As an employee, his manager and supervisor guided most of the steps on his career path.

But things were different after he left the corporate world and became a trader.

Fred enjoyed the freedom that trading gave him. He could start work at almost any time in the day, and had the freedom to decide how many hours he would work. Not having to turn up at an office meant that when he felt that he needed more rest, he could take a few hours off from work; having no project milestones to hit meant as long as he worked to his satisfaction, he felt fine. (He did set some earnings targets. But since he was his own boss, when the targets were not met, it was easy to tell himself to "just try harder next time.")

To his friends and family, Fred seemed to be a dedicated trader. His trading activities took up at least 80 percent of his waking hours. He was glued to his desk, busy looking at charts and analyzing the market, busy deciding whether to enter or exit trades. And when he was not making trades, he was participating in online traders' forums to exchange tips with fellow traders, researching the markets, and visiting trading gurus' websites or blogs to get their advice and inspiration. He had practically no time for a life outside of trading—no time for a physical workout, no time for his hobbies, and no time for family and friends.

Deep down inside, Fred knew something was wrong. He was not making money consistently. His trading account was not growing, and he saw no significant progress in himself as a trader.

He started to wonder whether he was doing things right. As an intelligent young man, he soon realized that most of the hours he spent on trading were unproductive hours. He was spending his time aimlessly, not knowing where to head.

Fred was not really *working* most of the time. He was only slacking.

■ The Life of a Trading Mom

At another corner in the same city, Stacey was living a more fulfilling life than at her previous sales job. Juggling between trading and her duties as a wife and mother was not easy. It tested Stacey's time management and multitasking skills—but Stacey was doing well so far. And she was enjoying every moment of it.

Stacey held herself accountable for her trading career. She knew that she only had limited time, so she planned well. She would show up at her work desk at the same time every weekday (after settling her baby down for a nap), worked for a fixed number of hours, and called it a day punctually—unless anything unexpected cropped up in her trades.

She was a methodical person, and this character showed in her trading. She knew she did not have the luxury of time or extra capital to waste, so even before she quit her job and launched her trading career, she already had her trading system set up, tested, and proven. In addition to that, with the advice of her coach, Stacey had written a business plan. It was just nine pages and not exceedingly elaborate, but the process of designing her plan had allowed her some space to think through how she intended to conduct her trading. Consequently, she was clear about her short- and long-term goals, her daily work schedule, the methods to track her performance, and how to manage money—even before she started trading.

All these efforts to "systemize" her trading seemed tedious and dull at first—and indeed, at some point Stacey questioned the rationale and necessity to do so—but she pushed through it anyway. At the end of the process, Stacey appreciated that she had laid out all the components involved in a trading business and she knew that her goals were achievable.

And she was right—in fact, more than that. Not only was she doing well in her trading career (and motherhood), she earned more money than she did when she held a sales job—while spending less time at work and more time with her family.

■ The Question You Need to Ask

At this point, it should be clear to you who among these two traders are more likely to make it big in trading, and who is more likely to fail.

The question is: "What makes the difference between them?"

CHAPTER 2

The Technical Trader's Trap

In my 30-year career as a professional trader and trading coach, I have rubbed shoulders with traders of different calibers at all levels of success. Frankly speaking, many are mediocre, at best, but a small group of traders enjoys the perks of a successful trading career; moreover, a handful of them are successful beyond most peoples' imaginations.

I was interested in finding out what made the difference between average traders and high achievers. So, throughout the years, I observed and surveyed my fellow traders, students, and coaching clients. It did not surprise me when I found out that the traders' intelligence, education, prior experience, and personal caliber all play a part in their levels of success. However, a trader who lacks some of these qualities can do equally well, and in some cases better, with hard work.

So, I asked myself, "What can I conclude from this?" More importantly, I was curious to find out if there is a single deciding factor that determines whether a trader will succeed or not.

It turns out that there is.

■ Revisiting the Cases of Fred and Stacey

Previously, we looked at the different behaviors of two traders: Fred and Stacey. Let's review their cases again before we move on to discussing some of the lessons we can learn from them.

Fred was a highly paid engineer who was sick of being stuck in the cubicle nation. Perhaps it was out of desperation or impulse or simply because of the groovy "life of a trader" story that his ex-colleague had told him that attracted Fred to trading. He took the chance and jumped in with both feet.

A year after he started in this profession, Fred remained in the seeking mode, endlessly going after every "secret strategy" that trading gurus guarantee to bring success. He was not even earning consistent income, let alone doing as well as he wished. He was at a loss. What he was doing seemed to be meaningless and unprofitable. He started to suspect he had made the wrong decision and he couldn't earn a living by trading full-time.

At the other end of the spectrum, Stacey started her trading career slowly and steadily. It took her months to settle on a system and run tests to prove her strategy, one with which she was finally comfortable. Although selecting and testing her system was a long and painful process, as a result of this legwork, she had been making consistent income to support her parenting plan.

At the same time, the freedom that trading provided had allowed her to be a stay-at-home mother. If things continue to go well for Stacey, she might decide not to rejoin the workforce after her baby has grown up. At this stage in her trading career, trading seems to offer more flexibility, intellectual stimulation, and reward.

■ "Technical Junkie" versus Entrepreneurial Trader

There is no significant difference between Fred and Stacey in terms of intelligence, education, prior experience, and personal caliber. They are professionals (albeit in different fields), and they are young, intelligent, ambitious, and highly dedicated to making their career a success.

But there is a real difference in the way they treat trading.

Fred is like the majority of traders, who are caught in the *Technical Trader's Trap*. These traders are "hobbyist traders" or "technical junkies", regardless of how many years they have been in the industry, how well versed they are in all sorts of trading techniques and tricks, how much training they have received, how much time and effort they seem to be dedicating to trading, and how much money is involved in their daily transactions. They are not the professional players in the trading field because they lack a business sense in trading.

Stacey belongs to the rare group of traders who treat trading as a serious business and run it meticulously. These are the Entrepreneurial Traders. They know what they are doing, have an end in mind for their trading business, plan their trades and trade their plans, and hold themselves accountable for their trading career. Most successful traders belong to this group, and this is not a coincidence. Figure 2.1 summarizes this difference.

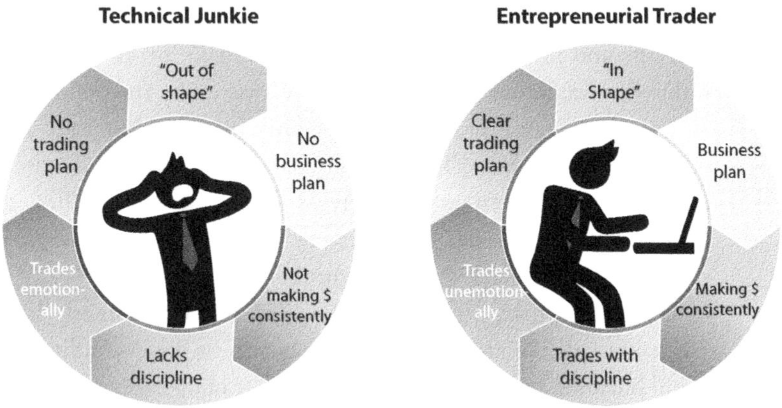

Technical Junkie

- "Out of shape"
- No trading plan
- No business plan
- Trades emotionally
- Not making $ consistently
- Lacks discipline

Entrepreneurial Trader

- "In Shape"
- Clear trading plan
- Business plan
- Trades unemotionally
- Making $ consistently
- Trades with discipline

FIGURE 2.1   "Technical Junkie" versus Entrepreneurial Trader

The Hobbyist and the Business Owner

Traders who are stuck in the *Technical Trader's Trap* do not understand that trading needs to be run as a serious business. Therefore, they do not bother to set up a business plan for their trading. They typically hop from one system to another (with a mantra like, "Whatever works!"), never finding one that suits their personality and preference. Not having a system to follow means they frequently make the mistake of trading emotionally, not logically. They rely on *gut feelings* on important decisions like when to enter or exit the market, how to cut losses, and how to manage their capital.

These traders are not interested in engaging a coach to advise them on their actions or provide them with external accountability. The freedom that the trading career gives them might actually spoil them to the extent that they lack discipline in their work. There is no fixed time to begin work, no fixed number of hours to work, and no clear targets for their daily work. Despite this, some of them seem overworked because they fail to design their trading around their lives. But the amount of hours they put in is not in direct proportion to their income because most of these are nonproductive hours.

Entrepreneurial Traders approach the game differently. They treat trading as a business, which needs to be well-planned, well-executed, and well-managed. They "own" the business, and they take the initiatives to keep it under their control. For a start, they design a business plan that details the important aspects of their business, including the short- and long-term goals, their preferred tactics and strategy to achieve the goals, and their resource (time and money) management plan.

All traders ride the pendulum, sometimes on a daily basis. The way a trader treats her ride can make or break her trading business. A successful trader with an entrepreneurial spirit considers the ride, no matter how rocky, as part and parcel of the business. She takes advantage of the pendulum swings to be in sync with the markets and finds good opportunities to make profit from it. On the contrary, a hobbyist or amateur trader tends to be swayed by the pendulum swings.

Entrepreneurial Traders are not only planners but they are also obsessed with executing their plans. They usually have a system that dictates the input, process, and expected output as precisely as they can. This is their recipe for successful trades. When they put their system to work, they do so in a highly disciplined manner. Emotions have no place in their execution.

On top of that, Entrepreneurial Traders understand the need to maintain a work-life balance and to keep their health in good condition. This way, they can avoid burnout and go a long way in their trading career.

■ Are You in the Technical Trader's Trap?

What if, after reading the stories of Fred and Stacey, you are still not sure into which category you fall? Table 2.1 lists the three common pitfalls that traders in the *Technical Trader's Trap* commonly face and their direct consequences.

As you examine the items listed in this table, you might find that you exhibit some of these characteristics. If so, I have two pieces of advice for you:

1. Fret not because almost all traders are guilty of committing some of them, including the highly successful Entrepreneurial Traders.

2. Understand that you can do something about them.

TABLE 2.1 Common Pitfalls in the *Technical Trader's Trap*

Pitfall #1: Lack of Discipline	Pitfall #2: Hobbyists' Trading Practice	Pitfall #3: Not Treating Trading as a Business
Wasting time on the Internet constantly looking for new trading strategies	Overtrading	Not treating trading as a serious business but only a hobby
Becoming a "technical junkie"	Moving between greed and fear	Not having clear goals or a business plan
Exerting scattered effort	Reacting emotionally to the market	Not tracking performance
Giving up too soon	Having no clear strategy	Not having a team for accountability
Having no patience	Setting no clear rules and boundaries	Not using a coach
Having a get-rich-quick mentality	Setting no trade plan	Not striving for a work–life balance
Continually looking for the Holy Grail of trading		Lacking of entrepreneurial skills and habits
Consequence: Waste time and effort	Consequence: Lose money	Consequence: Do not achieve full potential as a trader

How to Get Yourself out of the *Technical Trader's Trap*

Now that you have had an overview of the common traits of the traders in the *Technical Trader's Trap* as opposed to common traits of the Entrepreneurial Trader, you need to ask yourself the following questions:

- Are you trapped in the *Technical Trader's Trap* or are you an Entrepreneurial Trader?

- Do you want to be a "technical junkie" in trading or start treating your trading as a serious business?

If you find yourself in the *Technical Trader's Trap*, how will you move yourself out of it and transform yourself into an Entrepreneurial Trader?

The answer is by changing your habits.

The next question is "How?"

There is no easy way to change your habits. Some of the key ideas in Charles Duhigg's highly acclaimed book, *The Power of Habit* (Duhigg 2012), gave me a clue as to the answer to this question:

- Habits cannot be eradicated, but they can be replaced. There are three steps in a *habit loop*: the cue, the routine, and the reward. The *golden rule* in replacing a habit is to replace the old routine with a new one, while keeping the cue and reward intact.

  For example, if you have the habit of drinking coffee (the routine) when you feel sleepy (the cue) to regain your energy (the reward), you could probably replace the routine of getting a cup of coffee with the routine of doing some light exercise when the cue arises to get the same reward of feeling energetic again.

  In the case for traders, for example, whenever you are overwhelmed with the feeling of insufficiency (the cue) and look for the next trading strategy that promises unrealistic results (the routine) to relieve yourself from the bad feeling (the reward), why not revise the system that you have proven is working and get yourself really familiarized with it for the same reward?

- When you want to change a habit, start by quickly getting small wins first. Many habits have been ingrained over many years, and it is impossible to change them overnight. Break down the habit into small, digestible steps, and then *divide and conquer* each of them. Collectively, the feeling of victory from these consistent small wins will give you the momentum and convince you that realizing your bigger plan is doable.

- There are some small changes or habits that people introduce into their routines that unintentionally carry over into other aspects of their lives and, thus, create an avalanche of change in their lives.

For example, an overeater who cuts out sugar products (this is considered the "small change" although in practice it might not be) can unintentionally trigger a chain of other positive changes, like getting into a workout routine, becoming more disciplined at work (and therefore receiving a promotion), and turning oneself into a more attentive parent. Duhigg calls a small habit that brings forth a series of other changes a "keystone habit."

■ You can change any habit. Any behavior can be changed, regardless of how old you are or how ingrained the pattern is.

■ Eating an Elephant a Bite at a Time

The following chapters in this book discuss 10 habits that you need to model to turn yourself into a successful trader. It is certainly overwhelming when you try to incorporate all 10 habits at once into your trading life, but the lessons from *The Power of Habit*, suggest that you might do the following:

■ Do it one at a time and attempt the easier ones first for the sense of victory from "small wins."

■ Identify the *keystone habit* that will trigger the rest of the changes.

Now the questions are the following: How do you plan for the changes to take place? How do you know which are the ones you should attempt first as the candidates for your small wins? How do you identify the keystone habit?

And when you have identified the candidates for small wins and the keystone habit, how do you design your battle plan for cultivating these habits?

The chapters in this book provide you with detailed descriptions on what these habits are and how you can implement them, along with anecdotes (portrayed with our favorite protagonists, Fred and Stacey) that illustrate the behaviors and mentalities of traders who exhibit the 10 best habits, as well as those who don't.

After reading these chapters, you will have a complete picture of these 10 habits. With some planning and soul searching, you will have no problem identifying your strengths and weaknesses as a trader and start drafting out your action plan to implement your change in habit. (Remember, do it one at a time.)

This is not going to be an easy process, especially if you have formed a stubborn pattern of habits. But as Duhigg points out, a habit can be changed. While fighting against your old habits and pulling yourself out of the comfort zone they create, you are going to face a lot of challenges and resistance. Push on, warrior, I assure you that you CAN do it with determination and your eyes on the prize!

Chapter 3 provides an overview of the transformation process from "technical junkie" to Entrepreneurial Trader by changing your habits. But first, think about these:

- How do you minimize the fruitless effort in your attempts to implement your habit change?

- What is the fastest and surest way you can transform yourself into an Entrepreneurial Trader?

- You don't need to do it all by yourself.

Becoming an Entrepreneurial Trader—The Process

You might ask, "If I am stuck in the *Technical Trader's Trap*, how will I get out of it? And how do I turn myself into an Entrepreneurial Trader?"

Or in other words, in the context of this book, "How do I transform myself from a *Frustrated Technical Junkie Fred* into a *Successful Entrepreneurial Stacey*?"

Steps to Transform from a "Technical Junkie" into an Entrepreneurial Trader

To start on the right path, here are three broad areas that will require work.

Planning

First of all, make sure you have entered the trading business for the right reasons. It is true that successful trading can reward you with more money for less work and an independent lifestyle, but you need to understand that trading is not a get-rich-quick scheme. It takes hard work and dedication to get there.

To be a successful trader, you need to run your trading as you would run a serious business. Define your trader's business plan, including personal and business goals. This will help you to clarify the steps you need to take to fulfill your expectations, and make it possible for you to set your sights on the prize from your trading. You will also know how to react in case of any contingencies.

Execution

As an Entrepreneurial Trader, you need to go through the process of finding a trading style that suits you the best. It does not matter whether you eventually land on momentum trading, day trading, swing trading, or position trading as long as the style fits your personality and preference.

You should also set up trade plans based on your proven trading system that will capture trades in different market cycles and guide your actions, so you will not trade emotionally. Stick to the plan and system consistently and learn the correct process to tweak them if you find some flaws in them.

Continuous Feedback and Improvement

Getting everything right in the first few attempts is impossible. It is okay to encounter hiccups in trading, but when they happen, you have to make sure you know how to track them to learn the lessons. Similarly, you will want to track your good performance, too, so you learn how to repeat your successes.

Most successful businesspeople engage coaches or mentors at various points in their business development to help them grow, and as an Entrepreneurial Trader, you should do the same. At the most basic level, observe what top traders do in their trading business and model their habits of success.

The following chapters detail the 10 habits that you must cultivate to take you out of the *Technical Trader's Trap*, and into the group of Entrepreneurial Traders who consistently "win big" in the trading game. Before you get overexcited about your transformation, let's stop for a bit to examine where you are now and where you want to be.

■ The Trader's Quadrants: Where Are You Now, and Where Do You Want to Be?

Depending on your level of experience in trading and your trading habits, you fall into one of the quadrants in Table 3.1.

The question you need to ask yourself is this: *"Where am I now, and where do I aim to be?"*

TABLE 3.1	The Trader's Quadrant	
	Trader in the *Technical Trader's Trap*	Transformed Entrepreneurial Trader
New Trader	I Unsuccessful (developed negative habits)	II Successful (developed positive habits)
Experienced Trader	III Unsuccessful (developed negative habits and kept them)	IV Successful (replaced negative habits with positive habits)

If you have just started trading, your job might be easier because you are not set in your ways. If you follow the advice in this book and get external accountability and guidance if you need to, you will soon see yourself form positive habits and modeling the way successful Entrepreneurial Traders run their trading business. Start strong and start in the right direction, and you will be well on your way to success.

If you've been trading for a while, do not fret if you find out you have formed some negative habits in trading, no matter how long you have been practicing them. Any habit can be replaced, and it is never too late to improve it. The same advice for the complete beginner applies to you: Follow the advice in this book and get external accountability or coaching if you need to because it might be difficult to do it on your own, especially if you find that the habits are already deeply rooted in you.

Some words of caution: Transformation is not a one-way process; it is easy for you to get into the successful quadrants II and IV, only to find yourself falling back to the unsuccessful quadrants I and III if you are not mindful or do not have a process to hold yourself accountable. This is the reason why I highly recommend you learn these habits.

■ Trading Habit Cultivation

Getting organized and ready to trade is as important as the trading itself. In this section, let us examine the seven up-front setups involved in getting ready for your trading business.

1. The Business Model

See if the following ideas look familiar to you:

- Purchase a dilapidated property at a bargain price, renovate it, and sell it at a profit using those profits to purchase further properties.

- Purchase large rolls of paper, cut them down to small sizes and sell these, at a profit, in packs for use with computer printers.

- Buy a car and make it available to take people, at a price, from A to B within your local city.

Each of these ideas is a business model that businesspeople rely on to make profits from their businesses. All businesses conform to a model, and trading is no exception.

For example, a trader's business model might be this: get to know the behavior of a currency pair or a stock and monitor it for three hours each day; take trades when you believe there is a high probability of making a profit; gradually increase the trade size as your account balance grows to take advantage of the compounding effect.

This is one of many possible business models that a trading business is based on. Each model will depend on the individual trader's circumstances, which are a combination of the time available for trading, the size of the trading account, and the environment in which the trading must take place for example.

If you are unsure of how to identify the business model that suits your unique circumstances, then your coach will be able to help.

2. The Business Plan

All successful businesses have a business plan, and so should your trading business.

A trader's business plan outlines the stages that a trader must work through to arrive at success. Each of these stages typically consists of a series of actionable steps, as well as specific and measurable goals. Some of the earlier stages are the following:

- Obtaining suitable computer hardware and software

- Familiarization with the chosen trading tools

- Finding a suitable broker

- Obtaining the right training

- Identifying a coach

- Growing a demo account

All these have to be done before the "live" trading takes place. Once your trading goes live, you need another set of plans that commits you to the "official trading hours", agreed risk, money management objectives, and so on.

In fact, money management is a subject within itself and that makes up a large part of your business plan. You have to figure out your approach to compounding, draw down, withdrawal of funds as a salary, multiple accounts, and so on.

3. The Physical Environment for Trading

When setting up your physical environment (i.e., your workspace, trading desk, and the necessary facilities), consider the following:

■ *Personal comfort*. Even a short time spent in an uncomfortable position can affect your ability to concentrate. You need to be following the ergonomic advice available for using a keyboard and screens. If you are comfortable and relaxed, you can give all your attention to your trading job.

  Make sure your working environment allows you to take regular physical breaks to stretch and bend. Believe it or not, this helps to keep the mind sharp. Consider temperature, light levels, and nourishment. You will not be at your best if you are too hot or cold, blinded by the sun, thirsty, or hungry.

■ *Noise levels*. Are you intending to trade in a place where noise from other people or machinery will be a nuisance? Research has shown that high noise levels have detrimental effects on a person's cognitive process and concentration (Göran Söderlund 2010). So, choose an environment where the noise levels are low at your workspace.

■ *Distractions and interruptions*. If you are working out of a home office, make sure other members of the family treat your trading time as seriously as you do. Arrange for someone else to take phone calls and answer the door while you are trading.

Make sure your technology hardware is up to the task. Here is a checklist to help with this:

■ *Fast Internet connection*. This is important if you want to take part in video conferencing or webinars.

■ *Sufficient screen space*. Many traders employ more than one screen.

■ *Computer with sufficient capacity*. A computer with reasonable performance (e.g., with fast processor, sufficient memory, large and fast enough disk) is essential. Streaming data from the web to go to the disk first before you can use it.

Make sure the software is up to the task, too:

■ Your choice of charting software must do everything you require.

■ Your trading platform, if different from your charts, should be easy to understand and use.

■ You need adequate note-taking and recordkeeping software.

■ The trading tools to assist you should run without a hitch.

4. The Broker

Due diligence is required to research the broker you choose to trade through. First, you must decide in which markets you will be trading and select a broker accordingly. For example, if you are trading stocks, find a full service or discount stock broker, depending on your needs. Futures trading requires working with a broker that offers futures contracts. Finally, forex brokers not only offer currencies but most provide contract for differences (CFDs) on commodities and stock indices, as well. There are also brokers that offer trading access to stocks, options, futures, forex, CFDs, ETFs, and bonds through one account and trading platform.

Second, research how capitalized the broker is to make sure your money is secure and the firm can endure through all market cycles.

Third, look at the costs involved and the margin requirements for the markets you plan to trade.

5. The Trading System and Strategies

It is impossible to be consistent unless you have a trading system and know it well. Your trading system may consist of a number of different strategies that apply to different market conditions. You need to be familiar with these. Don't worry if you are unsure about this now. Chapter 9 of this book will guide you on this.

6. The Money Management Strategy

The money management strategy is one of the most important parts in your business plan. It should cover the following considerations:

- The maximum percent risk you are prepared to accept across all trades

- The maximum percent risk you are prepared to accept for a single trade

- The rules for moving your stop loss to break even

- The rules for breaking the rules (advanced trading only)

Chapter 10 of this book walks you through planning the money management strategy.

7. The Psychological Preparedness for Trading

You must follow the rules of your system and each strategy therein. This involves patience and forming strong habits, and you must absolutely avoid making decisions based on emotion. You must develop the ability to recognize when you are about to make a decision that is not based on analysis, and put a stop to it immediately.

Trading is a waiting game. Your intention is to ambush the market when the conditions are right. If you are not patient and do not have the discipline to follow your rules, then you are a gambler and not a trader. Traders beware, you could earn large sums of money. Gamblers beware, the market will relieve you of your cash in an instant.

It might seem like it requires an overwhelming amount of effort from you to get yourself set up even before you start trading, but do not skimp on the effort for this. You owe it to yourself to give yourself the best chance of success. This level of readiness is essential, and attention to the points outlined above will surely help you on your way.

What Kind of Trader Do You Want to Become?

As we have reached the end of this chapter, ask yourself if you now have a clear idea of what a "technical junkie" is versus what an Entrepreneurial Trader is, and what kind of trader you want to become? Are you clear about the preparations you need to do before you jump into the trading business with both feet?

Now we are ready to cut into the *meat* of this book.

Habit #1 will be presented to you right after the first episode of another key content of this book: the Pendulum Scenarios.

Pendulum Scenario 3.1: Fear versus Greed

"Be fearful when others are greedy. Be greedy when others are fearful."
—Warren Buffett

Fred was still undecided. He must have been staring at his screen for two hours, hesitating whether he should take action or just wait. Since he had first spotted the indication that the market was coming to the end of its downward trend and would soon turn bullish, he had been fixated on the real-time chart.

His analysis was telling him not to delay buying this market anymore. The trend reversal could happen anytime soon, and by hesitating, he might miss the entry point. Fred had a certain confidence in his analysis. After all, he spent one whole year immersed in the methodology and rigorously testing it on paper. He had done everything within his means to prove to himself that he had in hand a "lethal trading strategy" that he could rely on to produce laser-like accuracy in analysis, trade after trade.

But he wasn't entirely sure now. It was not his analysis that he had doubts about. It was something else.

An Outrageous Trade Plan

For this month, Fred had set a high earning target, and expected himself to stake a large sum of capital to achieve it. Half a month had passed and he had only hit around 30 percent of the target. Seeing himself running short of time, he figured that the best plan was to focus on taking a few trades only and aim at making the most profit out of each trade.

This worked at first. Fred ripped the market apart and analyzed it, and confirmed over and over before he entered any trade. And when he did, he risked a sum of money so large that it gave him cold sweats every time. "High risk, high return" he reasoned. And it was a "calculated risk" anyway, so he assumed he would have no worries.

The results were encouraging. Fred managed to reap good profits for the first few trades and was on his way to achieving more than 65 percent of his monthly target. At this rate, he would not be far from exceeding his monthly target in another week.

When the First Major Loss Hit

On Wednesday that week, the market moved in the opposite direction soon after it "lured" him in with what seemed to be an unmistakable uptrend move. Soon after Fred poured in his capital, it went wayward.

Shocked by this sudden turn of events, Fred was at a loss. His chart clearly screamed at him that his analysis was inaccurate, but he was in denial. After all, the consecutive wins in the week were the best proof that his plan worked. His analysis was also definitive, and his strategy robust or so he thought. And he could not make sense out of the subsequent market behavior that unfolded before his eyes.

To make matters worse, he was naive enough to suppose that if he gave the market some time, it would adjust itself to fit into his expected pattern. Sure enough, the market did not please Fred; rather, it plummeted all the way down, way past his imagined stop-loss level (which he had not actually set). But still holding on to some hope, he refused to take action to protect his capital.

When he finally did throw in the towel, he had taken a big hit. With just one trade, he lost 63 percent of the profit he made this month, thus widening the gap between his target income and his profit. Stress was building up again, and he felt remorseful for his reluctance to react to the unexpected situation. But remorse was not the only emotion that overwhelmed him. Another threatening emotion quietly crept in.

The Emotion that Paralyzed Him

It was fear. Fred had not set up any other trade since his last grievous loss. Losing 63 percent of his profit in one trade was a major hit.

He was in fear that the market would behave irrationally again, beyond reason. Whenever he was presented with an opportunity to enter a new trade, he hesitated. He was in fear that his analysis was pointing him in the wrong direction again. Worse, he started to doubt his capability as a trader, as he just witnessed his own indecisiveness in making the right decision at the right time.

So there he was, staring at the screen, paralyzed, and not entering any trade again. He was not doing just nothing. In fact, whenever he saw an indication that a trend move was brewing again, he performed his due diligence to study and restudy the daily chart, weekly chart, and even monthly chart. He wanted more confirmations before he launched into another trade. He would not forgive himself for making another mistake. He could not take another loss.

And he ended up being paralyzed by analysis and took no action. He was in fear.

Trader in Her Fever Mode

Four consecutive wins later, Stacey realized what she was in: a so-called *winning streak*.

She knew that it was not entirely luck. She had spent the past few days and nights watching the market, patiently waiting for the market move to set up. When the right time to enter the market struck, she took the right position size, placed a sensible stop loss that she vowed to obey (even though she was nowhere near her stop loss level throughout the trade), and exited the market when her profit target was met. Rinsing and repeating the same steps for all four trades, she made heart-throbbing profits every time.

Maybe the market was proving to her that her analysis, strategy, and trading system worked. Maybe she had accumulated enough skills and experience. Or maybe some luck was at play. Stacey reckoned that the market was on her side, and wanted to strike while the iron was still hot.

A Decision Beyond Reason

She felt unstoppable and intended to increase her position size and adjust her stop loss to an aggressive one. That went outside the parameters of her trading plan, but she was prepared to take the risk. "Just one more trade! I need to win just one more trade, and that's it!" she thought.

So, she was all eyes on the market and waited to enter her fifth trade. When the market showed that an end of trend and a reversal was imminent, she got herself ready to pull the trigger. Her heart started to race as she thought about the position size she was going to take, which was disproportionate to what her analysis instructed. That was impulsive, she realized. It was almost like a gamble, but it was one that she did not think she could lose since luck was on her side and she had won four trades in a row.

Deep down inside however, something kept reminding her that she was doing the wrong thing.

Fear and Greed

At some points in our trading journey, we were all Fred or Stacey. Fear and greed are the two most powerful emotions that can overcome a trader's logical reasoning and confidence in trading. Just think of how many times doubtful thoughts immobilized you when your analysis told you to enter a trade. Or how some senseless false hope prevented you from cutting a loss even though it was obvious that the market was not in your favor. Finally, how you relied on your gut feeling to place a position size that was not supported by your analysis, expecting to make more money out of your trade.

These could all be caused by fear and greed.

Nonetheless, these two emotions are not always bad. They can be a barrier to your success and your motivator. Traders who have a reasonable amount of fear are cautious. Fear is what causes them to confirm their analysis over and over before making trading decisions. Fear halts them and forces them to reconsider before gambling their money away. And fear reminds them to be more careful during the next trade after they suffer a loss.

On the other hand, greed is a motivator that makes a trader trade. It often pushes the trader to go beyond the mental boundary that he set for himself to achieve more. The right amount of greed is necessary because it moves a trader forward in his trading journey and allows him to grow.

Fear and greed coexist in trading. Not only do they drive the market dynamics in general, but they also affect every trader on a personal level. We all fear losing and yearn for making more out of our trades at the same time.

These two emotions are at the two ends of a pendulum swing. Each individual has a different risk-reward tolerance, and therefore a different tolerance level for fear and greed. The key to succeed in any trade is to position yourself somewhere in the middle of these two extreme emotions, maintain a balance between them, and not let one of them overcome you.

Tips to Tempering Fear and Greed

Here are three tips that can help you to temper your fear and greed:

1. Instead of focusing on the money, learn to appreciate the rewards of trading.

   - To most successful traders, trading is not only about making money. The process of applying prudent analysis on the market, objectively and accurately forecasting the move based on the understanding of human psychology and the economy, taking the most fitting actions in a snap, managing inflow and outflow of money, and so on, can all offer an enormous sense of intellectual fulfilment to traders.

- The trading process can be quite enjoyable if skills are learned and the markets are respected. It does not matter whether you are making a winning or losing trade today because every trade can be treated as a lesson. There is always another trading day.

- In the long run, if trading is run as a business, the profits will come.

2. Trade with money you can afford to lose and manage the risk so you can accept the worst-case scenario of every trade taken. Understand the risk before a trade is taken and sign off on it.

3. Develop or adopt a proven trading system. When you execute your trade, trust your system and follow it to the tee. This will help from being overcome by fear and greed.

PART II

Out of Hobby into Business Mode

CHAPTER 4

Habit #1: Establish a Trading Business for the Right Reasons

39

Todd Murphy glanced at his watch and realized that it was already 8:30 p.m. He quickly took a sip of his cappuccino, rushed to the sink, and splashed cold water on his face. Some instant refreshment was what he needed after a long day.

He had just ended a long and tedious appointment and had to get ready for the next one. Todd was a personal financial planner, specializing in retirement planning. His weekday nights never ended before 10:30 p.m., and most weekends were also lost to appointments. For the past few months, he had hardly taken any breaks.

He was physically exhausted, but the sense of fulfillment from his job was the reason he kept going. He remembered what he had gone through just six months earlier.

The Negative Motivator

Six months ago, Todd realized he no longer found meaning in his job. He did not understand why he could allow himself to be bound to the office chair when his real strength and interest were in interacting with people and helping them to solve their problems. His job was not paying him well either. Despite the hours he dedicated to his work, he was earning barely enough to cover his expenses. And it was close to impossible to save for rainy days.

An infamous slave driver, his boss would spare no thought to squeezing every drop of energy out of her employees. She thought unless she micromanaged them, she would not get the best returns for every cent she paid them. Every minute at work had to be accounted for, and every minute had to be a productive minute. What Todd found uncomfortable was the scheming look his boss maintained throughout the year and the disturbing aura that she constantly exuded. With this kind of atmosphere around her, who dared to say no to her?

Eventually, Todd did. When he was introduced to the job of a retirement planner—its career perspective, the freedom to control his own life, the opportunity to help people who need help, and the attractive remuneration—his eyes brightened. It was everything he was looking for.

■ Reasons for His Fight

Todd still felt tired after his brief wash but felt better after gulping down the remaining coffee in the cup. He was ready to run again.

He had good reasons to work his tail off. He had fought his way out of the cubicle nation and would defend his freedom with every ounce of energy left. This job offered everything he wanted out of a fulfilling career.

■ What Excites Successful Traders (It's Not All about the Money)

Successful traders are clear about why they launched their trading career.

Undeniably, the possibility of earning good money for less work is the number one motivator for most, but it is never the only motivator. Successful traders are also inspired by the following:

- The intellectual challenges that trading offers.

- The possibility of getting in the market with a sum of money, and out with it multiplied.

- The freedom to have a say—usually, the final say—on what career they want, as well as how, where, and when they want to do it.

- The exciting career perspective and somewhat heightened social status that comes with the glamorous title of a professional trader.

Each trader might be excited by a different combination of reasons. What about you? Do you know why you are in the trading business? Do you have solid reasons to be doing what you are doing now?

The Main Reasons Why Traders Are Traders

Figure 4.1 shows you six main reasons why traders get into the trading business. You might be a new trader who has not found his stride in trading yet. At this stage, money may be your sole motivating factor. Or you are not even sure why you are in this business. Take a look at these reasons. They will change your perception about trading.

On the other hand, if you know your reasons, you are still encouraged to compare them to these six reasons. This exercise will remind you of the aspirations you once held (or still hold), and refresh your motivation as it gives you new insights into the reasons why you are still in this business.

Financial Independence

As a trader, your income is not fixed. This means the following:

- *You pay yourself.* The bad news is you have to earn every cent yourself and will not receive money for checking Facebook or Twitter during office hours. The good news is if you dedicate more time and effort to your trading business and they turn out to be productive hours, you will be paid fairly.

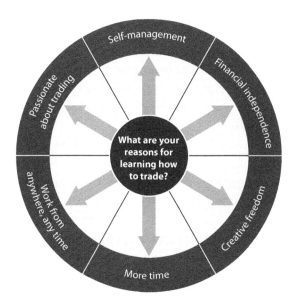

FIGURE 4.1 Six main reasons why traders get into the trading business

- *You are responsible for how much you earn.* There is no boss to whom you can beg for an increase. You no longer need to worry about pay restructuring. No one else has a say on how much you should be paid but yourself. If you want a pay raise next month, you can work hard toward it, and give it to yourself!

- *You can decide when you get the money you need.* Need an additional $1,000 this month? You can earn it. Now you do not just get extra pay during the bonus payout season but virtually any month of the year if your trading business goes well. You don't even have to be paid only at the end of the month as you are free to stagger your income withdrawal to a few times in a month. You also enjoy the freedom to decide if you want to focus your work this month to earn sufficient income, so you can take the next month off.

Trading can provide you with the financial independence that fixed-income earners can only dream about. No wonder the earning potential is the biggest motivating factor for most traders. Nevertheless, here are some words of warning: Although as a trader, there is no ceiling as to how much you can earn, there is also no floor as to how much you can lose. It is possible for traders not to earn money for months, or even lose their capital within a short time span.

It takes skills and dedication to excel in trading. Traders should not view financial independence to be a promise that trading offers. (There is no guarantee!) The truth is, trading is a risky business. If a trader cannot stomach the risks, he should resist the temptation to be lured into trading by the potential financial independence. In fact, he should not be trading at all!

Self-Management

A trader is on her own. She is her own boss and her own employee simultaneously. She takes orders from no one and is, thus, not accountable for how she spends her time, or how well or miserable her performance is. No one will scream at her for the mistakes made, and no one is going to give her a pat on the shoulder when she has done well.

She can choose to work with anyone she likes or not work with anyone at all. She can follow the working style that suits her best and not follow some set-in-stone archaic company policy if she doesn't want to. She can even design a flexible work schedule to fit into her personal calendar.

To do well, a trader has to wisely manage herself and her resources (e.g., money, energy, time). She has to set her performance targets and motivate herself to achieve them. The perks received when trading goes well, and the financial (and emotional) penalties that resulted from losing, are all her responsibility, not anyone else's.

If these scenarios describe you, *self-management* is one of your reasons why you want to become a trader.

Passionate about Trading

Not many things are more rewarding than spending our waking hours working on something we can call a passion. Many successful traders dedicate hours and hours honing their craft to near perfection, plastering their eyes to the computer screen all day long to study charts, and reading financial journals and online articles until late into the night, not because they are forced to but because they enjoy doing it.

Because of their love for trading, some successful traders landed in this business. Passionate traders can usually go a long way on their trading journey. To some of them, money has even become a side product that comes along when they do what they are passionate about.

Work from Anywhere, Any Time

Perhaps you cannot hold a day job because of a family commitment; you might have decided to start a lifelong backpacking trip, and no company in the world will allow you to work away from the office; or you are just tired of being deskbound for 40 hours a week. That is why you choose to earn a living by trading, a career that allows you to work from anywhere at any time.

With the advancement of technology, trading offers you the freedom to choose your working location and hours. All you need is dedicated work hours in a day or a week, a working computer (or just a smartphone), a reliable Internet connection, and on top of that, a robust business plan, lots of self-motivation, and strong self-discipline.

Being able to work from anywhere also means you do not need to spend hours commuting to work. For many traders, all it takes is a short walk from their kitchen to their work desk to start their day. You are free to work in the comfort of your dining room, a cafe, or even on your bed. If you choose not to, you do not need to dress up for work. It is possible to reap huge profits trading in your pajamas!

More Time

In today's modern world, our occupations can take a big bite into our life. It seems the higher up one moves, the more demanding the time requirement becomes. In most well-paying jobs, if you are not totally dedicated to the job, it is hard to advance.

This is not entirely true of trading. While most dedicated traders spend a big chunk of their daily life on their business, too, they do enjoy the prerogative to schedule their days to suit their lifestyles.

A trader's performance is not judged by the number of hours she spends staring at her screen or being tied to her office chair, but by hard numbers, meaning the profits she makes. A trader who is skillful at managing her business and life might be able to free up more hours to do the things she wants: taking care of her family, pursuing a hobby, getting herself trained on other skills, or even running another business.

Some words of advice here to ground you back to reality: Yes, it probably does not require you to be glued to your seat all day long to be successful, but trading does require attention, no matter whether you are doing it full-time or part-time. A trading session ranges from several minutes to many hours. When you trade, make sure you spend your time fully dedicated to your trading.

Just remember, as well as you can pocket good money within minutes from trading, you can also lose it within minutes. Unless you devote constant surveillance and make sure everything is properly in place during your trading session, success can be far-fetched for you.

Creative Freedom

Trading is not about being "right" but about bringing in money to your account. It is not as constraining as some jobs, where there is only one right way to do things, standard operating procedures to follow, or rigid steps to follow to eliminate chances of errors (which kill the expression of creativity at the same time).

There is no *one* right way to trade or *one* way to trade successfully. Traders are encouraged to explore and find the trading style and strategy that fit their personalities the best. As their skills mature, with experience and innovation, they are free to modify the current trading systems or even develop ones for themselves, to fit into their unique needs.

It is for this creative freedom that some traders love trading.

■ What Are the Reasons You're Trading?

After reading these main reasons why traders are in the trading business, it is time that you ask yourself this question:

"What are the reasons I am trading?"

Trading is never smooth sailing. More often than not, it is a bumpy ride with stormy weather looming. There are times you feel exhausted after a long day at work, down as your win/loss ratio drops or anxious when you start losing money and the situation is not improving. Before you give up, remember your reasons for entering the trading business. It will give you a jolt of motivation to persevere until the gloom is over.

As with Todd, the financial planner that we talked about in the beginning of this chapter, he reminded himself of his reasons not to give up. You might not have the same convenience of having the image of an ex-boss's scheming face to remind you that you cannot afford to fail, but everyone is motivated by something.

◼ Pendulum Scenario 4.1: Get Rich Quick or Go Broke Quick

> *"Get-rich-quick schemes are for the lazy and unambitious. Respect your dreams enough to pay the full price for them."*
>
> —Steve Maraboli

Fred read in a trade magazine about how some traders entered the trading business with only a few hundred dollars in their accounts and expected to make big dollars with this small amount of capital. The report said that some of them were even hoping they could achieve financial freedom within the span of one or two years.

Every once in a while, reports like this would make headlines. Readers eventually lost interest in these stories. Fred wondered why reporters still continued to write get-rich-quick articles.

What Trading Is Not

"Fat hope they have," he scoffed at these traders unreservedly when he thought about how naive they were. "What do they think trading is? A get-rich-quick scheme?"

He was well-aware it is not. In fact, he read a list of "what trading is not" before he became a trader, and wholeheartedly embraced every point in the list:

1. *Trading is not for anyone who cannot lose money.* That means if a person has only enough money to afford his living expenses, pay his credit card bills, or give to his family, he should use the money to buy his meals, pay his bills, or afford his family expenses and not to use it for trading. He should also not use the savings he has for emergency or special occasions (e.g., savings for the arrival of his baby, his child's education fund, or health insurance fund) for trading. And the worst advice? Borrow money to trade. In short, a trader must only trade with money that he can afford to lose.

2. *Trading is not for anyone who does not have enough money to trade.* No one should start trading with an account with only a few hundred dollars and dream of making tons of money from trading. Fred read that to be earning real money from trading, one needs to have at least $10,000 that he can afford to lose in his trading account. "To make money, you have to have money first," he concluded.

3. *Trading is not a sure-win game.* No one should enter any trade expecting he can definitely make profit from it. No matter what the trading gurus claim, no trading strategy or system can guarantee winning. In fact, the only thing that is guaranteed in the trading world is losing. All traders lose money regularly; the difference is those who survive the game and even "make it big" either win

more often or win more money than they lose. It is impossible to expect anyone to be winning all the time.

4. *Trading is not for perfectionists.* As mentioned above, trading involves losses. It is also unavoidable for traders to make mistakes in their analysis and trade execution. What is more important for them is to learn from their mistakes, and not repeat them. Considering that mistakes and losses are part and parcel of trading, perfectionists might have a hard time adjusting to trading. If they cannot accept the mistakes they make and move on, they will not progress in trading.

5. *Trading is not for those who are afraid of making wrong decisions.* It is not for those who seek to "get it right" in the decisions they make. The ultimate goal of the game is to be profitable and not to be making right decisions all the time, which the trader can go brag to his friends about. It is not unusual for a trader to be wrong 70 percent of the time but still make money in the end.

Trading Is NOT a Get-Rich-Quick Scheme

More importantly, Fred appreciated that trading is not a get-rich-quick scheme. A get-rich-quick scheme usually promises that everyone can generate an avalanche of money, sometimes from a tiny amount of capital. But trading is different. For trading, it takes money to make money. Think of making a return on your investment, which is the capital at risk. With interest rates at rock bottom levels, investors are thrilled with a 10 percent return on capital. So, why should traders with get-rich-quick mentalities expect to double and triple their capital in a short period of time?

Moreover, no trader should expect to make quick money from trading. Trading is not easy, and it takes years of conscientious practice to master the necessary skills. It also takes developing positive habits to succeed in trading. There is no shortcut to this, and no one should dream about getting rich overnight by stepping into the trading business.

Fred understood all these points, and he despised those who treat trading as a get-rich-quick scheme as they give the industry a bad name. He learned his lesson from a painful experience he had when he was a new trader.

Going Broke Quickly

There was a period of time when Fred was misguided about the true meaning of the famous saying in the trading world, "Trading is a numbers game."

The instruction manual that came along with the new trading system promised a certain win/loss ratio. All he needed to do was to take enough trades, and the probability would be in his favor. There would be some losses, as there are trading any system, but the profits he made would eventually outweigh the losses.

Fred was a newbie trader then and thought the experts behind this system were credible. He trusted everything that the promoter said and was sold on the idea of entering as many trades as possible to take advantage of the win/loss ratio without much investigation.

The excitement began right from the first trade taken. Fred followed the system, and entered a trade when all the entry rules were hit. The system required him to take a position size that was larger than what he could stomach and push his risk level from the usual 1 percent to 5 percent. He felt a twinge of uneasiness having to trade this way, but having unexplainable faith in the system, he did it anyway.

He was also bothered by how he was asked to get out of the trades once "some" profits were made and quickly enter another trade again. Analytically, he knew that if he held his positions for a longer time, he would reap higher profits. But the system kept asking him to get out of trades early, claiming that "trading small but trading fast" is the way he could enjoy a high win/loss ratio and make money quickly from the market.

Of course the win/loss ratio was high. But did he make money at the end? No. All it took was a handful of losses to wipe out all the money he won from the winning trades.

Applying the system for just two days had caused Fred to go broke for the rest of the month. The instruction manual that gave him the bad advice ended up in the garbage can by the second day. Fred learned a good lesson from this experience. From then on, he started steering clear of systems that make "too good to be true" claims and promise a get-rich-quick trading method.

▪ Pendulum Scenario 4.2: Realistic versus Unrealistic Trader

> *"I have to be realistic about what I can and can't do. So whatever I do has to really be worth it. I like to master the things I do."*
>
> —Queen Latifah

A new trading system was taking the traders in the city by storm.

On the advertisement, the trading guru behind this system spun a story of how a group of part-time traders who were all retirees had been secretly using this "underground trading system" to multiply their retirement accounts. It was after much effort that the guru was able to reverse-engineer their system, and for the benefit of all traders, he was willing to let the secret out even though the veteran traders were violently protesting against this.

The system had a fancy name called the "little guy's way" to grow a trading account. It advocated that a trader only needed to achieve a 0.9 percent profit every day, and by the end of the first four months, he would be on his way to doubling his account size. The account would be doubled again in another four months, and again in four more months, and so on.

The most amazing thing was that the system was talking about less than a 1 percent daily profit. That didn't sound too difficult! Moreover, the system laid out every step the trader needed to take to achieve the profit target, specified the time of day that he should trade, what he should be trading, and how much he should trade.

A safely guarded trading secret that a closed group was afraid to leak. A methodology by which even retirees could achieve success. A promise of consistent daily profits. A workable system to double a trading account every four months. Plus, a complete trading system that was formulated by a famous trading guru. These claims were too irresistible for traders to pass up. No wonder the sign-up rate skyrocketed. What's more, the guru later announced that he would only take in a limited number of students and vowed not to open up more seats until the following year. This created a nice level of commotion among the traders as they rushed to sign up.

The Traders' Reactions toward the System

Fred got excited by this announcement of the new system and handed in his subscription fee at just a glance of the advertisement, like everyone else.

But not Stacey. For a short moment, Stacey was tempted to find out about the system, too. But when she looked more closely at the promises, she knew she could safely ignore this offer.

A quick calculation told her so. Given that Stacey traded only on weekdays, 0.9 percent of return everyday would compound to 4.58 percent per week. In other words, at this rate, by the end of the year, Stacey's account would have grown around 8 times. As much as Stacey wished to achieve this kind of growth for her account, it did not appear to be realistic. In addition to that, the system promised a consistent profit every day. She knew it was beyond any system in the world to do that, so she did not take the system seriously.

Fred looked at it differently. He went into a frenzy over this. Earlier in the week, he thought he had tired of his current trading system, and it was time to cast it away. And by coincidence, he chanced upon this new system. "Coincidence, or is it the *law of attraction?*" Fred thought. Either way, this was a new light he saw in his trading business.

Reaping a 0.9 percent profit every day seemed so achievable to him. "It's not even 1 percent! Surely it won't be difficult, right?"

The advertisement was illustrated with a full-colored diagram depicting how a trader's account can double every four months just by growing it at 0.9 percent a day with compounding. Fred was sold on this idea. He was amazed by how this system broke down a task that previously seemed so farfetched into a series of small steps that he could take every day. He rubbed his hands together with anticipation as he was waiting for the course package to arrive at his home by courier.

But if he had taken a few steps to analyze the claims in the advertisement, he would have realized how unrealistic they were and might not be so excited anymore.

Unrealistic Expectations of a New Trader

Fred could be habitually unrealistic about his expectations. He had shown this trait since the beginning of his trading business, as when he planned for his earning targets. He set out to replace the monthly salary of $7,500 within half a year. Table 4.1 shows how he broke down his milestones but he left out an important element: his starting capital.

Moreover, these milestones were not set according to any published statistics but based purely on Fred's own vision and his trust of his capability. He figured that it was reasonable to start with the $1,000 target because this was the minimum performance he would expect. Thereafter, the earnings must grow at a rate of at least $1,000 per month, again, because he would not expect less from himself.

With all the prior study and paper trading he had done before making the leap out of his day job, he felt he had prepared himself well and was full of confidence that with full dedication to his trading business, he could be on his way to replacing his complete income within six months.

But in reality, did that happen? No, far from it. Fred's first miss of the targets happened in the second month, and he was not able to catch up on the subsequent milestones. As he repeatedly missed his target, he grew more lenient on himself and accepted missing the targets as his reality.

Eventually, setting targets or goals but not having the discipline and determination to achieve them became his habit. This jeopardized his trading business.

TABLE 4.1 Fred's Milestones to Replace His Income	
1st month:	$1,000
2nd month:	$2,000
3rd month:	$3,500
4th month:	$5,000
5th month:	$6,000
6th month:	$7,500

Realistic Expectations of a New Trader

Stacey researched well and did thorough planning before she launched her trading business. She chose a low starting profit target of $1,500 a month and aimed to hit this target in the first three months.

She took into consideration the amount of time she could devote to her trading business, the initial capital she started with, her risk appetite, her trading capability, the expected profits the trading plan could produce, and so on, when she set this target.

It took her well over three months to reach that target, but she was OK with that because she understood that the profit target was only a reference, and that a gap might indeed exist between her target and actual goals.

After hitting the first earning milestone, she then pumped up the target higher, but still kept it within a realistic range. She learned along the way and fine-tuned her trading plan to help her achieve the target.

At the end, after repeating this process several times, and with strong determination, guidance from a qualified coach, and support from her family and peers, she finally managed to replace the last-drawn income from her previous job in slightly more than one year.

This would not have been possible had she not set realistic goals for herself.

CHAPTER 5

Habit #2: Complete a Trader's Business Plan

In his book *Think and Grow Rich*, Napoleon Hill said, "Wishing will not bring riches. But desiring riches with a state of mind that becomes an obsession, then planning definite ways and means to acquire riches, and backing those plans with persistence which does not recognize failure, will bring riches" (Hill 1937).

That same wisdom can be applied to trading. Just wishing will not bring success to a trader. To be successful, a trader has to have an obsessive desire for success, have a definite plan with actionable steps to achieve it, and take massive action with persistence that does not recognize failure.

Successful traders know this well. They have a habit of clearly defining the goals for their trading business and setting up a business plan to guide their actions. In this chapter, we will discuss the habit of defining goals. For now, let's take a look at how establishing a trader's plan will help you succeed in your trading.

To begin, we will address a few important questions.

■ "Why Do I Need a Business Plan?"

Why do you need a business plan? You need one for many reasons, but here are nine good ones:

1. To take the time to thoroughly consider your view, right and wrong, about trading and your trading business.

2. To check your expectations: Are they realistic or mostly idealistic?

3. To clarify the reasons you are in this business. Your strong reasons will carry you through the highs and lows in trading, giving you a better chance to persevere during stormy times.

4. To establish your mission and vision and internalize them.

5. To honestly assess your personality, strengths, and weaknesses.

6. To dissect your current financial standing and plan for growth once you start your trading business.

7. To decide the trading strategy and system that you will use.

8. To foresee the financial, technical, and emotional hurdles that you will face when your trading business is in operation.

9. To define the metrics you will use to test your trading system and measure your performance.

All in all, you have to have a blueprint. Your trading business is not on autopilot just because you are clear about your destination and are steering your business toward it.

■ "But What if I Don't Have a Trader's Business Plan?"

What if you don't have a trader's business plan? The short answer is this: Many uncertainties may arise along your trading journey. If you have not given your trading business a thorough planning before you launch it, in the face of such challenges, you might be paralyzed or end up making emotional decisions that you will regret later.

The longer answer is this: If you do not have a trader's business plan ready before you start your trading business, four things might happen:

1. *You will forever be in the trial-and-error mode.* You will always be doubtful of the analysis methodology you employ, busy jumping from one trading strategy to another and endlessly experimenting with system after system.

2. *You will not be able to manage your money as well.* There will not be a proper strategy to protect your account when you run into a disaster; heck, you might not even be able to detect it when it is happening right before your eyes! Consequently, your capital will be at risk early on.

3. *You will trade when you are "in the mood" to trade.* You will not dedicate 100 percent attention when you trade. There is no system to hold yourself accountable for

your wins and losses. You do not manage yourself properly. Since you are the only player in your business, when you fail, your business fails, too.

4. *There will be no accurate way to track your performance.* You will not exactly know how to account for your gains and losses in your account. Your trading performance is likely to stay stagnant since you will not be able to objectively measure that performance based on your trading strengths and weaknesses.

■ "What Should My Business Plan Cover?"

Your trader's business plan should cover four main aspects of your business: the *what*, *how*, *why*, and *when* as illustrated in Figure 5.1:

What: Establish your realistic trading goals and objectives.

How: Propose a series of actions to reach your goals. Define your trading tactics and strategies.

Why: What are the reasons for your business? Why are you trading this year?

When: What are your milestones, and by when will you accomplish them?

Make your business plan a holistic approach to trading and to life. Think about incorporating your plan into your daily life to really make it work.

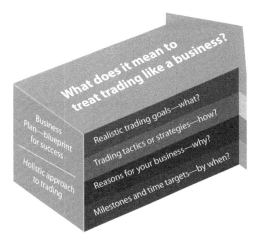

What does it mean to treat trading like a business?

Business Plan—blueprint for success

Holistic approach to trading

Realistic trading goals—what?

Trading tactics or strategies—how?

Reasons for your business—why?

Milestones and time targets—by when?

FIGURE 5.1   What should a trader's business plan cover?

■ "How Do I Set up My Trader's Business Plan?"

So how do you set up your business plan? First of all, don't be intimidated by the idea of having to plan for your trading business. You do not need a complicated,

90-page plan. It just needs to be comprehensive enough to cover all the aspects of your business. You don't need to follow a strict format. If you want to skip any parts that you find in a formal business plan (e.g., the table of contents, executive summary, and business overview), you can because it is just for your own use!

There are explicit steps taught by business schools in setting up a business plan. You can choose to follow their highly systematic and research-intensive way to plan your trading business (information on this is just a few Google searches away from you). Or if you prefer to have a simple plan that works, you can follow the FX Trader's EDGE™ nine-step business planning process.

■ Nine Steps in the Business Planning Process

Each step deals with an aspect you need to consider when you start your trading business.

Step 1. Establish Your Goals

You must know why you are in the trading business and what you want to get out of it. As an Entrepreneurial Trader, you have to make your short- and long-term goals as clear as possible. This allows you to focus your attention, time, and energy on what you want to achieve so you are not getting into the business blindly and walk on the path of trading blindly. Besides determining your financial goals, it also helps for you to establish your business goals, personal goals, and development goals as a trader.

Step 2. Define Your Trading Personality and Preferences

At the beginning of this step, you need to ask yourself a series of questions that will help you to understand your trading personality. Perform an honest self-assessment of your strengths and weaknesses, what you like to see in yourself as a trader, how you plan to fit your trading business into your life, how well you manage your stress and emotions, whether your daily routine is helping your trading, and so on.

You will also want to ask yourself about your preferences for trading—for example, whether you prefer to do momentum, day, swing, or position trading—and why; what markets you like to trade in; which currency pairs, stocks, ETFs, indices or commodities are you targeting; and how much time you plan to trade every day and do you even plan to trade every day?

This knowledge of your personality and preferences will help you to determine your trading style.

Step 3. Define Your Trading System

Your planning gets "technical" at this stage. Following the previous steps, you should have a detailed description of how you want to trade, what you want to trade, and what you are targeting to get out of the trades. Now, you will define your trading strategy and tactics, profit and loss parameters, specific criteria for trade entry and exit, and stop-loss procedures.

When all these are clearly established, you will produce a *pro forma* estimate of your weekly, monthly, and yearly trading revenue and eventually estimate your return on investment from trading.

Step 4. Define Your "Typical Trading Day"

This is where you put your imagination to work. Visualize what your "typical trading day" looks like. Establish how you implement your trading system in a step-by-step manner from the beginning to the end. Walk through every step in the process as if you are putting it to use in a real trade. If you plan to make a certain number or types of trades every day, walk through each trade to its completion.

Besides getting your mind prepared for the real "battle" when you implement your trading system, having a mental dry run on how your system works might also help to capture any weakness in your system before you fire it off.

Step 5. Define a Performance Tracking System

Weekly and monthly, you need to track and analyze the performance of your trading strategy and yourself. Not only will this help you to plan for improvement accordingly, it can also be helpful for your self-accountability or help your coach to evaluate your trading performance.

You will identify the key performance tracking metrics most suitable for your trading system, as well as a methodology to collect and analyze the data. (Most trading platforms will already evaluate the trades taken through a built-in performance module.) Metrics that you can use for performance measurement include, but are not limited to, win/loss ratio, profit targets, ROI, and risk/reward per trade.

Step 6. Design a Reward and Learning System

Most committed traders are good at holding themselves accountable when things go wrong, but they forget to reward themselves when things go exceptionally right! As a trader, since you are your own boss, you are responsible to motivate yourself to keep going. A reward system provides you with constant self-motivation and self-recognition, to fuel yourself with the energy to move on in this journey.

In addition to that, you have to make it a point not to stop improving yourself. Write down regular and dedicated learning activities in your business plan and make learning an essential part of your business. You should also engage a coach or mentor no matter what level you are at, to receive guidance to shortcut the development of your trading business, objective insights of your performance, and external accountability.

Step 7. Establish Your Money Management Strategy

No matter how much capital you have in the beginning of your trading business, you might lose every cent of it if you do not have a robust money management strategy. Plan the amount of capital you set aside for trading, how you will set up your trading accounts, how many resources you will allocate to each trade, what your profit-taking strategy is, what your stop-loss plan is, and how you will preserve your capital.

Step 8. Plan for Steps to Maintain an Energetic Mind and Body

You will achieve your optimal trading performance when you trade "in the zone." You can only get into "the zone" and stay there when you have a clear head, a healthy body, and an active mind. All these are only possible when you insert work-life balance in your business execution.

Plan for that balance. Make positive affirmations, a healthy diet, exercise, sufficient rest and relaxation, and meditation part of your plan to help you achieve trading success.

Step 9. Plan for Your Work Environment and IT Infrastructure

You might be deskbound for extensive hours by your trading business, not only during your trading session but also when you perform your research, study, and planning. For the workplace setup to support the efficiency of your trading activities, you need to make sure that it is comfortable, safe, and free from distractions.

You will also need to plan within your budget to equip yourself with efficient IT infrastructure, including but not limited to your workstation, data feed sources, backup procedures, and so on. Get professional help if you are not familiar with this.

■ An Important Research Discovery That Can Help You Achieve Your Goals

Dr. Gail Matthew, a psychology professor at Dominican University of California, conducted research to find out how goal achievement is influenced by three factors:

Putting down the goals in writing; having written plans to achieve the goals; and being accountable for the goals (Gail Matthew 2014).

She divided 267 participants into the following groups:

Group 1: Participants were asked to think about what they wanted to achieve.

Group 2: Participants were asked to write down their goals.

Group 3: Participants were asked to do everything that Group 2 did, formulate plans to achieve them, and write them down.

Group 4: Participants were asked to do everything that Group 3 did, and send what they wrote to their friends.

Group 5: Participants were asked to do everything that Group 4 did, and report their weekly progress to their friends.

At the end of the study, it was found that on average:

- Participants who wrote down their goals achieved 64.4 percent of their goals, and those who did not achieved only 42.8 percent.

- Participants who did not have a plan accomplished only 51.8 percent of their goals, and those who did accomplished 63.6 percent of their goals.

- Participants who received external accountability achieved 76.0 percent of their goals; that's 21.3 percent more than those who did not.

You can see how having a plan, putting your goals and plans down in writing, and getting external accountability can help you accomplish what you set out to achieve.

Interestingly, similar observations can be seen in my coaching students: Those who have their goals and trader's business plans in writing consistently outperform those who operate "out of their heads." Here are five reasons why this is happening:

1. The process of putting the business plan in words forces us to clarify our thoughts.

2. When we are tangled in the decision-making process, it is natural for us to run away, thinking we will come back to it after some time. In reality, we don't go back and habitually make these decisions "as and when" we trade. Completing a business plan in writing forces us to make definite decisions no matter how difficult the process is.

3. We can regularly review the written goals and plans. This encourages us to take action.

4. We get to capture the *reasons why* behind the plan. This prevents us from constantly changing our mind on the decisions made.

5. Even if we do need to make changes to the plan, a written plan lets us understand the process we have been through and learn from it and not keep reinventing the wheel.

Those who remain accountable, whether to a coach, a trading group, or a trading buddy, consistently outperform those who don't.

Take Action!

Now that you have seen the benefits of having a business plan and how to set one up, it is time for you to take action and create your own trader's business plan. I created a *Trader's Business Plan Workbook* to guide you on this. Download the workbook at www.wiley.com/go/traderspendulum.

As mentioned above, there are nine steps in the trader's business planning process. The workbook provides accompanying instructions to walk you through these steps.

Also, in each of the following chapters in this book, you will find a section like *this*: "Take Action!" Each of these sections corresponds to a step to create your trader's business plan. Follow the guidance, and by the time you finish reading this book, you will have a complete business plan ready!

Remember, you have to write down your plan for maximum effect. Even if you are not entirely sure about everything you want in your trading business, plan it anyway. Just come out with a minimal plan to have something to begin with. It is perfectly okay to change it or add in more details later in your trading journey.

Don't just *read* this book. Take action!

▉ Pendulum Scenario 5.1: Clarity versus Muddled Thinking

"Children are remarkable for their intelligence and ardor, for their curiosity, their intolerance of shams, the clarity and ruthlessness of their vision."
—Aldous Huxley

One thing about being a self-manager is that one gets to manage his or her own time. Some use this to their advantage, and some to their disadvantage.

Stacy wore many hats. She was not only a stay-at-home mother, but also a wife, the manager of her house (the cleanliness of the house, the laundry, prompt payment of household bills, making sure the environment was absolutely safe for the baby, and countless other things, were all her responsibilities), a resident chef, and of course, a 24/7 personal attendant to her husband and baby.

A Trading Edge from the Disciplined Life

At first, Stacey thought it was crazy to even think that she could tackle so many tasks in a day, especially when she was also trading part-time. But the mad rush she went through in the first few weeks after her baby boy's arrival forced her to learn.

She learned to multitask and prioritize. She learned that being impatient about getting things done and fretting over every little small hiccup were only going to cause more damage and not help at all. More importantly, she learned that once she figured out a schedule for everything and abided by it with discipline, she could move from one task to another seamlessly, completing every one of them like a true pro.

Unexpectedly, the discipline to stick to her schedule gave her an additional edge in trading. Barring some rare case that kept her awake until midnight, she went to sleep early and woke up early. The schedule allowed her to get enough sleep almost every day. As a result, she felt energetic almost all day long. This level of energy was almost a luxury when she was in her previous job as she could only get little time to rest and the immense stress level easily exhausted her.

The now-healthy body and clarity of mind became her winning edge in trading.

Lack of Habits Ruined a Young Man's Life

Fred became the self-manager of his time, too, after he started trading full-time. He was single and did not have a family to tend to. All he needed to take care of were himself and his trading business.

On the first few days when he was in this business, he screamed to himself, "Freedom! Freedom!" He envisioned himself trading for a few hours a day, "closing shop" before evening, and starting to enjoy his leisure time for the rest of the day. Unfortunately, things were starkly different from his expectations. What he had imagined never happened even for just one day.

Strangely, in his previous job, Fred was a highly disciplined worker who turned up punctually, completed all his tasks neatly on time, and demonstrated laser-sharp concentration in getting the work done. But as the boss of his own trading business, Fred was no longer disciplined. On the first day in the business, when trying to plan out his life, he visualized what an "ideal day in trading" would be like: He would wake up early, start trading when the market opened, stop before the evening, go have some fun, and get to sleep early. Unfortunately, his plan was not realized.

His life became a mess after launching his trading business. Every day, he only started trading one or two hours after the market opened. He stayed at his "trader's desk" for extended hours even after the market closed, probably just to "feel less guilty" as he knew he had not been productive during the day. By the time he called it a day, it was usually late in the evening. Using the excuse that his day ended late, he rejected almost all his friends' invitations to meet up after work.

The only entertainment he got? Returning back to the "trader's desk" again, eating his dinner alone, and watching videos on YouTube for hours on the big screen he bought with the intention of making it easy for him to study charts. Most of the time, he watched program after program until late at night. And not surprisingly, he woke up late in the morning and missed the market open almost every day. For months, this was what he called his life.

The messy daily routine not only took a toll on him, but also severely affected his health. Now he felt tired easily. He was no longer the energetic man he once was. His poor habits affected his trading performance, too. After months of abusing his own body, he could no longer stay sharp and think clearly when he needed to. In fact, he was always in the muddled mind state.

Trading with Clarity of Mind

As a day trader, when taking a position, Stacey always looked at three time frames: the 15-minute, 5-minute, and 1-minute time frames. Additionally, she confirmed her directional view using Elliott Wave analysis with an hourly chart. When all three time frames were in alignment, she would be clear about the action that she needed to take. When they were out of sync, she stayed out of the market and waited.

Because the time frames she used were short, she needed to stay vigilant and have a clear mind when she traded and act without hesitation when the opportunities to trade surfaced. She had a whole checklist of things she did to identify high-probability trades, confirm them, and select the proper position sizes to take. She had to do these systematically and meticulously because a slip in any of these steps could mean profit loss.

All these were only possible when she was trading with a clear mind. She knew she had it, thanks to her need to stick to a strict routine with her son, which indirectly allowed her enough rest.

Trading with Muddled Thinking

Fred tried to stay sharp when he traded, too, but that was nearly impossible. The consistent lack of sleep, unhealthy lifestyle and diet habits, and negative emotions did not help his brain to function optimally. But he struggled. He tried squeezing out his reserved energy with artificial stimulants, such as, coffee and tea, regardless of the fact that he knew he would break down once the reserve depleted.

Lack of energy aside, he was also not organized in his trading business. For example, he maintained three live accounts and had not properly defined what each one was for; he had not studied the features of each of these accounts and was therefore, not maximizing trade execution; he lost focus easily, as he stretched himself too thin when he traded, trying to accomplish dozens of things at the same time.

All these practices did not allow him to think clearly, but still he dared to vow, "One day, I will become a successful trader, more successful than Stacey!"

■ Pendulum Scenario 5.2: Forgiving versus Angry Trader

"Anger makes you smaller, while forgiveness forces you to grow beyond what you were."

—Cherie Carter-Scott

Fred had become an angry man. He was losing on his trades, and witnessing his capital leaking to the market. The angrier he got, the more money he lost; the more money he lost, the angrier he got. Not admitting defeat, he continued trading even more furiously, and losing even more money.

Consequently, he trapped himself in the vicious cycle of anger and profit loss. He thought there was nothing he could do to salvage this situation. Is that so?

A Standard Operating Procedure to Deal with Anger

Although every experienced trader will agree that losing is part of the game, it is not hard to get traders to also agree that no one likes losing money trading.

Once, Stacey got really angry with the market. Confusing indicators were flying around, causing Stacey to make several costly mistakes in her analysis. The market refused to move according to her wish, and this was nothing short of maddening, not only because this had caused her to lose close to 3 percent of her total capital within hours, but because it was hurting her pride. That was the period during which Stacey wanted to prove to herself that she had attained a satisfactory level of trading competency, and the market was seemingly trying to prove otherwise.

Stacey could not take it anymore when her anger was overpowering. But like a miracle, a quick self-awareness moment flashed by and Stacey realized she had stopped thinking clearly about the market. That was when she decided to execute her standard operating procedure to deal with situations like this: taking a break from trading.

She exited all the remaining positions, closed the trading platform, switched off her monitor, left her workstation, and went out for a walk. She promised herself to not return to the workstation until her anger and other emotions had subsided. She thought it would only take her at most an hour, but after an hour, she could still clearly feel her anger.

As it was close to the market closing time, she decided to call it a day.

Paying Back at the Market, or Paying Back to the Market?

Fred would not agree with how Stacey handled the situation. To him, a lost day in trading was a lost day in making profits. He held the opinion that Stacey should have kept in the market and kept trading, trying to make back her loss, and not giving up before her trading session ended.

"Such an emotional decision," he chided. But was he right?

When it was Fred's turn to be trapped in the vicious cycle of anger and money loss, he indeed "practiced what he preached" and stayed in the market, desperately trying hard to recoup his losses but failed in every attempt. Sure enough, his anger went over the top, and he lost control.

The angry trader found himself taking additional trades impulsively to "show the market." In this state of mind, he could not think clearly, let alone plan his trades. He entered and exited trades so furiously as if he was launching an attack on the market, or taking what the trading world called *revenge trades*. But of course, this was a futile effort. The market was not a bit affected, but Fred himself was. Hard-earned money was thrown into the drain with Fred's irrational actions.

Forgiving Oneself—Let Bygones Be Bygones

When Stacey was back to trading the next day, after running away from it because of anger, she felt relieved. She was now in control, and anger was no longer steering her trading.

Although she lost money the day before, Stacey chose to let bygones be bygones. She had learned an important lesson from her emotional outburst and vowed to be more mindful of her emotions, but she did not have remorse about the money lost. Between blaming herself and forgiving herself, she chose the latter, and moved on.

"I don't choose to carry around emotional baggage anymore; it just cramps my style and steers me in the opposite direction from where I ought to go!" the wise trader commented. She chose to continue to grow in her trading.

How to Avoid Angry Trading

Stacey and Fred discussed how their anger took over the control of their trading, and came out with the following steps to prevent the same incident from happening again:

1. A trader has to be constantly mindful of the emotional state that he is experiencing, and be in the driver's seat instead of letting his emotions get the upper hand.

2. If he loses control, it might be a good idea to take a break or call it a day, and come back when the emotion subsides. There is no point in trading when he is overwhelmed by emotion, because he will not be able to stay focused, think clearly, and make appropriate trading decisions.

3. The trader has to suppress the desperation to win back or take "revenge trades" out of anger. He has to remember, when this happens, he is always the loser, and the market does not care how hard he is trying to hit back—the fact is, there is no way he can hit back.

4. The trader needs to temper the anger by forgiving himself and, if he thinks so, forgiving the market. He has to learn the lesson anyway, but move on. It will be a bright new session or day the next time he sits down at his trading desk.

5. Lastly, apply the same old wisdom in trading, which is, "Plan the trade and trade the plan." If he finds himself overpowered by his anger or emotions and cannot follow his trade plan anymore, he should do the right thing—and stay out of the market.

■ Pendulum Scenario 5.3: Courage versus Conformity

> *"Every man has his own courage, and is betrayed because he seeks in himself the courage of other persons."*
>
> —Ralph Waldo Emerson

"I wonder what other traders are saying about this stock," Fred thought as he held off his decision to trade because he needed to check his favorite online trading forums for fellow traders' opinions, "just to take a quick look to confirm my judgment."

But a "quick look" like this could sometimes sway his decision.

Following the Crowd

Fred was not lazy. He never cut corners in performing the required analysis when he was deciding which trades to take. As a former engineer, he knew he could trust his analytical skills and be confident with the results of his analysis. Still, he got butterflies in his stomach almost every time he needed to commit to a trading position.

Perhaps this was caused by his strong desire to be *right*, or his fear of losing money, or most probably both. Fred often wished he could find something to support his decision, or someone to agree with it, before he entered a trade. The easiest way to do that was to check out online forums to see what other traders were saying about the same stocks.

As a well-informed person, Fred knew he could not trust everything he saw there. But he always found it challenging to resist the temptation to alter his decision based on the active forum discussions. Everyone seemed to know what they were talking about, and everyone sounded so convincing. So, even if Fred was confident with his own analysis, he might sometimes consider following fellow traders' recommendations.

Trusting the Gurus

And it was not only fellow traders that Fred listened to. Fred was also a diehard fan of several famous trading gurus. Not only did he subscribe to every course and trading system under their names, but he also spent a few hours every day submerging himself in their websites, reading every word of authority from these experts.

To Fred, their opinions were not just opinions. They were more like instructions. These traders seemed to have a strange power over Fred, and he found it hard to go against their recommendations. This loyal follower of the gurus would follow whatever they said even when their advice went against his own judgment and trade plan.

Fred had unwavering faith in these experts. He did not understand where it came from either. It was not as if their advice had helped him win his first bucket of gold. He just trusted them.

Conforming to the Market

Like most dedicated traders, Fred kept a keen eye on the market. But unlike most accomplished traders, he allowed his trading decisions to be led by the market without first understanding the trend.

Fred commonly entered a certain trade because he observed an increasing number of traders undertaking the same action whether his analysis supported the trade or not. Equally common was when his analysis told him to trigger a trade and he did not because he saw the crowd was doing the opposite.

Besides, Fred took signals from institutional trading groups and fund managers too, wary that every move they made could possibly shake the market. He thought it was better to be safe and follow what they did although sometimes this went against his own prediction and his understanding of how the market worked.

The "Unshakable" Trader

Stacey was a hard-headed person. She was not easily affected. This personality showed up in her trading.

Like Fred, she did not spare any effort in analysis before deciding on every trade she took. She tended to want some confirmation for her decisions, too, so she would also visit traders' forums, read trading gurus' advice, and see what the crowd and the big players were doing. However, different from Fred, she did not blindly believe in what she learned from them.

As a matter of fact, when the information she received flew in the face of her analysis, having excessive confidence with her analytical skill, she would most likely become skeptical. Faced with opposing information, she would roll her eyes a bit and go ahead to run the same analysis she did again, not to prove herself wrong but to prove the information wrong.

Sometimes to make doubly sure, she would analyze the trade with a different methodology and overlay the result with her original analysis. For example, she often verified her Elliott Wave analysis with candlestick analysis. Looking at the same trade with a different lens and getting the same results gave her peace of mind.

Once she gathered enough confirmations to support her analysis, she would stick to her decision and pull the trigger without further hesitation. She then ignored the "peanut gallery" in the trading forums.

The worst that could happen would be a trading loss. But since she usually traded with a conservative position size using strict money management and had stop losses protecting her, losing was not an issue. Stacey knew she had the courage to make the appropriate move and not feel pressured into following fellow traders, heeding the trading gurus' advice blindly, or conforming to the market masses.

She knew she could confidently make her own decisions and stomach the outcome, no matter if it was good or bad.

The Opposite of Courage

Most people think the opposite of courage is cowardice, but this is not always true. When it comes to business, personal development—and yes, trading—the opposite of courage in most cases is conformity.

The majority of people do not have the courage to make independent decisions. They will look for a leader who decides for them and shows them what to do; they will follow his instructions and recommendations—sometimes with a disproportionate amount of faith. Or they will do what *everyone else* is doing, with perhaps the only reason being, "If so many people are doing it, it cannot be too wrong."

Blindly following advice and conforming to the market can be deadly in trading. Traders who do not make independent decisions, understand every move they choose to take, substantiate the information they receive with analysis and confirmations, and most importantly, have the courage to act according to their own judgment cannot go far in their trading business.

CHAPTER 6

Habit #3: Define Your Goals

The summer vacation was over, and Susie was going back to school. The night before, she tidied her school bag, selected her outfit, and even chose the hair band she wanted to wear the next day. The next morning, she woke up before the sun rose, talked with her mom over breakfast in a tone of hyper-excitement about the kids she was going to meet, and left home with a big smile on her face.

That was an encouraging start to her first day of junior high school, her mom thought. But she was shocked when her daughter came home crying. "What happened, Susie?" her mom asked, as she settled her down. "Did something bad happen? Did somebody bully you? Or was it your teacher?" Fortunately, it was none of those. Instead, Susie showed her mom the timetable and activity plan for that semester.

"There are so many subjects for me to take this year and so many activities. How am I going to manage, mom?" she sobbed. The perfectionist personality that she had inherited from her mother had put her under pressure. For the first time in many years, she displayed deep distress in her now teary eyes.

When her mom checked the timetable and activity plan, she immediately empathized with her daughter. There were indeed more subjects and extracurricular activities than Susie had ever taken before, but her mom knew she could handle it. All she needed to do was to set her priorities right, and make efficient use of her time. So Susie's mom gave her the best parental advice, "Set your goals, and do one thing at a time."

■ "How Did We Do That?"

Susie's mom's advice to her daughter brings us to the third habit of successful traders. But before that, let's equate what Susie went through with what we all did as students.

Remember when you were a high school student? Each year, you had to take at least eight subjects. The nature of the subjects were so varied that each required its own effort since the subject matter did not overlap. Regardless of the large amount of homework, you were still managing well. How did you do that? The following two main factors could be at play:

1. *We received help from our teachers.* They would set goals for us and guide us along the way to achieving them. We just needed to heed their guidance to advance us one small step at a time. With them holding our hands, we would eventually reach the goal.

2. *The grading system provided visible targets for us.* We had an idea of the kind of grades we wanted to achieve and knew how far we were from them. We could then gauge how much effort was required to get there and work accordingly.

And you might ask: How are they relevant to you as a trader?

■ Tackling the Subjects in Your Trading Life

Now that we have grown up, we lose the luxury of having teachers to hold our hands and lead us toward our goals, and unlike employees who are under supervisors or managers, we do not have someone to set goals for our trading business. As traders, we have to define our own destinations, and find our own ways to reach them.

Our goals are what we consciously or unconsciously set out to achieve in our life, in a relationship, in our career, and in all meaningful work. They provide a target that we can set our eyes on and a direction that we can move toward. Wise people have often said: Without knowing where we are heading to, we are heading to nowhere. This might sound clichéd, but it remains true generation after generation.

Successful entrepreneurs have a habit of setting goals: They envision the kind of profits they want to earn, the scale with which they want to grow their businesses, and the business areas they want to venture into. Successful traders have a habit of setting goals, too: They know what they want to achieve from trading, their short- and long-term development targets, and the kind of lifestyle they are going to achieve.

And you, as an Entrepreneurial Trader who runs your trading as a serious business, should set your goals, too, and let your trading journey be guided by your goals. How do you do that? I suggest you first ask yourself the following questions:

- Do you plan to trade part-time or full-time?

- What time of day will you set aside for trading on a consistent basis?

- What specific goals do you have about daily, weekly, and monthly profits?

- What trading strategy will you employ and what are the rules?

Let's look at each of them.

Do You Plan to Trade Part-time or Full-time?

The reason why you must decide is this: You need to plan your trading business around your life, and sensibly allocate time for your trading business. As I have repeatedly advocated in this book, when you execute your trading sessions, whether on a part-time or full-time basis, you need to be fully focused. You cannot be doing nine other things simultaneously because when your attention sways, you tend to make mistakes or miss profitable opportunities.

Deciding whether you will trade part-time or full-time also prevents you from becoming overambitious or underachieving: If you are trading part-time, you will not set targets that are beyond your means to fulfill within the limited hours you devote to trading each day; if you trade full-time, you ought to maximize your trading hours and go the extra mile to reach targets that you would not be able to otherwise achieve.

What Time of Day Will You Set Aside for Trading?

When you are trying to decide on the time of day you will set aside for trading on a consistent basis, besides considering the inherent constraints imposed by the opening and closing hours of the markets, you can take your personal preferences into account, too.

Perhaps the sharpness of your mind is at a peak after your morning workout, or you are only "ready to rock" late in the afternoon (or after the fifth cup of coffee); perhaps your day is filled with other commitments that leave you with a few hours before bedtime to trade; or maybe you just prefer to trade on a foreign market that opens at 3:00 a.m. your local time. No matter what factors you weigh in, decide the time of the day that you will run your trading business and make a habit to stick to your schedule. This will help you to achieve consistency in your trading. Try to fill in your calendar a week in advance to schedule your trading times.

What Specific Goals Do You Have for Daily, Weekly, and Monthly Profits?

Going back to the beginning topic of this chapter, when your teacher taught you a subject, did she impart all the knowledge to you at one go? No. She designed a semester-long syllabus, broke down the content of the subject into digestible parts, and guided you to conquer them one at a time.

Your ultimate goal as a trader is to achieve successes in trading. Do you believe you can achieve them in just a few steps? Unlikely. You break them down into yearly, monthly, weekly, daily, and even per-trade goals. And then you take on each of them, one step at a time, to reach your final destination.

But why are these goals needed at all in the first place? First, they provide a direction for a trader to work toward. Second, they are important metrics for a trader's performance evaluation for accountability purposes. If a trader cannot hold herself accountable for the goals she establishes, things can go south for her in a hurry.

What Trading Strategy Will You Employ, and What Are the Rules?

After you have established your goals, you need to figure out your *plan of attack* to achieve them, and that is your trading strategy.

Think about the rules that you plan to employ. For example, you need to decide whether you should be a momentum, day, swing, or position trader and why. You have to discover the trading style and time frames that are optimal for you. You have to identify the key indicators in your trading system and understand why you use them, and so on.

Right and Wrong Goal Setting

Year after year, I have students who tell me,

"I set a goal to double my account every month."

"My goal is to achieve financial freedom within two years."

"I will replace the income from my job by September (two months from now), and double it three months after."

When I hear goals like these, knowing that they are unrealistic goals beyond the reach of these students, I will try to nudge them back to reality in the least hurtful way possible.

Don't get me wrong. I do encourage my students to set goals that can push them beyond their current limits, but at the same time, they have to be realistic and set goals that are achievable.

Peter Drucker, a world-renown management consultant, educator and trainer, suggested the SMART criteria for goal setting (Drucker 2006). According to him, each goal that we set must be:

S: *Specific*. For example, instead of saying, "I aim to earn a lot of money from trading," we should set a goal to "earn $10,000 from trading in five months."

M: *Measurable*. The example above is also measurable: You either attain the goal by the specific date or not. You should also want to measure your progress and not just the final result. For example, you can keep track of your accumulated earnings on a daily basis, so you know how far you are from the goal.

A: *Actionable*. Having a goal without figuring out the actionable steps to achieve the goal is equivalent to just making a wish. Break down the process to achieve the final goal into small actionable steps or milestones. Using the same example above, you can aim to earn $2,000 per month for a total of five months, or $100 every day (assuming you trade 20 days in a month).

R: *Realistic*. If your performance track record shows that you have been pocketing $1,650 a month and you trade with around the same amount of starting capital, it is unrealistic to set a goal to earn $10,000 by the next month. Hitting the total profit of $10,000 five months from now (that translates to $2,000/month), however, is still beyond your current earning capability but could be considered realistic.

T: *Time-bound*. A goal is a dream with a deadline. Set a deadline for your goal, and you will work hard to achieve it.

■ Working out the Numbers

Having specific measurable goals is extremely important. These numbers are the only real measure of performance and accountability. However, if a trader is unable to hold himself accountable to the metrics he establishes, things can go south in a hurry. That is why it's good to have a coach or another person to force the issue of accountability to the metrics.

One of the most important aspects of setting goals is to make them realistic and achievable. Start by establishing a reasonable rate-of-return (return on investment or ROI) on your investment. For instance, is 1 percent per month reasonable? What about an 8 percent per month profit target? I would argue that a 1 percent

ROI calculated on the notional amount traded is reasonable as is an 8 percent ROI calculated on the trading account balance. Let me explain why.

The trader's ROI depends largely on the vehicle being traded and the amount of leverage it affords. For example, if you are trading forex, you only need a small amount of capital to earn a good return. This is possible because the leverage factor affords you position sizes that are 50 or 100 times the amount of capital in your account. However, traders should only risk a maximum of about 6 percent of the trading account balance for actual trading across all positions. This brings down the actual leverage used considerably.

Example 1: Profit Goal Calculations, Leveraged and Unleveraged

Let's say you have a trading account balance of $30,000. The maximum amount a trader should risk at any one time should be about 6 percent, or $1,800 over several positions, risking 1 to 2 percent on each position. Remember, trading is a numbers game, and you need to conserve capital and stay in the game long enough until the win/loss ratio eventually works in your favor.

(To simplify the illustration in the following examples, the effect of *compounding* has not been taken into consideration in the calculations.)

Using our $1,800 risk limit, we could purchase about $200,000 in currency pairs with a generous 90-pip stop loss ($1,800/$20 per pip). If the trader manages to make a net profit of 120 pips in one month, the profit would be $2,400. That works out to be a return of 8 percent on the $30,000 account balance. Annualized, that becomes 96 percent ROI on the trading account balance. However, what is the return on the notional capital traded, the $200,000? It is 1.2 percent per month, or 14.4 percent annualized.

The risk/reward of 1.33:1 ($1,800 capital risked to earn $2,400) is conservative. Most traders will consider trades with at least a 2:1 risk/reward (in our example, that would be $1,800 capital requirement to earn $3,600 (180 pips) profit). That being the case, the ROI calculated on the account balance would be 12 percent or 144 percent annualized.

With a 2:1 risk/reward, the monthly ROI calculated on the $200,000 notional capital is 1.8 percent or 21.6 percent annualized. Of course, it is always better to be conservative in goal setting, so setting a 1 percent monthly trading return on notional, which is an 8 percent return on the trading account balance, is reasonable. The key is to accept losses and set tight stops and let profits run to best achieve your goals.

Example 2: How to Improve the Trading Results

Let's say you have a win/loss ratio of 65 percent. If you make 20 trades per month where you have 7 losses (35 percent) with an average 50-pip loss and 13 winning trades with an average 85-pip gain, you would have a net gain of 755 pips (1105 pip gains – 350 pip losses). This risk/reward in this example is 85-pip gain/50-pip loss or 1.7:1. The dollar amount would depend on what size contracts you were trading. If you were just trading one $10,000 contract each trade, you would net $755 for the month. If you had traded $20,000 contracts for each trade, you would net $1510 and up it goes, depending on contract or lot size.

The keys to improving the trading results are the following:

- Increase the win/loss ratio (65 percent in this example)

- Increase the risk/reward (1.7 profits versus amount risked per trade in this example)

- Reduce the proximity of the stop loss through good analysis, thus increasing the trade size and still staying within the acceptable risk tolerance

Indeed, a trader could have a 50 percent win/loss ratio and still be successful if the profits per trade exceed the losses per trade.

Example 3: Profit Goal Calculations with Different Account Sizes

Let's say you make 20 forex trades per month where you have 9 losses and 11 winning trades. This implies that for the 20 trades, you are 55 percent successful and 45 percent unsuccessful, and your win/loss ratio is 11:9 or 1.22. In other words, you are making 1.22 profitable trades for every losing trade.

Let's also say you employ a 50-pip stop loss and have an average 75-pip gain. The risk/reward is therefore 1.5:1. This means the size of the win is greater than the size of the loss by a factor of 1.5, or for every pip lost (risk), you will gain 1.5 pips (reward).

So, now we have two useful numbers that we can use to assist us when calculating profit goals: win/loss ratio and risk/reward ratio.

In this example of 20 trades, we have:

- 9 losses of 50 pips = 450 pips

- 11 wins of 75 pips = 825 pips

This gives a net profit of 825 pips – 450 pips = 375 pips.

The dollar amount would depend on what size contracts you were trading (function of leverage) and the size of the starting equity in the account. If you were trading $10,000 each trade, you would net $375 for the month. If you were trading $100,000 each trade, you would net $3,750. Let's work backward to see the size account necessary to make various income streams assuming the above assumptions hold true.

We will start with three different account sizes: $1,000, $10,000, and $100,000. Making 375 pips per month translates into 94 pips per week and 19 pips per day. These projections are reasonable. In fact, I encourage traders to look to make between 200 and 400 pips per month for a position taker, which is the equivalent of 50 and 100 pips per week for a swing trader, or 10 and 20 pips per day for a day trader. The totals come out to be the same and all that differs is the trading style implemented.

Table 6.1 shows the profit goal calculations with these account sizes. Notice in the table that the leverage used is only 4:1 (as per the position size), not nearly the 50:1 allowable leverage in the United States. The leverage is low because the 2 percent capital at risk calculation was used to figure out the position size.

All of these calculations have to do with managing the risk of the trade by first identifying a position size based on the starting capital and capital at risk. The key terms learned so far are:

- Win/loss ratio

- Probability of success

- Risk/reward ratio

From the above examples, we can see that the win/loss ratio does not show a complete picture of the performance of a trader because a trader can still be

TABLE 6.1	Profit Goal Calculations		
Account Size	$100,000	$10,000	$1,000
Capital at risk (2 percent)	$2,000	$200	$20
Stop loss	50 pips	50 pips	50 pips
Position size	$400,000	$40,000	$4,000
Total monthly pips	375	375	375
Risk/Reward	1.5:1	1.5:1	1.5:1
Win/Loss	11:9	11:9	11:9
Probability of success	55 percent	55 percent	55 percent
# of trades	20	20	20
$ amount per pip	$40	$4	$.4
Monthly profit ($)	$15,000	$1,500	$150

profitable even with a low win/loss ratio if his profit per trade is high, and vice versa. We will look into this in more detail in "Chapter 11, Habit #8: Measure Your Performance."

■ Checklist: How Your Profit Goals Give You a Framework for Trading

We have looked at three examples to get a better understanding to calculate profit goals. Let's recap what we have discussed by going through the following checklist:

- Start with your trading account balance and establish an annualized return target.

- Divide that annualized target by 12 to establish a monthly target.

- Calculate the dollar value of that monthly target.

- Calculate the stop-loss dollar value for each trade risking 1 to 2 percent of your trading account balance (1–2 percent × trading account balance).

- Estimate the average stop loss in pips for forex or dollars for stocks.

- Calculate the average trade size based on the average stop loss calculated above.

- Figure out how many pips (for currencies) or dollars (for stocks) you need to make your monthly target using the trade size calculated above.

- Estimate the average pips per trade you expect to achieve, and divide the monthly target in pips by that number to arrive at the estimated number of net-positive trades you need to make in the month (dollars for stocks).

- Calculate the risk/reward based on the average stop loss and the average profit per trade estimated above.

- Start with a 50 percent win/loss ratio and the calculated risk/reward and work backward to determine how many winning and losing trades you need to make to meet the monthly target.

- To improve the results, focus on either increasing the win/loss ratio or increasing the size of the winning trade versus the size of the losing trade.

Of course, the real world is a moving target, but setting goals gives you a framework. You are not going to exit a trade just because you hit your target; you will let profits run unless your trading system dictates exiting at predefined levels. Ideally, your trading system will require confirmation before entering.

This allows you to set close stops because if the trade moves against you, losses are cut quickly. Yes, it may hurt your win/loss ratio and your ego, but this is where the discipline of your system will allow you to keep emotions and ego out of your trading and let the numbers work in your favor. Without specific goals, you will flounder, just as a ship at sea without a star to navigate by.

■ The "Grading System" in Your Trading Journey

You might have noticed that I was equating the goal setting habit of successful traders with how our school teachers helped us to tackle the many subjects during school time. I mentioned breaking down a huge subject into a digestible syllabus and having a grading system to help us track our progress.

Yes, we traders need to have a "grading system", too, to track our progress and measure our performance.

These are the questions: How do we do that? And what kind of metrics should we use? The first obvious metric is our profits. This can come in the form of our per-trade earnings, the balance in our trading account, or our year-over-year profits, for example.

True enough, the profits we make from trading, being quantifiable data, is a convenient metric that tells us objectively where we are now and how far we are from our goals. But is money the only metric we can use? Can dollar amounts measure everything related to our goals, or are there other valuable metrics?

We will talk about all these in "Chapter 11, Habit #8: Measure Your Performance."

Take Action!

Define your goals by asking yourself these questions:

1. What are your professional goals today? (Not limited to trading)

2. Why are you trading?

3. What are your trading goals?

4. Where do you want to be in your professional life five years from now? (Not limited to trading)

5. What do you see as your greatest strengths as a trader?

6. What strengths do you have that you can make even better and how can you do that as quickly as possible?

7. What are your greatest weaknesses as a trader?

8. Can you overcome those weaknesses by focusing on your strengths?

9. What do you see are your greatest roadblocks to your success as a trader?

10. What actions must you take to overcome these roadblocks?

11. Are you enchanted by the image of being a trader?

12. What do you tell people when they ask you what you do for a living?

13. How does your trading business fit into your life?

14. How much time can you commit to trading each day?

15. What are your personal goals for the next 18 months?

16. Where do you want to be in your personal life five years from now?

17. How do you deal with stress in your life?

18. How do you deal with stress in your trading?

19. Do you have a plan in place to keep healthy in mind and body?

20. How do you plan to keep as positive an attitude as possible?

21. Do you have a daily routine to keep physically and mentally alert?

◼ Pendulum Scenario 6.1: Taking Action versus Feeling Remorse

"If you spend too much time thinking about a thing, you'll never get it done."

—Bruce Lee

How would you feel if the market makes a huge move and you are not involved? Would you regret not getting in the trend and blame yourself for this?

What would you do when you miss the start of a trend (and, therefore, the opportunity to reap the maximum profit), but your analysis clearly indicates that if you still want to get in, you can because the market is still in a trend? Would you give up on this trend and wait for the next one, or enter the trade anyway to make some profits?

When the market continues with its trend move and you keep waiting for the correction to jump in, but it does not happen, how would you feel? Will you sit there wishing you could turn back the clock or take action to make the best out of the current market development?

A Day Beginning with Remorse

Stacey jumped out of bed when she saw the chart on her iPad showing a strong downward moving trend in the EUR/USD. She ran to her workstation, pulled out her trading journal and a few more charts, and got herself ready to take action even though it was a few hours before her "official trading hours." The trend started in Europe when she was still comfortably tucked up in bed. She missed the start and the potential to add around 80 pips to her profit. As much as she wanted to kick herself for this, she was aware that it was too late to feel remorse. So she did not let her negative emotion hold her back and got herself together to plunge into action.

After some analysis, she sprang into the "take-action" mode to catch up with the trend move. She was eager to make up for the missed opportunity but did not rush into making trading decisions. A brief trade plan was quickly formulated because she was mindful that she could get too emotionally involved while trying to "redeem" the lost pips. Having missed the best opportunity for profits, she would not forgive herself if she missed the rest of the potential move. She made it a point that she must trade the plan. Anxiety would have no place at any point in time.

When everything was ready, she carried out her plan. First, she moved to an hourly time frame, waited for a retracement in the direction of the trend, and sold with a reasonable stop loss. For the next few hours, she kept her eyes on the trend movement and continued to make timely decisions. Her trading session only ended in the afternoon when she needed to switch her attention to her baby. Even so, she regularly checked her trading platform for updates in the market, wary that she might miss another large trend, until the end of the day.

It turned out to be a good day for Stacey. The EUR/USD continued to plummet, and Stacey's hard work added 55 pips of profit into her account. By taking action and achieving a positive trading result, the remorse felt earlier in the day for missing the first move quickly dissipated. She was also proud of herself for taking action with calmness.

An Opportunity Missed During the Lunch Break

At another corner of the same city, Fred witnessed a huge upward move in the market, right up to the next resistance zone, with mixed feelings of regret, annoyance, and shock.

The upward trend did not surprise him. In fact, his analysis indicated that it was imminent, and he had been expecting it since last night. However, what he did not expect was its early arrival, and coincidentally, it happened right when Fred was taking an early lunch break. He cursed himself for going for lunch when the market had its "timely move". Now he felt he had missed the boat to make his profits for the week and did not have any idea when a similar move of that magnitude would arise again. It was his bad luck, it was a joke that the market was playing on him, and it was perhaps even a punishment for whatever he had done.

While he continued to mourn for his misstep, he could not think clearly enough to decide how he should move on. So, he just continued staring at the chart on his screen. Amidst his inaction, the price bounced off the resistance zone and continued to move lower. His anxiety kept building up; he was at a loss, still undecided on the action to take, until he could not stand it anymore and finally sold at the bottom. Massive regret overwhelmed him. "Why didn't I just do it earlier!" he blamed himself.

The Post-Mortem in the Evening

At the end of the day, Fred reflected on his trade. He realized he was too influenced by the powerful emotion of regret. Mourning over the first missed opportunity, he was unable to think logically and take the appropriate steps to make up for his loss. He did not like that he could not pocket the maximum profit when his analysis was clearly accurate. He was so obsessed in blaming the missed timing, the "untimely" market move, and his lack of attention, that he did not calm himself down to make the best out of his situation.

He was also in fear. He was afraid of losing money if he entered the position too late even though his analysis ensured him that he could still make profit at a late entry point and virtually screamed at him to act "NOW! NOW! NOW!" He just could not because his fear had incapacitated him.

If he had learned from Stacey, he would understand it is better to win (or lose) small than not get in the trade at all. Stacey's decision to ride the trend although she missed its start was made in a timely fashion. Though she was feeling remorseful, too, she did not let her emotion get the better of her and remained calm when strategizing her trade. She waited patiently for the move to set up, and once it did, she was in.

She was not obsessed with regretting the profit opportunity she had missed although that was 80 pips, enough to buy a month's supply of baby products! Her attitude was that she could still catch the next round of pips. She had no time to feel remorse because she was eager to take action. As a proactive trader, Stacey's mind was wired to promptly react to the situation rather than sitting and feeling regret for not being able to turn back the clock. "As soon as the market shows its hand, I am in!" she had promised herself.

Think about the Questions Again

In the beginning of this Pendulum Scenario, I asked you a series of questions related to the situations that Stacey and Fred faced. Now let's revisit them:

What will you do when you miss the start of a large trend move?

Will you be able to act calmly like Stacey or get overwhelmed by regret like Fred?

Would you rather be mourning over a missed opportunity or take timely action to catch up?

Think about it.

Pendulum Scenario 6.2: Enthusiastic versus Apathetic Trader

"Flaming enthusiasm, backed up by horse sense and persistence, is the quality that most frequently makes for success."

—Dale Carnegie

Stacey had just welcomed a new member into her family. She and her husband had decided she should stay at home to personally take care of the baby instead of entrusting him to a random babysitter. Though they both agreed that a mother's personal caretaking in the tender years was one of the best gifts for their baby, Stacey's giving up her job meant a major cut of income to her family.

Fred, on the other hand, quit his job after hearing about the potential to earn a huge income from trading. With a resolute determination to "make it big," he entered the game and did not bother to make a back-up plan. He had enough savings to last him for more than a year and had envisioned that, in less than a year, he could earn enough to replace the salary from his previous job. The idea of supplementary income never once crossed his mind.

Stacey and Fred started trading for the same motivation: money. But a few months down the road, an intricate difference showed up.

Trading Beyond Money Making

Trading was no longer only a means to bring in income for Stacey. For one thing, it replaced the sense of career achievement that Stacey lost since she left her sales job; for another, it fulfilled her need for intellectual challenges. Even though caring for her son *was* an intellectually demanding and fulfilling task, Stacey needed a different kind of intellectual stimulation and satisfaction, something that she could only get from a successful career. And trading provided it.

Her enthusiasm in trading flourished as she dove deeper into it. Part of it was because of the "feel-good" factor. As she grew more skilled and experienced, her win/loss ratio continued to climb. Winning in trades meant having extra money for her household and proved she was still highly competent and career-wise.

Another reason why her enthusiasm developed was that after only a few months in the trading business, she could share her knowledge with fellow traders. It started off with her seeking advice when she was new. When she realized she had accumulated some knowledge, she was eager to share it with fellow traders. Eventually, positive feedback and appreciation started rolling in, and this encouraged her to take the initiative to offer guidance to new traders.

She gave her advice freely because she treated this as a way to improve her knowledge. Teaching gave her the chance to look back regularly on what she did, review her trading journal, and revise the technical theory behind her trading system. "Call it good karma if you want," she said. "I did see further improvement in my trading after I started guiding the newbies."

But she knew it was not only good karma. By sharing her knowledge passionately, her enthusiasm in trading rose, and she became more determined to hone her craft.

Trading as a Means to Make Ends Meet

After a few months in the field, Fred was still treating trading only as a means to earn an income. He was not as "lucky" as Stacey and had not had enough successes to make him thrilled for his trading business. He was interested in learning new trading strategies and systems. As a matter of fact, studying the technical aspects of trading was almost the only thing in trading that excited him, and he did not mind "religiously" investing huge sums of money to get his hands on the latest trading programs.

Having said so, at times he would come to some sober realization. He could see that endlessly studying one course after another would not help him to progress in trading. However, within a short period of time, he would inevitably brush that thought away.

Escaping seemed to be his habitual way of dealing with his problems. There were times when he would ask himself, "Where has my enthusiasm in trading gone?" only to end up with him "getting back to business" before he thought of a decent answer. He would rather numb himself with the trading activities, staying apathetic throughout, than to confront the issues and sort things out.

Not feeling a sense of achievement, not finding meaning in this business, and not making enough profits: Fred began to worry, and asked himself, "How do I carry on down this path?"

Trading as an Enthusiastic Trader

Stacey won again. Although it was only a small win, she was happy. ("Here we have it, another contribution to my baby's *baby product fund!*") She started to look for another opportunity to enter the market just minutes after taking profit from the previous one.

Stacey maintained comradeship with a team of like-minded traders that she took a trading seminar with. She enthusiastically traded with them daily and exchanged thoughts and trading tips with them on a regular basis. She just could not wait to tell them about the setups that she found in the markets and the many clever decisions that she made, sometimes the silly ones, too. Her teammates saw no bounds in her enthusiasm in trading and were inspired by this.

Unavoidably, some days, Stacey lost more than she won. Even so, she would still hold up to her enthusiasm by getting moral support and positive energy from her teammates. Soon, she would recover from the falls, and by the next day, she was ready to go all out in her trading business!

Trading as an Apathetic Trader

Fred lost the "fire" in the trading business when things started not going well for him. Like today. A few wins in the beginning, followed by successive losses, sent Fred into the apathetic mode. There he was, staring at the charts again motionlessly.

Trading was not about getting him closer to his dream lifestyle anymore. The title of a "full-time trader" and the intellectual stimulation that once made him excited were of little relevance now. It was about earning enough money to make ends meet, with no enthusiasm to speak of.

Emotions sometimes took control of Fred. He might decide to take a leave from trading when he was "not in the optimal mood" to trade. He might become apathetic of his trading performance, not willing to take it through proper reviews. This sounded funny because on the one hand he claimed trading was how he chose to earn a living, but on the other hand, he had ceased to care about what kind of living he was earning from trading.

Fred was a lone wolf in trading. Unlike Stacey, he did not work with any other traders. He had no outlet for his emotions, positive or negative, and he had no one to speak to about these. No one else could lighten him up when he was discouraged. Sure enough, failure after failure later, he lost the fire he had in the initial stage of his trading career.

Fred was not indifferent about his apathy in trading. The question, "How do I carry on down this path?" still lingered in his head. What he could do was to seek help from a coach or trading buddy. Otherwise, he could do what Stacey did: Actively involve himself in the trading circle and build comradeship with fellow traders.

If he had gotten moral and emotional support from these people, his enthusiasm in trading might have returned. He could have become enthusiastic about other aspects of trading beyond monetary gain.

PART III

Becoming an Entrepreneurial Trader

CHAPTER 7

Habit #4: Commit to Your Education with a Trading Coach

Have you ever wondered how successful traders do it? How did they know what the right path to take was and what to do at each step on their journey to achieve success?

Some of them figured these out on their own, some took the arduous route of "trying it until you get it," and a handful got lucky and chanced upon the right path. But most others sought external help through advisers, coaches, or mentors.

This is true for high achievers in all industries. Top performers in sports, for example, always train with a coach. It is not so much that the coaches know more about the games than the athletes or perform better than them. It is not that there are any rules that say all athletes must be trained under qualified coaches. It is also not that the athletes will be completely at a loss and cannot figure out on their own how to perform better without the guidance of a coach. The need for direction from a coach lies within the wisdom of having outside, objective, and truthful input.

Here's a specific example: Tiger Woods, formerly the World's No. 1 golfer, received coaching from numerous coaches throughout his career. Questions like the following might enter your mind: Since he was already the World's No. 1, who could be qualified to train him? Wouldn't it take a better golfer than him to train him? Where would he find such a person, or did such a person even exist since Woods was the top player?

Here's something even more puzzling: Could all the coaches beat him in any round of golf? No, of course not, otherwise the coaches would have been the world's top players and not Woods. So, why then did Woods entrust his golfing career to them? Why did he have to follow the coaches' instructions and guidance, knowing that they were not as good a golfer as he was?

Was Tiger Woods even thinking logically?

The fact is he was. He trusted the coaches because they were experts who could provide him with professional support and perspective. Although they were not as skillful as Woods, they were the *critical observers and advisers* he could seek advice from. Among other things, they analyzed his techniques and strategy, provided guidance and solutions when his performance suffered, and kept the golfer in a peak performance mindset.

Now imagine you, too, as a trader, have a coach who will do the same for you: analyze your trading techniques and strategy, provide guidance and support when you fall or pat your back for your exceptional performance, and keep you in a winning mindset.

How do you think having a coach will transform you as a trader? Wouldn't you agree this will accelerate your success or heighten your success rate? Can you see what kind of difference this will make for you in your trading business?

■ What Can a Trading Coach Do for You?

The following are some guidance tools that you should expect from your coach.
On learning and development, a coach will do the following:

- Guide you in finding your *trading personality*. Are you more suited to be a scalper, day trader, swing trader, or position trader?

- Question what skills you should acquire. What shouldn't you waste time on, and what skills are you still lacking? Are you learning and applying your trading techniques correctly?

- Find out what trading system fits your personality and preference the best.

- Critique your trading strategy. How do you verify it, especially if you are new and do not have enough experience to know what you are doing is right or wrong?

- Ensure you are applying *best practices* in your trading. What are you doing well now? What are you not doing well yet that can significantly improve your winning rate?

- Plan ahead to help you grow as a trader. What milestones should you be aiming to achieve? Every trader has a different scenario, so run-of-the-mill growth plans might not be suitable for everyone. Your coach should advise you based on your unique conditions.

On accountability, a coach will do the following:

- Question if you are using your time wisely and efficiently. What *else* can you do to maximize your time management strategy and, therefore, potentially increase your profitability from being more efficient?

- Question if you are a well-disciplined trader. Are you doing fine managing yourself and your resources? Should you tighten up your self-management or cut yourself some slack to avoid trader's burnout?

- Ask if you are holding yourself accountable for your trading business. If not, your coach can provide external accountability! Is your accountability plan working? Has it helped to keep you on track with your financial, business, and personal goals?

On goals, a coach will do the following:

- Question the goals you should set for your trading business. How do you even know what you want? Your coach can guide you in discovering your true inner desire. In the process, don't be surprised to find out you might not be 100 percent sure about what you want.

- Ask if your goals are realistic and achievable or just overly idealistic and farfetched. Are the milestones you set constructive, redundant, or downright destructive to your trading business?

- Help you plan for your actions to achieve your goals. How do you break down the daunting task of achieving a goal into small, attainable, and actionable steps, which you can take one at a time?

- Question if you are prioritizing your goals and milestones effectively. Remember, you have limited time for your trading business each day, so you must sort out your priorities.

- Help you measure your trading results. What metrics should you use to objectively and accurately tell you whether you are close to achieving your goals?

- Guide you to stay on track to achieving your goals. Your coach can tell you when you are deviating from your plan and pull you back on the right course.

  On motivation, your coach will do the following:

- Ask what motivates you to be in the trading business. What motivates you to do better? How do you stay motivated?

- Ask if you have a positive mindset. Are you cultivating wholesome habits that will help you develop and maintain a positive mindset?

- Question what it takes to be consistently "in the zone" for trading. How do you salvage the situations when you consistently fall out of *the zone?*

- Ask if you are in the business for the right reasons or if you are like most traders, who entered under an illusion that a trading business is the "magic pill" to solve all their problems.

- Guide you when the going gets tough in case you fall short on motivation. Your coach will be there to find out what it takes to prevent you from giving up prematurely.

  On problems you face, your coach will do the following:

- Help you to spot the traps on your trading journey and foretell if a storm will brew. With the help of your coach, you might be able to stop them from coming your way.

- Guide you after a major setback in your trading. Do you have the emotional, psychological, and financial stamina to stand up after a fall and even emerge as a stronger trader after that?

- Question what the lessons are that you can learn from your wins and losses. How do you formulate a system to repeat your winning trades and a *prevention plan* to avoid falling into the same pitfalls over and over again?

- Help you keep a clear head when confronted with problems and your own weaknesses. Can you prevent your emotions from getting in the way? Are you still able to stay logical and rational when facing adversity?

- Question if you are prepared to face the financial, technical, business, emotional, and psychological challenges in trading by yourself. Don't you agree that it would be helpful to have someone to provide guidance and support when you need it the most?

  On your perspective, your coach will do the following:

- Question how well you have been performing in trading. How do you even assess yourself?

- Help you question whether your view is narrow-minded judgment or a legitimate perspective coming from your experience, which is helpful in your trading.

- Point out if you are locked into your own head and your own ideas. Have you stopped listening to advice and absorbing new information, thinking you are already "enough"?

These are a few of the areas your coach can help you with. When you work with the right coach with the right experience and right style for you, your probability of succeeding in trading will be higher. Think of this as taking a shortcut that leads to your destination. And if you face any problems on your trading journey, the answers you are looking for are often just a phone call or an e-mail away!

How Do You Find a Trading Coach?

Unfortunately for traders, no "association of trading coaches" exists from which you can hunt for your coach. There isn't even any well-established structured coaching development program as they have for swim coaches, personal development coaches, and career coaches. Needless to say, no certification process exists for trading coaches.

So, how do you find your coach?

This question has no clear-cut answer. You need to do the legwork of gathering recommendations from fellow traders or do your own research. You might want to check out trading groups that offer coaching services or approach veteran traders with a demonstrated knowledge in trading and the markets.

Remember that with today's technology, your trading coach does not need to be located in your local area. You might be living in Europe but the coach you wish to engage is in North America, which is no problem. Setting up coaching sessions with her is easy through online meeting rooms, conference services, or VOIP calls. You can even engage in daily communication with her using messenger services or e-mail.

Engaging a Coach Is an Investment, Not an Expense

Here are some final remarks on committing to your education with a trading coach. Working with a qualified coach is going to cost you some money and the coaching fee is usually not cheap. To top it off, usually you have to work with your coach for an extended period of time, six months to a year at a minimum, for optimal results.

Nevertheless, you should not treat this as an expense. Rather, you should think of it as an investment. At the end of the day, working with the right coach could be the investment that will bring you back multiple times of the money you invested. It will be, as mentioned again and again, the shortcut to your successes in your trading, your business, and even your life.

Take Action!

1. Now that we have reached the middle of this book, it's time for you to check the following:

   a. Have you completed the trader's scorecard? (This is an important step. Remember, you will do it again at the end of this book so that you can witness first-hand the changes in yourself as a trader.) If you haven't done so yet, go to www.wiley.com/go/traderspendulum to complete the scorecard.

   b. Have you been making progress toward becoming an Entrepreneurial Trader by following the suggestions in this book?

   c. Have you been implementing the suggestions in the "Take Action!" sections in the previous chapters?

2. Besides making a plan to engage a coach, you should also plan for continuous learning. The following questions will help you to figure out how you can do that:

   a. How do you plan to improve your performance?

   b. How do you plan to constantly monitor the validity of your strategies and game plan?

   c. Under what circumstances will you make changes to your trading strategies or game plan?

   d. How will you make changes to your strategies or game plan?

   e. How will you use your trader's business plan?

   f. Do you find it valuable to exchange information with others?

   g. How do you plan to connect with other traders?

   h. How do you plan to acquire new knowledge?

   i. Have you budgeted funds for continuing education in trading?

◼ Pendulum Scenario 7.1: Foresight versus Hindsight

"Hindsight plays tricks on our minds."
—Jeremy J. Siegel, The Wharton School, Stocks for the Long Run

"Show me your crystal ball," Fred demanded.

"Crystal ball? What crystal ball? I don't have one," Stacey replied.

"I don't believe you, Stacey," Fred insisted, "If you don't have one, how do you always manage to forecast the market with such accuracy? How do you know exactly when to enter and exit the market and what the correct position sizes to take are?"

"Fred, seriously, I don't have a crystal ball." Stacey rolled her eyes. She then looked into his eyes and said, "I am using tarot cards."

Tools That Provide Market Foresight

Of course, Stacey was not serious about her claim, but she did have several tools up her sleeve that helped her to predict the market moves.

Before entering any trade, Stacey would use Elliott Wave analysis to forecast the large market moves. She first counted the waves on the 1-hour time frame to see the big picture for her day trading time frame, which was the 15-minute chart. Usually, she targeted the wave 3, as it was the strongest and most profitable wave. Using Fibonacci, she would project how far wave 3 could travel and that provided the context for her day trades. (See Figure 7.1 for the big picture.)

Once she had confidence in the direction of the market, Stacey would then move to a lower time frame for day trading, normally the 15-minute time frame, to look at the more immediate market move. When she found that the 15-minute chart was aligned with her prediction, she knew there was a high probability her forecast would be correct. (See Figure 7.2.)

Stacey used Elliott Wave analysis to have foresight into the market cycles to a high degree of success and would not trade without it, but she relied on other tools. For example, sometimes she used moving average convergence divergence (MACD) to confirm her buy or sell decision in conjunction with Elliott Wave analysis.

Let's look at the previous 15-minute chart again to see how the MACD complements Elliott Wave analysis as a trigger for a buy/sell signal. (See Figure 7.3.)

Why does she use MACD along with Elliott Wave analysis? This combination provided her with more precise foresight into the market. Stacey had faith in Elliott Wave analysis but agreed with most traders that the greatest challenge was to count the waves accurately. Adding MACD to her analysis was like examining her wave

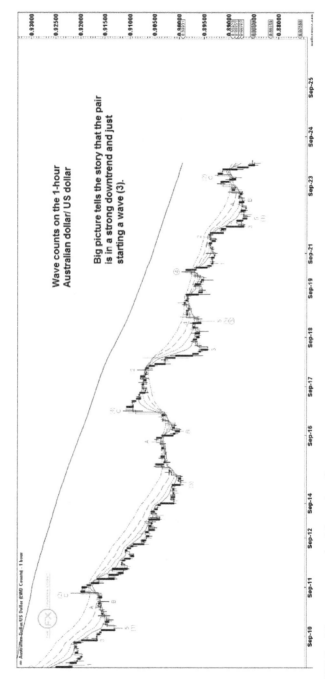

FIGURE 7.1 Wave counts on the 1-hour time frame

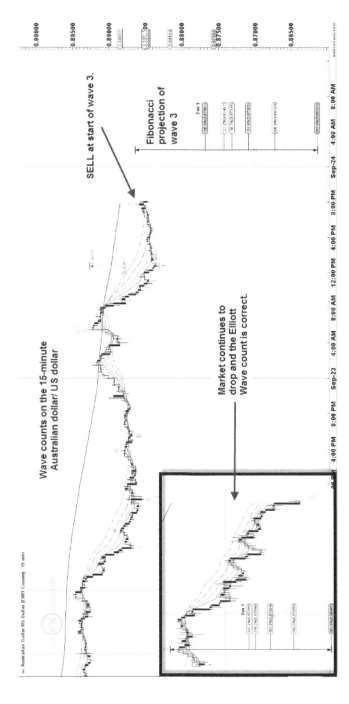

FIGURE 7.2 Wave counts on the 15-minute time frame

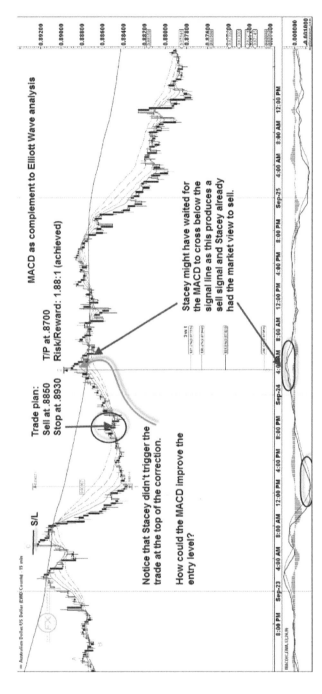

FIGURE 7.3 MACD complementing Elliott Wave analysis as a trigger for a buy/sell signal

counts through extra lenses. She could trade with more confidence knowing the setups she identified with Elliott Wave analysis were of high winning probabilities.

The "Woulda, Coulda, Shoulda" Mindset

Fred never knew traders were learning these analysis skills to gain foresight into the market until Stacey introduced them to him. He admitted to Stacey he was a "woulda, coulda, shoulda" type of trader, who was forever looking back and replaying those trades he had not taken. His hindsight always showed him what he missed in the market and what he "would have, could have, or should have" done if he had seen these earlier.

However, when Stacey showed him how she forecasted the market, he realized he had overestimated his ability to make predictions. In fact, all the predictions he made would not materialize because they were all based on his "gut feelings" about the market and not a proven analysis methodology. He did not even know these analysis techniques existed until Stacey showed him.

That brought him back to a trade that happened months ago, captured by the chart in Figure 7.4.

The market was at point A when Fred looked at the markets during the evening. With his analysis, he correctly predicted there would be a large upward move, so he entered the trade at point B the next morning. The market did not disappoint him. It was an upward move! But now he was faced with these questions he did not have an answer for: "How long will the upward trend continue? When will the reversal happen?"

To play it safe, he sold at point C, way before the reversal. He regretted this conservative decision, seeing how much more he could have earned if he just held onto his position until the price was closer to the peak. "It was unlikely that the market trend would reverse so early. I should have seen that," he thought.

Now that the market was moving downward, when would it reverse? Fred was guessing it would happen when the price moved back to the 50 percent Fibonacci retracement level, but he was not sure. He took no action because of this. As it turned out, his prediction was accurate. Fred's "woulda, coulda, shoulda" thinking sprang out again, and he blamed himself for his inaction. He was agitated, but he knew better since it was just a guess that turned out to be correct. Nothing could justify why he should have taken a position in that trade.

Fred spent his afternoon looking at the market movement, repeating the "predicting the reversal, prediction came true, regretting and blaming" game in his mind. A conversation with Stacey revealed how pointless this game was. He did not know how to forecast the market. All he was doing was making wild guesses.

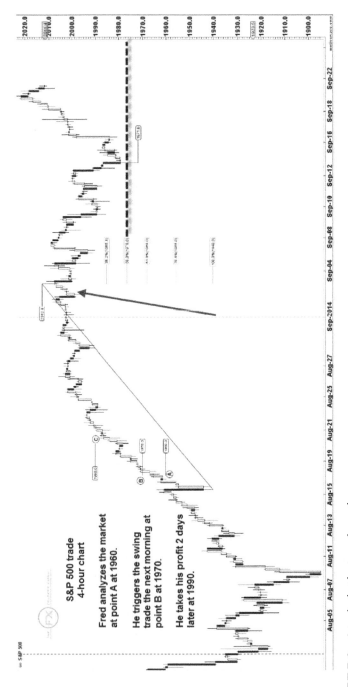

S&P 500 trade
4-hour chart

Fred analyzes the market
at point A at 1960.

He triggers the swing
trade the next morning at
point B at 1970.

He takes his profit 2 days
later at 1990.

FIGURE 7.4 A trade that happened months ago

Before their conversation ended, Stacey threw another bomb at him. She pointed out something that Fred was not aware of.

Stacey asked Fred to look at the right side of the chart. She analyzed it for him. (See Figure 7.5.)

She told him that if she had seen this setup, she would have traded it and earned some extra cash from it. It was a perfect confirmed setup!

The Lesson That Fred Learned

Fred read a quote by Jeremy Siegel that says, "Hindsight plays tricks on our minds," and he finally appreciated what this means.

He saw how his hindsight had caused him to blame himself for trades he "would have, could have, or should have" taken, not knowing previously that his predictions were only speculations, and he was right to have not taken any actions based on them. His hindsight was playing a trick on him, blaming him, and trying hard to make him regret.

He saw he overestimated his ability to forecast the market. When he reviewed the trades he did not take, he thought he should have been able to predict these moves, not knowing that this perception was formed by his hindsight. He did not know any methods that could help him to make the prediction.

He understood this after he found out how Stacey had internalized various patterns and trade setups and was freely using them in her trading. He realized these were the tools she was using to predict the market movement.

■ Pendulum Scenario 7.2: The Lucky versus Unlucky Trader

> *"Many an opportunity is lost because a man is out looking for four-leaf clovers."*
>
> —Author Unknown

Stacey and Fred looked at trading in many different ways.

For example, Stacey planned her trade and traded her plan. She was not afraid of revealing to fellow traders that she feared losing on trades because she really did. Her fear of loss made her tread with extra care. Each step she took was calculated because she needed to know what she was doing. She did so because she was a control freak (she openly admitted so) who enjoyed micromanaging her trading activities and because doing so gave her a sense of security.

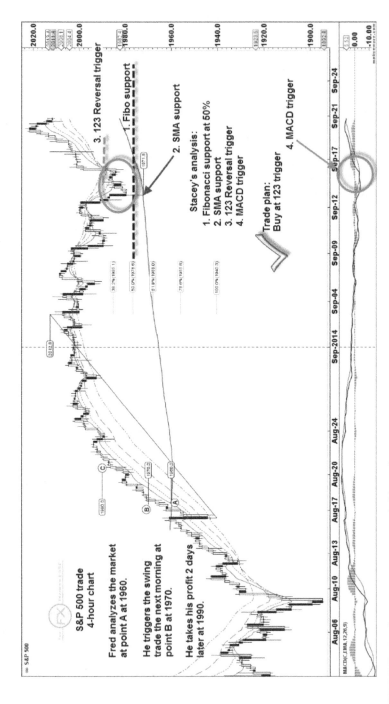

FIGURE 7.5 Trading opportunities revealed by analysis

Is Luck an Important Part in Trading?

Fred held a different view. Like Stacey, in his initial stage in this business, he did go through the painstaking process of building up a good foundation in trading. Unlike Stacey, he loathed planning the details. He thought a skillful trader should be able to think on his feet in the face of market changes, and make the right decisions there and then instinctively. "Let the thinking mind work" was his guiding principle. To him, planning was a chore, and the effort was not worth it because he was never able to plan as fast as the market changed.

On the one hand, Stacey believed trading was a sequential and logical process. Most things, if not everything, happened for a reason and could be explained through well-formed analysis or post-mortem work. Fred, on the other hand, thought luck played a major part in trading. "If you're naturally lucky, you have a high chance of winning regardless of what silly actions you might take; if luck is not on your side, all your analyses and all your brilliant trade plans don't count. You're bound to lose." So, Fred was not as zealous as Stacey in planning. After all, since luck played a part and he could not control it, why should he plan?

What he did not understand was why Stacey always seemed to have an inexplicable abundance of luck with her trading. While he repeatedly failed despite the effort he dedicated to trading, Stacey seemed to often enter the right trades at the right time and take profit right before the market reversed. What was more infuriating was that he spent all day long in his trading business, but Stacey only traded for three hours a day.

Fred thought that everything happened effortlessly for Stacey. Looking at her superb performance in trading, Fred wondered how she did it. Was she more intelligent, or was she so much more technically skilled? He did not think so. She did not seem to have a secret trading strategy or system either. Everything she did looked so fundamental to Fred. "She's exceptionally lucky," Fred concluded. He could not think of any other reasons.

The Secret Behind "Luck"

This week, Fred witnessed "Lucky Stacey" gain close to a thousand dollars within three days. The EUR/USD pair practically devalued with a 3 percent drop, and that gave Stacey windfall profits in her account. She had also shorted some JPY pairs and realized hundreds of pips on those positions. Fred could only watch with amazement and envy as this series of lucky events happened to Stacey. Making profits from trading seemed so easy for her.

"Lucky?" Stacey responded when Fred expressed his envy to her. From the abrupt rise in her voice, Fred could sense a tinge of discontent. Stacey felt he had done her an injustice with that statement and was about to teach him an important lesson in trading.

She opened up her trading journal to show Fred what he missed: the prior fundamental and technical analyses that pointed her to specific markets to trade. A well-written trade plan that directed her actions turn-by-turn. Heaps of analysis and confirmations done before she pulled the trigger. A well-planned and well-executed stop-loss strategy. Annotated screenshots of past days' charts that confirmed her view to sell those markets. So on and so forth.

"And do you still think it's all luck?" she asked Fred.

Stacey believed that trading success came naturally when a trader did his homework and was well-disciplined and organized. From her experience, she concluded that if she traded systematically and planned her trade in a disciplined manner, her chances of success would rise.

A Lesson from Luck That Never Came

The conversation with Stacey made Fred recall what happened in one of his trading sessions last week. He was in a rut in his personal life and was distracted, and he missed the move in the market. He kept waiting for the stock market to retrace before buying a particular stock. He prayed, "Some luck please. This has got to happen," but his prayer was not answered.

Even so, somehow he obstinately refused to follow his analysis again. When his analysis revealed it was time to buy, he refused to take action. Instead, he was overwhelmed with unfounded hope his prayers would finally be answered and the market would retrace.

At the end, he bought high. He blamed it on luck for the retracement that he yearned for never arrived. Now, as he thought of the words from Stacey, he started reflecting that his failure was not due to luck. The main culprit was his lack of discipline and determination to follow a well-defined trading system. His false hope that he could get lucky also caused him to ignore the analysis.

Fred lacked control, not over his luck but over himself and his trading approach.

"Lucky Traders": Is That Possible?

Although my students know that I advocate that the systematic, slow-and-steady manner is the way to go to build up a serious trading business, they often still ask me, "Is it possible to make money from trading by being lucky?"

Yes, I must admit, it does occur once in a while. Sometimes, luck might play a part in trading (or it is something right that a trader does by chance), but more often what happens is this:

1. All "odd" or unexpected conditions that will set up a "lucky" trade are becoming apparent.

2. Only highly alert traders are able to identify such an opportunity.

3. Out of these traders, only those who are courageous will take action to grab the opportunity.

And when they win, people call them *lucky traders*. But as you can see, it is more of an ability to identify the opportunity and the courage to pull the trigger that brings winning trades.

Here is an example to illustrate my point. Look at the following chart in Figure 7.6. Average traders will see the market is dropping and will either stay out of it because it has "moved too much" or will look to go short with the trend.

However, students of my Elliott Wave Ultimate course will have a different view. By adding some Elliott Wave counts and a harmonic pattern, along with looking for divergence in the Awesome Oscillator and a 123 reversal pattern with the MACD crossing above the signal line, they will see that the market is about to change direction, and there is a major opportunity to trade.

All of these analysis tools provide confirmation of a change in trend, and one of the better ways to trigger the trade is through the 123 reversal pattern. Since this is a daily chart, many traders will move down to a smaller time frame to enter at a better price point on a 123 reversal. Figure 7.7 illustrates this point.

A strong analysis method, combined with a trading strategy for triggering the trade, is what it takes to be confident in taking a position and following it through. When an end of trend presents itself on a larger time frame, such as the daily chart, it is time to train the brain for the large move that will follow and *plan the trade* accordingly. The beginning of a new trend creates opportunities to get into the new trend early and to add to the position as it moves in the direction of the new trend.

When they take profits out of this trade, average traders call them "lucky" because it is beyond their imagination that money can be made here.

So you see, "lucky traders" might not be just lucky. They could be those who keep their eyes open for market moves and are skilled enough to spot and trade opportunities that are invisible to the crowd. This requires razor-sharp alertness, skillfulness, courage to act, and of course, a few ounces of luck are always appreciated!

■ Pendulum Scenario 7.3: Calm versus Nervous Trader

"To play well you must feel tranquil and at peace."
—Harry Vardon, notable professional golfer from Bailiwick of Jersey

"Just another day at work!" Stacey said to herself after a troubled day in trading. As with any traders, Stacey's trading journey had ups and downs. She rejoiced

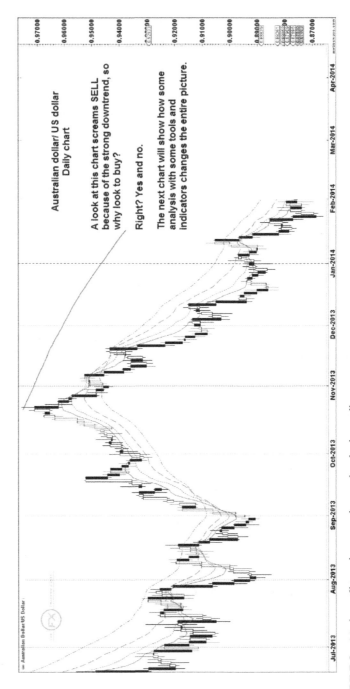

FIGURE 7.6 Market still in a downtrend so traders look to sell

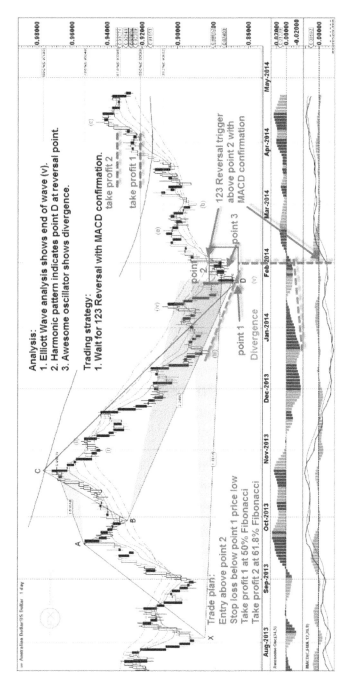

FIGURE 7.7 Trade entry opportunities revealed with Elliott Wave analysis and trading strategy

when she had good days, but when her trades went south, she could be affected emotionally.

However, Stacey cared about her performance in the trading business, but trading was not the only thing in her life. She was also a mom, a wife, and a homemaker. Not wanting to carry her emotions over from work to her personal life, Stacey toned down its impact by telling herself whatever happened during the three hours when she traded was "just another day at work."

By letting the day go, she could calm herself and save her baby from facing an agitated mom and her husband a grumpy wife.

A Plan to Temper the Nerves

Stacey understood she did not perform optimally when she was nervous. The problem was she became nervous easily. Recognizing this, she actively sought help for this. Months later, with the help of her coach and peers, she devised a plan:

1. *Be well-prepared before trading.* Nothing beats starting a trading session with abundant confidence as well as being armed with a roadmap for possible market trends. This was why Stacey did her homework the night before any trading day. The market was volatile: The information she gathered might well be outdated by the time she traded, the market might have changed, or her research might not be accurate. But knowing she came prepared every time she traded gave her a sense of calmness.

2. *Follow the trade plan.* The same advice that can be applied to almost every situation related to emotional trading can be applied to calming the nerves, too. Stacey knew when she executed her trade plan by rote, emotions—nervousness included—did not have a place in her trading. The emotions might arise as she traded, and when they did, she rarely maintained 100 percent calmness. However, when she followed her plan, she could usually temper her emotions until she closed her trades.

3. *Focus only on a handful of tasks.* Stacey tried not to multitask. She kept the number of trades she entered to a minimum, so her attention was well-focused. Though she had a habit of looking at a wide range of currency pairs for market insights, she only traded a few of them consistently. One of the reasons was since she was familiar with these currency pairs, she could more easily make profits when she focused on trading them.

4. *Cut down on distractions.* Avoiding multitasking also meant when Stacey traded, she focused on her work. She dedicated full attention to trading during her three-hour trading session and tried not to have another 97 things hanging over her head at the same time. The things on her to-do list could wait. If they

could not, Stacey would make a plan to settle them before she started trading. With full attention on trading, she could calmly tackle any positive or negative market conditions that arose during her trades.

5. *Avoid being too engrossed in trading.* No matter how immense her passion in trading, Stacey avoided becoming a 24/7 trader. This gave her the time and space to weather distress from a losing trading day, so she did not enter the next trading session carrying emotional baggage on her shoulders and could start the new day calmly.

Other techniques, including maintaining work-life balance, practicing meditation and yoga, as well as garnering a high level of confidence by repeatedly trading the trade plans on a demo account helped, too. One of her trading associates even taught Stacey an unusual way to deal with her nervousness: singing some silly ditty when she became stressed out or nervous.

Stacey was tempted to try it but not yet.

The Nervous Trader

Fred had never been able to tame the butterflies in his stomach when he traded.

He felt confident with his analysis skill, trading system and the research he had done, and by following his trade plan, he could get rid of certain noises from his trading. Yet none of these actions completely removed his emotions, especially the stomach-knotting nervousness he often felt when he needed to decide on a trade.

When the market moved according to his plan and he saw opportunities to get into trades, he was nervous; when the setup was coming to him and he needed to get himself ready to pull the trigger, he was nervous; and when the trend went against his analysis and he needed to decide whether to change the decision on his position, he was nervous, too.

Fred felt as if the market kept playing a game with him, trying to test his emotional threshold. Fred had no plan to concede defeat, but he did not know how to deal with the market.

What Can a Nervous Trader Do?

Fred did not realize that the real issue he had to deal with was not the market but himself. The market did not care about how he traded, whether he was making the right trading decisions or what kind of results he was producing, but Fred did. His concern about his performance and the fear of making wrong decisions caused his hands to shake when he traded. Fred needed to find a way to temper his nerves, so he could trade calmly and maximize his trading.

If he would listen to Stacey, she could give him a whole list of things waiting for him to try out, but that made him nervous, too!

Fred needed to spend time analyzing his personality to pinpoint what was causing his nervousness. It is difficult for traders to perform this high level of self-analysis on their own because they tend not to assess ourselves honestly. In Fred's case, it would be helpful to engage professional assistance from a trading coach.

CHAPTER 8

Habit #5: Understand and Exploit Your Unique Trading Personality

Do you know that the United States has an alarming high school dropout rate? It was reported that around 1.3 million students drop out annually (Monrad 2007). That's 1 every 25 seconds, or in other words, for every five students who enter high school every year, one of them will quit before completing their diploma.

Researchers around the nation have studied the motivations for the devastating dropout rate. One of the studies reported that the main reasons for students quitting prematurely included uninteresting classes, lack of motivation, financial issues, and academic challenges (Bridgeland 2007). Researchers generally agree these are some of the causes for the high dropout rate, but some of them ask, "So what are the causes for these causes?" or, in other words, what is the *root cause* for the issue?

Eventually, a group of researchers, educators, successful businesspeople, social activists, and highly successful figures in society suggested the root cause for the high dropout rate was a one-size-fits-all academic system failing the schoolchildren (Goyal 2012).

If you think about it, the school system is training everyone to become a professional even though not everyone is "naturally talented" to follow that path. Think about how the schools have made students sit through test after test, with no relevance to what students will do for a job as an adult. Think about how students are prescribed a "correct way of learning" when not everyone shares the same strengths and weaknesses, personalities, talents, styles of approaching issues, and so on.

This explains why some school kids do not find their classes interesting, lack motivation to study, or face challenges in keeping up with the class.

■ What about a One-Size-Fits-All Trading Style for Traders?

Average traders pick their trading styles based on recommendations from fellow traders, reviews they find on the Internet, the popularity of the styles, or their favorite trading gurus' promises. Some just pick the first one that appears in the search engine results page. They do not perform the due diligence to research the effectiveness of the style, whether it fits their personality, and what it takes to successfully practice the style. They do not have a valid reason to select the style, but they have an *intuition* about it. After all, "If the trading style works for everyone else, it should work for me, too."

Average traders think they should change their personalities to fit the trading style they pick. If the style requires them to be aggressive, they act accordingly, regardless of whether or not they can keep up with the speed. If the style requires them to wait and see for a prolonged period, they subdue the "fire" they have in trading and watch quietly, like turning themselves from a tiger into a tamed rabbit.

Following prescribed styles sounds like a good idea, especially when the traders are new and do not have a solid idea on how to trade. But how good is an idea if the followers have to alter part of their personalities to follow it?

For example, a day trader has to stay stuck watching the market during the entire trading session which could be anywhere from 2 to 8 hours. If traders prefer to look at the daily charts because either they don't have time to day trade or their temperament doesn't suit waiting for every move in the markets, then they shouldn't day trade.

On the contrary, some traders like to day trade because they want instant gratification, a quick fix, a quick profit, and they want to see results immediately. That's what you get from day trading and not from patiently waiting for a trade to come your way.

If traders force themselves to trade in a way that doesn't come naturally to them, how long before the traders will quit? How can the traders be consistently winning in trading if the styles they choose do not suit their preferences and personalities?

Doesn't this sound exactly like the case of the "one-size-fits-all" education system that is causing the high dropout rate in America? Could this be the same reason why many traders drop out of trading within the first year of launching their trading businesses?

Different Trading Styles

There are four different trading styles. Read the descriptions below and see which one suits your trading personality the best. Consider also your available time to trade when you choose your style. For example, some of these styles require you to respond quickly when alerts trigger, and others might offer more buffer time for you to react.

Scalping or Momentum Trading

This style is most suitable for traders who are thrilled at fast-paced, heart-pounding, and somewhat stressful trading. Every transaction happens within a matter of seconds or minutes, and scalpers have to think and act quickly. These momentum traders trade various time frames ranging from tick charts to 30-second to 5-minute time frames.

Scalpers trade only during the busiest times of the day, have to exercise high focus on the charts for several hours, make quick decisions in response to small price movements, and take as many trades as they see setting up. This trading style isn't suitable for those who cannot withstand the excitement and stress and prefer to make profits by patiently analyzing the markets. (See Figure 8.1.)

Day Trading

Similar to scalping, day trading is for traders who like excitement, prefer short-term trading, and want to see their trading results in a short time span. However, different from momentum trading, day trading involves holding a trade for a longer period of time, from several minutes to several hours. Nonetheless, day traders do not hold their trades overnight. Day traders typically trade 5-minute to 1-hour time frames.

This trading style is not suitable for traders who have day jobs because it requires them to constantly monitor the markets. Like scalping, it is not suitable for traders who do not favor buying and selling swiftly and making profits from small price movements. (See Figure 8.2.)

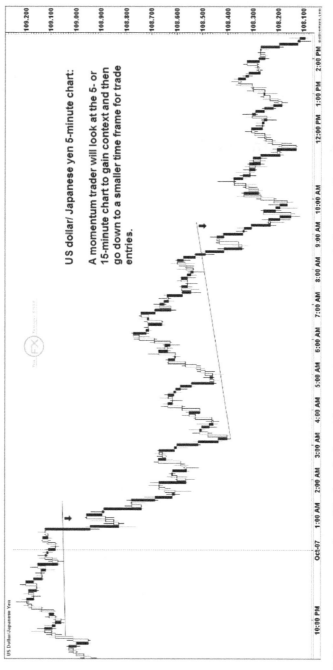

FIGURE 8.1 A momentum trader will look at the 5- or 15-minute chart to gain context, and take trades off a smaller time frame chart to fine-tune entries

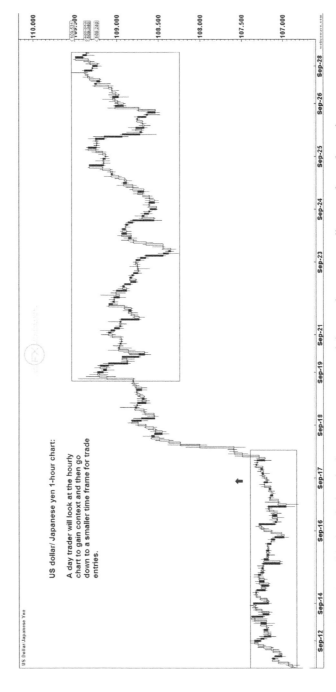

FIGURE 8.2 A day trader will look at the hourly chart to gain context and then go down to a smaller time frame for trade entry

Swing Trading

Swing trading is suitable for traders who are patient and are willing to hold their trades for days. It is ideal for those who have day jobs or can only dedicate a limited amount of time for trading every day. A swing trader typically chooses between trading off the daily, 4-hour, and 1-hour charts. Sometimes the trade is triggered in the direction of the trend on the larger time frame but taken on the smaller time frame to get better price entry. The trade can be managed on either the larger time frame or the time frame that triggered the trade.

As swing traders trade a longer time frame, they need to make sure they employ good setups and have larger stop losses in place to weather short-term market fluctuations. Swing traders need to think medium-term, from a few days to several days, depending on the market volatility. They must stay calm when their trades are going against them. This trading style is not suitable for those who are impatient and seek instant gratification, immediate results, and quick profits. (See Figure 8.3.)

Position Trading

Among all main trading styles, position trading involves the longest term. A position trader can hold a trade for several weeks to months, or even years, to capture a fundamental change in the value of the financial instrument that he trades. During the holding period, the trader has to think independently and ignore market noise. A position taker will likely look at the daily, weekly, monthly, and sometimes quarterly charts to analyze the trades to take. (See Figure 8.4.)

Position traders need to have good foresight of the markets. They predominantly employ the understanding of fundamentals in addition to their technical analysis. They have to remain patient and calm when the market fluctuates and cannot be swayed by small price movements. Moreover, they must have enough capital to stay in the game until the "grand reward" or ROI arrives. (See Figure 8.5.)

■ How Do You Choose Your Trading Style?

Successful traders take the necessary steps to study the styles, find out about the inherent strengths and limitations, and learn the conditions under which the styles work. Most importantly, they take time to understand and exploit their unique trading personalities before deciding which trading style suits them the best.

When looking for a trading style for yourself and examining whether it aptly fits you, you should take into account the following:

What type of trader should you be? A general guideline is this: If you enjoy sitting in front of the screen watching the market action all day long, you may prefer

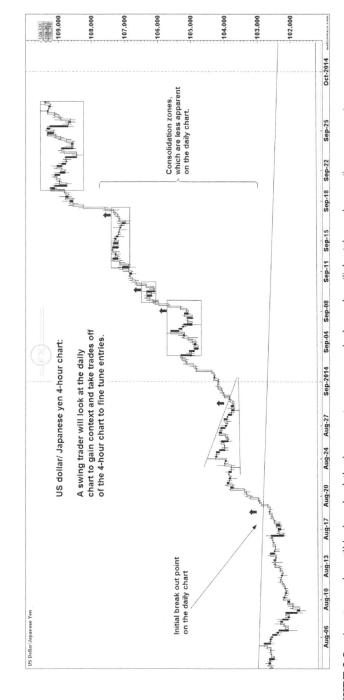

FIGURE 8.3 A swing trader will look at the daily chart to gain context and take trades off the 4-hour chart to fine-tune entries

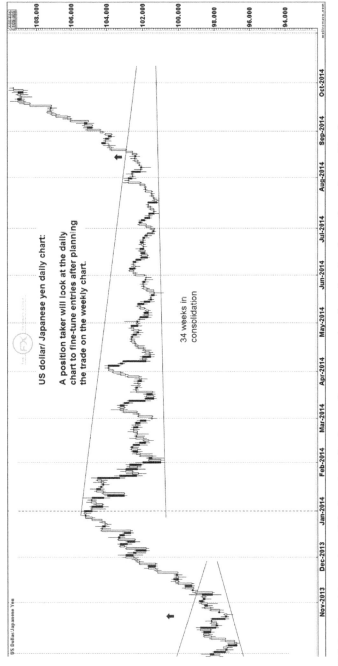

FIGURE 8.4 A position trader will look at the daily chart to fine-tune entries after planning the trade on the weekly chart

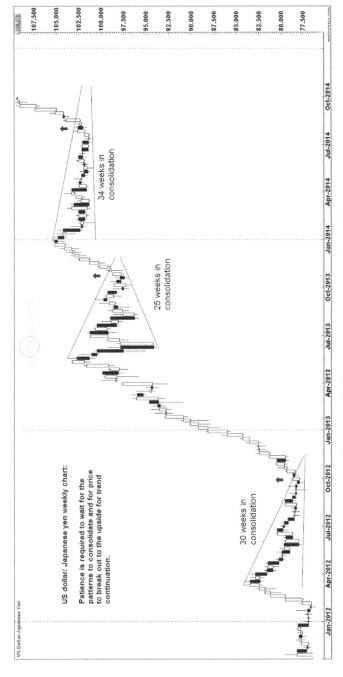

FIGURE 8.5 Patience is required of a position trader to wait for the patterns to emerge on the weekly chart

momentum trading or day trading; on the other hand, if you prefer to analyze the markets, establish your trade plan, and let your trade play itself out, you might be better suited to swing or position trading.

Short-Term or Long-Term Trader?

If you are a stay-at-home mom (or dad) or a full-time trader who has more flexibility with your time, you can perhaps concentrate on short-term trades; if you hold a day job and do not have that kind of freedom, you might probably be more suited for longer-term trades.

Discretionary or Mechanical Trader?

You might prefer your trading decisions to be guided by a set of well-defined and intentionally rigid rules, straying from which gives you a disturbing sense of insecurity. You might have a documented trading strategy and have promised yourself to loosely adhere to it, but when it comes time to pull the trigger, your experience, judgment, and intuition almost unmistakably kick in every time and force you to reevaluate the situation. If you are the former, you are most likely a mechanical or systematic trader. Otherwise, you are trading discretionarily.

Automated Trading or Conventional Trading?

Some traders favor automated trading. They will program the parameters for entry orders, stop losses, and profit-taking targets into an automated trading system and let it automatically monitor the markets and execute the trades for them. Using such a system removes the emotions from trade execution, because trade orders will be executed once the pre-programmed conditions are met, regardless of the trader's hesitation or emotions. Consistency can be achieved when the system trades the plans the trader has established through testing. Also, the trader is less likely to miss trading opportunities that arise over the 24-hour day or when the speed of entering orders is increased with the help of the computer program.

Algorithmic Trading, Black- Box Trading, and High-Frequency Trading

Automated trading is also known as *algorithmic trading* because the trading system follows an algorithm(s) pre-programmed into it to execute trades. Traders may allow the algorithm to trade completely automatically or intervene on occasion. Trading that is 100 percent automated where the trader doesn't know what is in the system is called *black-box trading* as the decision-making process is hidden from the traders.

Also, a special class of algorithmic trading that uses complex technology and algorithms to rapidly transact a large number of orders is called *high-frequency trading* (HFT). HFT operates at the millisecond level, and traders who employ this technique make profits from executing high volumes of trades.

Automated trading is widely used by institutional traders. On the retail side, many traders are employing it, too. However, retail traders have to be mindful of the execution costs such as spreads and slippage from the broker (the difference between the expected price of a trade and the price when the order is actually executed, especially in highly volatile markets) and factor it into their profit and loss.

On the other hand, there are traders who do not like to let go of the control of their trading and need to live through every price movement. They will not consider automated trading.

Having said so, does it mean that a trader must either be practicing automated trading *only* or conventional trading *only*? In other words, does she need to fall into one of these two extremes? Not necessarily so. Some traders are "somewhere in between" automated and conventional trading; they perform semi-automated trading.

For example, many forex traders use Expert Advisors (EA), which are integrated into the universal MetaTrader 4 or 5 (MT4 or MT5) platform in trading. The platform includes all the necessary components that allow traders to create, test, optimize, and run automated trading. They can control almost every aspect of their automated trading strategy and market analysis.

EAs are used to automate the analysis of forex and CFDs, and with many brokers, there is a wide range of CFD asset classes being offered on forex trading platforms. The high processing speed of these programs allows traders to write highly sophisticated codes to execute a large amount of analyses. Popular technical indicators such as MACDs, moving averages, and stochastics are typically applied to EAs as the basis for these analyses.

EAs can also be used to fully automate trade execution. However, some traders choose to retain certain control over the trading strategy. Instead of letting EAs place trades for them without their intervention, they might program EAs to just generate trading signals and then decide how to proceed based on the signals. These are the traders who perform semi-automated trading as previously mentioned.

While we are on the subject of trading platforms, the first question to ask is this: "Which broker will I set up an account with?" As a self-directed trader, many brokers offer forex, futures, and stock trading. Traders will research the following when selecting a broker: breadth of markets covered, number of instruments, speed of execution, reports and accounting functionality, account minimums, commission structure, support function, and the number of bells and whistles that fall under the tools and services category. Automated trading capabilities would fall under that "bells and whistles" category. So, if you are a trader requiring such functionality, research well when selecting a broker and test out the trading platform first to make sure the capabilities and "bells and whistles" fit what you want.

Micromanaging Trades or Staying Away?

For many traders, micromanaging their trades not only adds a lot of stress but also causes fear and greed to lead the trader away from their system. These traders prefer to set up their trades based on their trading system and to minimize their personal and emotional involvement by allowing the trade to run its course. On the contrary, the adrenaline rush from active participation in trades for certain traders might even be the primary motivation for their trading business. These traders prefer to actively watch their trades and stay close to the market throughout, almost micromanaging them.

None of these styles are strictly right or wrong. The key is to find the right balance that suits your preference, personality, and unique circumstances. That is why the first two steps in establishing a trader's business plan (Habit #2) is to understand who you are, your strengths and weaknesses, what you want out of trading, as well as your personality and preferences.

■ When Should You Get Help?

You might be a novice trader who does not have enough experience in finding a fitting trading style. You might be afraid you are "too close to yourself" and can be disillusioned by your hindsight. You might not be sure which trading style is suitable for you or whether your current trading style is the most profitable. This is when it will be beneficial to enlist the help of an experienced coach (Habit #4).

The correlation between trading style and your personality is one of the best things a trading coach can help you to determine. Once your "trading personality" is established, your coach can further guide you to establish an effective trading strategy around that knowledge.

Different Learning Styles for Different Traders?

Besides guiding a trader to find a suitable trading style, an experienced coach might also observe how the trader learns and customize a plan for him accordingly.

For instance, the trader might be a visual, auditory, or kinaesthetic learner. He may learn better by analyzing chart patterns, listening to audio tapes or lectures, or taking piles of notes while studying.

He might be a left-brain dominant person who is logically and mathematically inclined, analytical, and sequential, so he is attracted to learning trading system automation. He might be a right-brain dominant person who is intuitive, synthesizing, and tends to look at situations as a whole, so learning to make discretionary trading decisions will be his preference.

Also, he might feel more comfortable by stuffing as many techniques as possible into his brain before starting to trade, or he might prefer to learn as he trades.

These are but a few examples. There are countless possible learning styles a trader might adopt. It is up to him and his coach to find out an optimal one for him.

There are many ways to trade that involve certain special techniques you (and most traders) are not aware of. An experienced coach can point you to them.

Many traders make the mistake of wasting too much time exploring the different trading styles, only to end up landing on ones that do not fit them well probably because they only searched within their limited domain of knowledge or because they did not manage to profile their trading personality correctly to begin with. If you choose to discover your trading style on your own, make sure you assess your risk appetite, level of commitment, analytical capability, emotional stamina, time available for trading, and your trading strengths and weaknesses. All of these factors will help you determine which trading style suits your personality the best.

■ Reducing the Dropout Rates of School Kids and Traders

As we are reaching the end of this chapter, I had to return to the opening topic of this chapter: the high school dropout rate in the United States.

I asked myself this: Just how many children can be given a brighter, more secure, and more successful future if the system can be designed correctly. Imagine how much confidence we can instill in our children if we have a better system to identify and fully develop their talents and interests.

If only we can have enough well-trained and experienced experts to help the kids to explore their talents, preferences, and personalities, and fit them into an education system that suits them, how much things would be different. We might have happier kids and a lower school dropout rate.

Similarly, for you as a trader, if you can find a trading style that fits your strengths and weaknesses, preferences and personality, can you imagine how much your probability of "dropping out" from trading can be reduced or how much your chances of success will be heightened?

1. Answer the following questions. They will help you to define what you perceive your personality and preferences to be, and how it relates to your trading activities.

   a. Why are you trading this year?

   b. What style of trading do you prefer (momentum, day trading, swing trading, position trading) and why?

   c. What part of your trading system do you feel most uncomfortable with?

   d. What markets do you prefer to trade and why?

   e. What time of day do you prefer to trade?

   f. How long do you trade each day?

   g. How does trading impact your lifestyle?

   h. On a scale of 1 to 10, rate your risk aversion to trading. (1 = extremely risk averse, 10 = risk seeking).

   i. How well do you handle stress?

   j. What do you do when you feel burned out trading?

   k. If you don't see positive results quickly, do you become easily discouraged?

TABLE 8.1 **Matrix to Help You to Determine the Trading Style That Suits You**

		Trading Styles		
	Momentum	Day	Swing	Position
Conventional / Manual trading:				
Discretionary				
Systematic / Mechanical				
Programmable trading platforms for semi-automation				
Automated trading:				
Algorithmic				
Black box				
High frequency				

2. Use Table 8.1 to get an initial idea of the trading style that suits you.

   a. First, do you want to be a momentum, day, swing, or position trader?

   b. Second, what is your preference in trading? For example you might want to be a discretionary trader, systematic/mechanical trader, or one who performs algorithmic trading, and so on.

   Circle your preferences in Table 8.1 that correspond to your answers. You are allowed to choose more than one style. Review this chapter if you are not sure what any of these entries mean.

   This exercise provides a preliminary idea for you to find out more about the trading style(s) of your choice. You might want to work with your coach to further explore this.

◾ Pendulum Scenario 8.1: Self-Doubting versus Overconfidence

"Our doubts are traitors, and make us lose the good we oft might win, by fearing to attempt."

—William Shakespeare

This must have been the fourth trading strategy that Fred had tested since the beginning of his trading business. The previous three seemed promising at first. Rounds of testing on his demo account proved this. But when they were put to the test in the real battlefield, the results he saw were far from what he anticipated.

Fred thought there were too many uncertainties in the real world that these strategies did not address, and he had to modify them on-the-fly as he traded to accommodate for these uncertainties. Hard cash was on the line, and he had to do everything to protect his capital even if it meant he had to deviate from his original trade plan.

A Self-Doubting Trader and His Mistakes Repeated Over and Over

Fred ran another test after the first three failed him. Fred was optimistic about it because the system seemed to be extraordinarily well-rounded. The pitfalls he experienced in the past were all covered, and he saw no reason why he would fail this time. He was full of confidence when he sat down and started to trade in the morning. "All I have to do is to trade my plan!"

Then it happened again. Fred was expecting an upward move in the market, and it did happen. Based on the criteria listed in his trade plan, he identified a "near perfect" setup. He was overjoyed, was rubbing his hands together in anticipation, and could not wait to enter the trade when the time was ripe.

But as the time to pull the trigger drew closer, doubts brewed in him. "Have I chosen a good setup? What if there's something wrong with my analysis? Is it a right move to trust the strategy so well?"

He hesitated and repeatedly tried to evaluate the trade entry point. The consistent analysis results should have left him confident, but Fred was still frozen by his doubts. In the end, the trade flew by. Fred blamed himself as the chart showed him that the market moved according to the pattern forecast by his system. His failure to follow his plan taught him something:

"It was not the strategy that was at fault. It was me. What's wrong with me? Why do I keep losing in trading?"

A Trader Who Would Not Listen and Her Trading Failures Caused by Overconfidence

Stacey's peers warned her that she might have been overtrading, but she didn't listen.

After months of experimenting, she was confident she had developed a good understanding of the strengths of her trading system and was putting it to good use. The system was not perfect, but for every weakness she discovered in the system, she found a clever way to work around it. The hundreds of hours she devoted in studying her markets also gave her much confidence to the extent that she thought, "I could even predict the market move with my eyes shut."

All these gave Stacey a win/loss ratio that was significantly higher than her peers. That was part of the reason she was not willing to listen to their advice. She believed she knew better. She showed no interest in slowing down. After all, with so much time and effort poured into reaching this level of skill and grasp of the markets, it was time to reap the fruits of her hard work and make an onslaught in the market.

On Thursday afternoon, Stacey realized the well-meaning behind her peers' advice. For the past three days, she had achieved winning rates that were so high they blew her mind. She was now overdosed on confidence and felt almost invincible. "It's time to take a step beyond what I'm doing now," she determined. For a moment, that thought gave her an adrenaline rush, but she would soon find out it marked the beginning of a disaster.

Aiming to earn more from each trade, Stacey took a big risk by taking positions larger than she should. It worked. She repeated her success over more trades than her money management rules allowed. She could not exactly "clone" the success rate to all the trades, but she still managed to hit a high overall win/loss ratio. That was when she became overconfident and took a bolder move. Not only did she trade excessively, with larger than the supposed position size, but she also relaxed the stop-loss level.

At this point, she had stopped trading her plan and was almost trading according to her intuition. Soon, she found herself losing more than winning. But blinded by her previous successes, she was still high in confidence and would not admit defeat. In fact, she did it more aggressively, seemingly to prove to herself she was not wrong to trade that way. More trades were entered more quickly, even larger position sizes were taken, and the stop loss levels were so liberal that they were as good as nonexistent.

At the end of the day, Stacey lost around half the money she had made from her previous winning streak. During the end-of-day review, she found she had gambled the money away. She felt regretful and blamed it on her overconfidence. She shared this experience with her peers and apologized for not listening to what they said. Stacey vowed not to repeat the same mistake again.

But would she, especially when the winning streak comes to her again? No one would know.

Why Do Overconfidence and Self-Doubting Matter?

Traders who are overconfident tend to overestimate their knowledge of the markets, trading skills, and ability to react toward uncertainties. At the same time, they can underestimate the risks involved in each trade. These can temporarily blind the trader and cause oversights in the decisions they make when they trade.

Traders who are overconfident are likely to be trigger-happy and less likely to trade according to their plans. They will enter more trades than they should, take larger position sizes than they should, and risk more than they should.

Self-doubting is the opposite of overconfidence. It is caused by the lack of confidence in traders even though their trade plan, system, and analysis could have removed any possible doubts in their trading decision.

Contrary to overconfidence, self-doubt can cause inaction in traders. Remember the last time when the trade setup you were waiting for arrived but you were momentarily halted by inexplicable fear, and this caused you to miss a trading opportunity? This could be caused by self-doubt.

▮ Pendulum Scenario 8.2: Cautious versus Reckless Trading

"Risk comes from not knowing what you're doing."

—Warren Buffett

We have seen numerous times in this book how a trader's personality shows up in his or her trading, and we will take a look at it again in this Pendulum Scenario. For an example, let's look at the different ways Stacey and Fred approach driving.

A Cautious Driver

Stacey remembered how "timid" she was when she first learned how to drive. She knew the road was full of danger, so she did not want to be too confident about her driving skills. She clearly understood that lives might be involved every time somebody makes a mistake, so no one can afford to be reckless. Maintaining the "expect the unexpected" mentality when driving put her on high alert when she drove.

From those lessons, she made sure she checked the rear-view and side mirrors (no blind spots!), safety belts of all passengers, and the brakes before she hit the road. Sometimes she took these precautions repeatedly if she was not sure or she suspected she missed something. Making sure that things were all right gave her a sense of confidence and calmness.

Her husband would sometimes laugh at the precautions she took, joking that she was out there to win the neighborhood "drive safely" contest. This only caused Stacey to give him a disgusted look, and a few punches landing squarely on his arm.

Stacey abided by all traffic rules and driving etiquette, no excuses. Stacey knew the rules were there for a reason and violating them could mean disaster. By constantly reflecting on her mistakes she improved her driving.

A Cautious Trader

Stacey's "timidity" showed up in her trading, too. Since the first day she traded, she knew the trading journey was full of traps and unforeseeable circumstances, so she did not want to be too confident with her trading skills. She understood hard cash was involved in trading, and she could not be reckless. The same "expect the unexpected" mentality she had when she drove applied to her trading today.

For every single trade she wanted to make, Stacey checked to make sure all the setup conditions, entry, and exit criteria, and stop-loss limit were in place before she pulled the trigger. Sometimes, she checked again and again if she was not sure or suspected she missed something. Making sure she did this checklist right gave her a sense of confidence and calmness.

Her peers in trading sometimes laughed at her overcautious nature, but Stacey ignored these remarks. She knew better. This "timidity" gave her the edge to stay in the game and win most of the battles.

Stacey set up trade plans and strictly followed them. No excuses. She understood the rationale behind every rule in the plan and knew that deviating from them could spell disaster. She could easily review the bad trades she made and find weaknesses in her trading skill when she went by the rules. Constantly reflecting on the mistakes helped her improve her trading skill.

There was no question that "cautious Stacey" can go a long way in this trading journey.

A Reckless Driver

Fred had a conception that men were natural drivers. He thought he naturally drove well.

Fred understood the road was full of danger, too, but he believed in his ability to handle every situation that came at him on the spot, so he maintained a "spontaneous" mentality. He understood lives were in his hands when he drove, so he exercised a "reasonable level of caution" without overdoing it. "Being overcautious can just kill the fun in driving," he thought.

Fred did not check the condition of his car regularly. He had no reason to do this because the condition would not change much from drive to drive. As long as his gut feeling signaled to him the car felt fine, he would not pay extra attention to it.

Sometimes his passengers, out of fright, warned him he was driving too recklessly. However, he had confidence in his car-maneuvering skills and never heeded their advice.

Fred remembered how much effort he put in to study the driver's handbook and familiarize himself with all the traffic rules and regulations to pass the driver's license written test in the first sitting. However, he did not always go by the traffic rules. "These rules are only for reference," he once told his friend, "and it is more important to use your *thinking mind* to make decisions when you drive."

A Reckless Trader

Fred's character showed up in trading, too. As a self-proclaimed logical person, he prided himself as a natural trader. Having no doubt with his analytical and reasoning skills, he thought he was gifted with the natural ability to trade well.

Like Stacey, Fred treated trading as a battlefield with dangers looming around, but he believed in his ability to handle every foreseeable and unforeseeable circumstance that came to him, so he maintained a spontaneous mentality when he traded. Hard, cold cash was at stake when trading, he understood, but he thought that being overly cautious took out all the fun and excitement in trading, so he chose not to go down this path.

Fred did not regularly and thoroughly check his trade plans. He did not see why he should be testing his setup conditions, entry and exit criteria, and stop-loss limits since he could not see how one trade could be too different from the next. Sometimes, it crossed his mind that something might be amiss, but as expected, he would brush the suspicion away. As long as his gut feeling signaled him everything would be fine, he was not going to bother to pay extra attention to it.

Fellow traders warned Fred when they saw him trading recklessly and impulsively. However, having exceeding (but somewhat unproven) confidence in his trading skills, he never heeded their advice. In fact, he was unhappy about being advised because he felt he knew his situation and himself better.

In the beginning of his trading business, Fred followed the recommendations of the course he took to establish his trader's business plan and trading system and learned them by heart. However, he did not want to be tied to the rules in the plans. "They are for reference only," he once told a friend, "and it is more important to use your *thinking mind* to make decisions when you trade."

Good luck to "thinking" Fred. He probably won't go a long way if he keeps his reckless style of trading.

CHAPTER 9

Habit #6: Follow a System

Committed traders are avid learners. We regularly attend seminars, learn new skills from courses, and keep our knowledge updated by reading various publications.

These are all beneficial to traders. However, many are not aware that outside of seminar rooms, training courses, and published materials are other places we can draw practical lessons that will benefit our trading business from.

For example, have you ever wondered the following:

1. Why do servers at a fast-food restaurant always ask you the same questions when you order your meal? How do they minimize the queuing times for you? How do they manage to serve your meal within 10 minutes even during peak hours?

2. How do hypermarkets manage their inventory, when there could easily be thousands to tens of thousands of items stocked in a single store? How do they make sure they do not overstock or understock those items? And how do they even count how many items there are in their stores?

3. How does one of those large online bookstores manage millions of titles? How does it handle the huge number of orders, easily thousands of them per minute from all over the world? How do they deliver the right items to the right customers to minimize re-routing and complaints?

Simply put, how do successful large corporations function when they have so many resources to manage, with so many people getting involved, and the processes getting increasingly complicated? How do they keep track of what works and what does not work? And most importantly, how do they make sure everything they do is driving profits to the corporation?

The key is in their systems. Through years of experience, after going through countless failures and successes, they have derived winning formulas in every aspect of their businesses. They have established systems that fit into their business requirements, environments, and ecosystems, and will consistently follow the system. They keep a record of what is bringing them successes and what is failing them.

They will do the same thing the same way (and even at the same time) every day to ensure their business operations yield the outcomes that they expect until a breakdown in their system occurs. That's when they have their experts patch up or optimize the systems. After which, they start to apply the system consistently again to produce consistent results.

■ What Can You Learn from These Big Corporations?

Just like tested and proven systems do wonders for giant corporations, a robust system for your trading will help you consistently achieve the results you desire, too. Successful traders rely on well-defined systems for their trading.

If you have a system, ask yourself this: Is your system tested and proven? Does it consistently produce the results you desire? Are you executing it consistently, or are you still jumping from one system to another, like a typical trader who is in the *Technical Trader's Trap*? Can you trust it wholeheartedly? And do you have the confidence to follow your system?

If you don't have a system, consider setting one up, as this will give you a winning edge in trading. What does it take for you to find or establish a system? Do you need to engage the help of a coach?

When you try to set up your system—especially if you are still a novice trader—you may start out by experimenting with many different strategies, attending as many seminars as you can afford to, taking courses, and jumping from one guru's recommendation to another's. That's okay. However, at some point you need to settle down, take a step back, and develop your own system according to your trading style and temperament.

And when you have an approved tested system, *follow it*. A system is only as good as the paper it is written on, which is good to look at but practically useless unless you apply it in your trading and strictly adhere to it.

What Is the Difference between a Trading System, a Trading Strategy, and a Trade Plan?

A trading system is a collection of trading strategies. A trading strategy is simply a methodology that determines how a trader enters and exits trades based on price action, analysis techniques, a chart setup with indicators, or a combination of all. To deal with various market cycles, a trader often defines a number of different trading strategies. These strategies together make up the trader's trading system.

A trade plan is a set of rules formulated for an individual trade when a trade opportunity arises. It dictates the trade management actions a trader *plans* to take for that particular trade, including where to enter the trade, where to take profit, and where to take the loss. Each trade plan is unique to a trade. Actual price levels are used when defining these actions.

To further illustrate, let's look at what a trading system and a trade plan each consists of.

A trading system defines what you want to trade, how you want to trade, and what your specific trading strategies are within the system. It comprises the following elements:

- The markets you want to trade in
- The time frame you want to trade, e.g., 5-minutes, 15-minutes, 1-hour, 4-hours, 1-day, etc.
- The chart setup, including analysis trading tools such as Elliott Waves, Fibonacci, pivot points, and indicators to identify and confirm trading opportunities
- The position size based on money management rules
- The specific entry rules
- The specific stop loss procedures and risk taken
- The specific exit rules

On the other hand, a typical trade plan defines the following for a particular trade:

- Entry prices for the trade
- Profit taking exit prices for the trade
- Stop-loss level for the trade
- Trade management rules for the trade (trailing profits or stops for example)

These are four main trade management strategies:

1. Get in and out all at once.

2. Get in all at once and take profits at various levels.

3. Get into the position at various levels and get out all at once.

4. Get in and out at various levels.

Strategies 1 to 4 go from simple to more complex. Which strategy to choose is a function of the trader's experience.

Notice that a trade plan is brief and can usually be outlined in a few lines.

How to Set up Your Trading System

In Chapter 8, we mentioned that there are systematic and discretionary traders. The sample structure outlined in this chapter applies to systematic and discretionary traders because all traders need some defined rules to follow even if it is only a checklist.

Some discretionary traders trade on the fundamentals. However, having a plan is always better than having no plan. Even a discretionary trader should have a trade plan in mind, no matter whether it is based on a specific system. Discretionary traders might not have rigid fixed trading systems, but some form of *rule-based* discretionary trading will keep their trading in check.

The first suggestion for you when you set up a trading system is to follow it, so keep it simple and straightforward. Make it easy to refer to and not too complicated. Chapter 16 presents a more complete trading system for you to follow as a guide once you learn all the concepts in this book.

A minimalist recommended template consists of only four parts:

- *The specific chart setup*. The market(s), time zone(s), and time frame(s) that you want to trade in are defined here. You will also specify the indicators, tools, or price action (including candlestick patterns) that help you to identify a new trend, and indicators, tools, or price action that confirm the trend.

- *General rules*. This lays out a set of rules that hold true for every trade. It mainly serves as a reminder for you to stick to the trading system.

- *The specific entry rules*. What should trigger your buy/sell decisions? Be specific when you state them.

- *The specific exit rules*. These include the stop-loss and take-profit criteria.

Here's a tip that might be useful for you when you set up your trading system. Some traders write out a list of *general rules* they want themselves to follow before going into the more specific and "formal" rules. The following is a sample set of a trader's general rules.

---

10 General Trading Rules

1. Avoid buying or selling after a large move in the market.

2. Avoid emotional trades that do not follow the trade plan.

3. Do not change the trade parameters once they are entered in the trading platform unless it is part of the trade monitoring process.

4. If the trade is missed, wait for the pullback or Fibonacci retracement.

5. After a 5-wave sequence (in Elliott Wave analysis), determine the potential Fibonacci retracement and print out the chart to wait for the level to buy (or sell) so you don't miss the trade.

6. Trade with the trend. If the daily and trading time frame trends are up, look for buys unless the following occurs:

   - There is divergence in the oscillator (RSI, stochastic, or Awesome Oscillator, for example) signaling the price action is running out of steam.

   - The market has made a large move and needs to pause or retrace.

   - Price is way above the moving averages. Think of a rubber band analogy and the need for price to snap back to the averages before the trend continues.

7. Be happy taking losses and profits and don't focus on the money but focus on the set up instead.

8. The best way to minimize risk is not to trade. Do not feel obligated to be in a position all the time.

9. Do not undertrade either. Follow the markets even if a trade is not apparent.

10. Risk no more than 2 percent on any one trade for a total risk of 6 percent. When starting out, 1 percent is the amount you should risk. No more. Remember, trading is a marathon, not a sprint.

You should list your trading beliefs and affirmations that support successful trading, and allow them to guide you when you define your system. The next list shows you an example of some beliefs and affirmations.

Positive Trading Beliefs and Affirmations that Support Successful Trading

1. I learn through my mistakes and my successes.

2. There will be other opportunities besides this one.

3. The market provides me with oceans of opportunity and profits.

4. Risk is essential to reward.

5. My emotions are balanced on the fulcrum between fear and greed.

6. I love trading, as it is a privilege to trade.

7. I will do the necessary planning and journaling to be a superior trader.

8. I know my rules and I follow my rules.

9. I don't trade on other analysts' advice.

10. My trading rules are rigid but my expectations are flexible.

11. I create my life. I create the exact amount of my financial success.

12. I trade to win. My intention is to create wealth and abundance.

13. I am truly grateful for all the money I have now.

◼ Words of Caution for Traders in the *Technical Trader's Trap*

Nowadays in the market, there are about as many trading systems as there are traders and a myriad of variables and correlations discovered that boasts to help traders to "win big" in trading. Many gurus claim their trading systems will be the final answer to their followers' search for financial independence and can take away their money worries forever.

The nonexistence of a perfect trading system might sound discouraging, but this is where the excitement in trading comes into play. No one trading system is suitable for everyone. It is up to you, as a trader, to apply your creativity and insight to develop a system that fits your unique personality and preferences and to test it and tweak it until it produces consistent results.

The marketplace is a huge testing ground full of uncertainties and surprises. It is up to you to make new discoveries about it, experiment with what you learn, and make other exciting new discoveries.

I will also remind you that it is easy for traders in the *Technical Trader's Trap* to get caught up in the obsession of tweaking and adjusting their trading system to the extent that the amount of time and effort they spend on this overrides that of their trading. Remember, a trader's main job is to make profits from your trading business activities and not to get caught in the technical *chores* of overtweaking a trading system.

Take Action!

Define your trading system by answering the following questions:

1. Describe your trading system.

a. What are you planning to trade?

b. What is your trading style and time frame for trading?
   For example, you may be a day trader with a mechanical system trading off the 15-minute and 5-minute charts. You may also have a swing trading system for longer-term trades that you establish every evening. It is possible to use different strategies with different styles. The recommendation is to set up different accounts for different strategies. For example, a day-trading strategy will be traded in a separate account from a swing-trading strategy.

c. Identify the key indicators in your trading system and why you use them.

d. Describe your chart setup for each strategy. (For example, you may have a trend strategy for getting into the trend, and you may have an end-of-trend strategy for finding the end of the trend before the correction takes place.)

2. Determine the rules for your trading system.

a. What is your daily premarket routine?

b. How do you analyze the general market conditions?

c. How do you determine the position size traded (what is your percentage of capital at risk for each trade)?

d. What are your profit targets: pips[*], points, ticks, or dollars (cents) per trade per trading style (momentum, day, swing, or position)?

e. How many trades do you intend to take per week per given style?

f. How much time will you devote to trading in a given day or week?

g. Specify and print out your chart setup for each strategy.

h. What are your criteria for entering trades?

i. How do you determine your potential profit area for your exit strategy?

j. How do you determine your stop loss on each trade?

3. Create a *pro-forma* estimate for projected trading net revenue.

a. What are your estimated trades per week?

b. What is your monthly estimated win/loss ratio?

c. What is your estimated profit (pips, points, ticks, or dollars) on weekly and monthly trades?

d. What is your estimated loss (pips, points, ticks, or dollars) on weekly and monthly stopped out trades?

e. Estimate monthly and annual pip, points, ticks, or dollar profits.

f. Convert pips, points, and ticks to dollars.

g. Determine your return on investment (use total $ amount of unleveraged capital).

h. Determine your return on actual trading capital used in your account.

*Pip: In the forex markets, a pip is a unit of measurement to express the change in value between a pair of currencies. It is the smallest amount by which a currency quote can change. For example, for a US dollar-related currency pair, the smallest change it can make is USD 0.0001. Therefore, one pip for this currency pair is USD 0.0001. Now brokers quote to 5 decimal places, but the pip is still to the fourth decimal place, or 1/10,000th. For the Japanese yen pairs, the pip is to the .01, or the one-hundredths decimal place.

Point: For the futures markets, one point is a price change of one one-hundredth, or 1 percent of one cent. For example, if a futures contract experiences a price change from 1450.00 to 1451.00, a move of one point has happened.

Tick: A tick represents the minimum movement in the price of a security. The size of a tick varies for different financial instruments. For example, for stocks, a tick may be 1/8, 1/16, or 1/32 of a dollar; but for e-mini S&P 500 contract, the tick size is 0.25, which means each tick represents $12.50.

Dollar: For the stock markets, the price of a stock is expressed in dollars and cents. For example, the price for IBM stock could be quoted as USD 184.00.

▓ Pendulum Scenario 9.1: Optimistic versus Pessimistic Trader

"Optimism is the faith that leads to achievement.

Nothing can be done without hope and confidence."

—Helen Keller

It had been the third loss in a row since the beginning of her trading session and not even one winning trade yet. Stacey felt so anxious that she started to pace up and down in her living room.

Today was not her day. As usual, she had done her due diligence in analyzing the market before entering every one of her trades, but somehow the market was not moving in her favor. Either the position size she took was wrong or the expected trend reversals did not materialize, and this was costing her trades. The only fortunate thing was that she had set up proper stop losses according to her trade plan. That limited her losses before things got out of hand.

One week ago, Fred faced the same situation. After just one winning trade, the stock market started to move in the opposite direction to what he had forecast. Fred was quick enough to execute a stop loss and protected his earnings for the day. However, his trading went haywire for the next few trades. The market fluctuated in an irrational and unpredictable fashion. His analysis seemed to be continually failing him.

The market fluctuations did not make sense to him since he was confident that his analysis was correct. As he later found out, his analysis was not at fault. Some news came out that adversely affected the markets for which he was unprepared.

How the Optimistic Trader and the Pessimistic Trader Begin Their Days

Stacey and Fred decided to call it a day after losing the next three trades. The following day, they began their trading sessions again but with different outlooks.

Stacey was hopeful. Although she was still a little skeptical about the market movement, she knew she had every reason to stay optimistic because since she began trading live months ago, she had been weathering the storms on the journey well. Moreover, her tested and proven trading system had been serving her well. It had become her source of confidence in trading.

She fully understood that it was only natural to feel uncertain when she began her trading session today. After all, she had just gone through a full day of mishaps the day prior and had barely recovered from the emotional roller coaster ride. However, she kept in mind that trading is a psychological game, and unless she stayed optimistic and focused, she would be trapped in a losing streak. So, the first thing she needed to do that morning was to clear the "pessimistic air" around her.

Fred also was fully aware of the state of mind he was in after going through yesterday's tempest. A brief contemplation revealed that the emotion overwhelming him now was not fear. It was frustration. He was angry the news came out at such an untimely moment. "How could they have employed such unscrupulous means to rob us of our profits?!" he grumbled. Understanding that victims like him could do nothing against news coming out, he was upset.

Although the insider's report he received revealed that the big players had stepped out from the market after the news was released and the damage was done, he remained pessimistic. Would the market resume its normal behavior? He doubted it. He had lost hope that he could make any profits for the next couple of days even if the market regained its composure.

The fact was, even if he was skeptical, he could leave that market alone and try his hand on other markets, but he did nothing. The only thing that was stopping him was in his mind, his pessimism.

The Difference in Perspectives

Stacey was not an eternal optimist. Once in a while, during her "troubled trading periods," she lost sight of her direction and felt like giving up too. That was when the positive mindset, her so-called *internal rescue system*, kicked in.

Since Stacey knew her numbers, such as how many wins she received versus how many losses on average, she could easily remind herself that taking losses was all right. She told herself that winning trades would be on the way after the probability for the losing trades wore out. This logic made it possible for her to stay impartial with every trade and trade her plan consistently on the subsequent trades after losses. She accepted that losing was part of the trading game, so it did not bother her.

"The winner is just around the corner, waiting right there to pop up at anytime!" That was how she kept her spirits high and her optimism growing as she marched on.

As for Fred, he was not as fortunate as Stacey. When self-doubt overwhelmed him, no internal rescue system turned on to protect him. What kicked in instead was wave after wave of depression, anxiety, and self-doubt. His response to these? Inaction. He would stare blankly at the computer screen, sometimes for hours, when he was unsure about which trading action to take.

He did not choose to be pessimistic. In fact, when he first jumped into the trading business, he was full of hopes and high spirits. But his morale started to wear down after rounds of failure and nonperformance. Fred was consistently missing the targets he set for himself. If the situation persisted, he would run into financial strain before long. He had trouble being optimistic when all he saw was doom and a gloomy future.

"I'm not as good a trader as I thought I was. Maybe I shouldn't even be trading." That was a typical lament when pessimism crept in. Pessimistic thinking like this did not improve his situation and only made things worse. Pessimism begat pessimism.

What about You?

Do you think it is possible to always stay optimistic as a trader? Are you always able to see a half-filled glass as "half full" and not "half empty"? Or better yet, will you hold high hopes the half-filled glass will eventually be filled?

What we know about trading is that what shows up in life shows up in trading, too. So, an optimistic person will generally deal with her trading optimistically, and a pessimistic person will deal with it pessimistically.

An optimistic trader understands that losing is inevitable and tries not to be affected by it emotionally. She takes setbacks in stride and moves on. She might even confidently proclaim, "Yes, I've made losing trades, but so what? I've made more positive trades than losers, so take that!" A positive mindset becomes her edge in trading.

On the contrary, a pessimistic trader loses her motivation fast whenever she encounters setbacks. Her pessimism can cause her to doubt her capability to make profits from trading, stop seeing the reasons for pouring in time, money and energy in trading, and eventually close her trading business.

Tips to Temper Pessimism

Here are three tips to help you temper your pessimism:

1. It all starts with completing your business plan and testing your trading system to gain confidence in it.

2. When experiencing losses, stay emotionally neutral and go back to your demo account to practice or retest your strategy. Fine-tune it if necessary. When you fall into pessimism, practice, practice, and practice on the demo account to regain trust in your system and prove your trading capability to yourself.

3. Once your trading system is proven, hope and confidence will naturally return. There is no way you can feel pessimistic anymore!

In the long run, treat trading as a business. All the highs and lows in trading (including the emotional roller coaster rides) are part of your business. When pessimism comes knocking on your door, keep your cool, confront it, and deal with it!

■ Pendulum Scenario 9.2: Flexible versus Stubborn Trader

"Hope begins in the dark, the stubborn hope that if you just show up and try to do the right thing, the dawn will come. You wait and watch and work: you don't give up."

—Anne Lamott

Stacey and Fred, although one being an Entrepreneurial Trader and the other a trader in the *Technical Trader's Trap*, shared a few common traits.

Both of them were young, intelligent, and highly educated; they had stellar careers before quitting their day jobs to become traders, and to top things off, they had achieved an enviable level of success in life. With outstanding track records throughout their careers and lives, both believed in their capabilities and had faith they were gifted with qualities required to succeed in career, in life and in trading.

They were confident and had every reason to be so. Most of the time this feeling of confidence helped them in trading. They knew they had put themselves through the grind to pick up the necessary trading skills and felt comfortable with their craft. Both traders relied heavily on their technical analysis skill in trading, and time and again the markets proved their competency. Fred even once jokingly claimed it was not that his technical analysis was showing him the market moves, but the market was moving according to his analysis.

There was a flip side to their level of confidence, and sometimes, it went to their heads. For example, they did not like to admit their analysis could be wrong when fellow traders, or even the markets, clearly proved so. This happened especially when their profits took a hit. The loathsome feeling of losing often triggered their defensiveness and caused them to stop listening. They would fight back on the feedback and guidance offered to them in the same way that an obstinate old man defended an outdated custom.

Overconfident people like them tend to mistake kind comments from fellow traders as criticism or an open challenge, overreact against them and, therefore, lose opportunities to learn from them.

When Stubbornness Helps

When Stacey saw enough confirmations from the market, she knew she should get ready to enter the trade because her trade plan indicated so.

To verify, she ran the market through several lenses. She first overlaid a chart pattern onto the chart and found an imminent market reversal with Fibonacci. Going on to a larger time frame, she confirmed the market would retrace by counting the waves using Elliott Wave analysis. This was her first trade of the day, and she was elated this trade entry opportunity came to her so quickly, within only 15 minutes into the day!

But the peculiar thing was other traders in the same market did not seem to have the same view. They were still following the trend and showed no signs of taking the reverse move. Stacey got skeptical and quickly repeated the same analysis to make sure she did not miss anything. Her steps were correct. The same patterns were observed, and the analysis pointed her to the same trade to take.

When all the repeated verification was done, she was confident, and she made the decision to go against the crowd. If some of her peers saw her doing this, they might call her stubborn and advise her to take the lead from *the market,* which had not reversed yet.

But Stacey wouldn't. And at the end of the day, the market proved she did the right thing by being a bold contrarian and thinking independently. Her "stubbornness" paid off.

When Stubbornness Fails

Fred had faith in his strategy, but he had greater faith in his own insights. He believed the steps involved in the strategy were often fixed, lifeless, and rigid. As a rational person, he knew they were intentionally so to remove emotions from trade execution. However, he sternly believed that, as an intelligent human being, a trader should do the thinking. He would not accept that strategy should dictate his every move and do all the thinking for him. In other words, he wanted to use his intuition and gut feeling every time.

Although his trading was still largely guided by the trade plan and strategy, he would not hesitate to adjust his decisions when the "thinking mind" instructed so. This sounded logical because he could not find a good reason to allow a set of rigid rules to tie up his thinking mind.

The main problem was his "thinking mind" was more intuition rather than real logical reasoning. Fred did not always objectively check what his "thinking mind" dictated against indications from the market and his analysis. He did not agree this was necessary because as long as he could make even the slight connection between what he thought and what the charts showed, he would think it was fine. Did he prove the validity of the connection? Seldom. That's where the problem was.

Time and again, Stacey advised him against this gut-feeling trading style, but Fred became agitated whenever Stacey took the initiative to offer friendly reminders. He was aware of Stacey's kind intention to help him to improve, but it felt like criticism or an open challenge to the credibility of his skills. He was sure Stacey would feel the same, too, if someone did it to her.

Fred was stubborn and would not listen. He prefered to trade in his own way. Only his "thinking mind" could tell him the right way for him to trade. Others had better just watch out and keep their opinions to themselves.

Flexibility in Trade Plan Execution versus Blindly Following It

Stacey spent a good couple of months before landing on a trading strategy that aptly suited her personality and preference. She followed the trading strategy with discipline because this was the only way she could take her emotions out of trading. Being concerned about performance, she knew the trading results could sway her away from emotional neutrality, no matter whether they were winning trades or losses.

Like Fred, she allowed her "thinking mind" to work when she traded, too, but in a different way. Stacey did not make decisions by following her gut feelings. She was more cautious for fear of losing money. Although she allowed for a certain degree of flexibility in her trading, she followed her trade plan unless the market price action said otherwise.

For example, sometimes, she found the market was not playing out according to her trade plan. Instead of stubbornly continuing down the path that led to an unknown trading result, she would make a swift decision to close the position and move on to the next trading signal. Deviating from the trade plan might not be right, but she knew trading was not about being "right." There was no point being married to the trade plan when the market conditions changed all the time. She had to be flexible with her trades to ensure her survival and profitability.

Every day, at the end of her trading session, Stacey performed a post-mortem on her trades and analyzed the results of the day. One of the items she always checked was whether the flexibility she allowed herself was misused.

With this self-imposed system of checks and balances, the flexibility was almost always in her favor. She was glad she could rationally decide when to be flexible with her trading rather than just blindly following her trade plan. "This way, I don't get stuck on any one view or position!"

■ Pendulum Scenario 9.3: Accepting versus Willful

"Acceptance doesn't mean resignation; it means understanding that something is what it is and that there's got to be a way through it."

—Michael J. Fox

"The markets do not care about what you feel, think, or do. They will behave however they want. We have no control over them, no matter what we try or how hard we try."

This was a lesson learned in a foundational course on trading that Stacey and Fred attended. The traders were taught to understand the nature of the markets, accept what the markets had to offer them on a daily basis, and not to be emotionally attached to what they received from the markets.

They understood the profound wisdom behind this advice but appreciated it at different levels.

Surfing the Waves of the Market

Stacey was a consummate student of the market, and she looked forward to discovering what the market would throw at her on a daily basis, what she could learn from it, and how she could make profits from it. She appreciated she could not change how the market wanted to behave, but she could act on the behavior of the market.

For example, she learned that markets move in certain patterns. When she mastered the skills to analyze the markets based on these patterns and *visually saw* the rhythm of the markets, she could predict the market movement with a significant level of accuracy. (Refer to Figure 9.1.)

Two analysis methodologies that she frequently used were Elliott Wave analysis and Fibonacci. Using them, she saw when the markets were trending, measured some price targets, predicted when the reversal would arrive, and so on. With this knowledge, it was up to her to apply any appropriate setups to trade the trend or the end of trend.

Did she wish the markets would move according to her will? Well, sometimes she did because this would save her a lot of effort and make her ultra-rich. However, in reality, she had to accept the market movements as they were and trade accordingly.

Did she need to fight with the markets? No. She understood what she was taught that no one could fight them no matter what they did.

The way she traded, using her own words to describe it, was like "a surfer surfing." Just as a surfer riding the waves hopes not that he has the power to change the waves but see the waves, feel the waves, and act upon the movement of the waves. Stacey did the same when she traded.

Swimming against the Market Flow

Fred appreciated what he had learned about the market behavior, too, but he believed he had to be in control. This was how he got himself into a constant fight against the market.

At times, the general market trend was moving in a certain direction, but if Fred thought otherwise because his analysis somehow showed him or because his gut feeling told him, he traded against the trend and anticipated the general trend to reverse direction to prove him right.

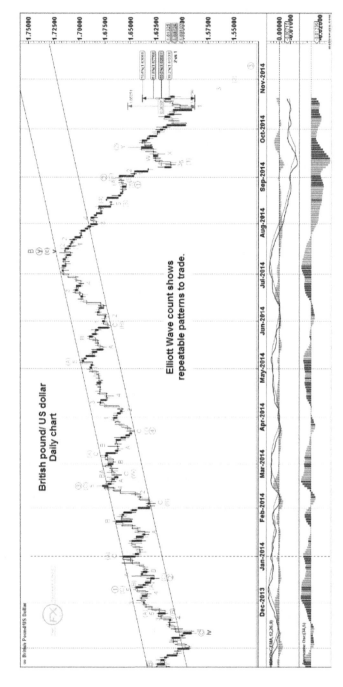

FIGURE 9.1 The market moves in a repeating and rhythmic manner

Sure enough, this almost never happens. Money will be lost, time will be wasted, and the chance to enter other higher-probability trades will be missed, but to Fred, these were not as important as proving himself right.

A meticulous trader will always look at higher time frames to verify her prediction of the trend direction. For example, if she is trading a 15-minute time frame, she will pull out the 1-hour, 4-hour, and 1-day charts to confirm the trend movements showed by these charts are in agreement before she pulls the trigger. If the position she plans to take is against the general trend direction, she will think twice.

However Fred, being a short-sighted trader, did not bother to do so. All he focused on was the time frame in which he traded because he believed that was all the information he needed.

Would he ever know if he was moving in trend with the bigger time frame or against it? Hardly. But did he care? No. He was trading in a willful manner, and this was causing his win/loss ratio and profitability to suffer.

Accepting Market Behaviors versus Rejecting Them

On some days, the markets are kind to traders, and on others they can be barbaric monsters. When Stacey reaped profits from the markets, she felt grateful; but when she suffered a setback, she actively thought about her next trade with a positive proper mindset.

As a mature trader (and person), Stacey accepted the behaviors of the markets as they were although she inevitably complained when she lost money. She thought, "I have realistic expectations and am a patient trader. The market setups that I expect will come to me; profits and success, too, will come. I have no doubt."

By contrast, Fred maintained the attitude that he had to win and had a strong desire to be right all the time. That was one of his biggest motivations in trading. Since winning mattered to him, he was unable to control his emotions of anger when his trading decisions were proven to be inaccurate or, in his own words, when the markets "went against his will."

Fred beat up on himself constantly after each setback. What was the bottom line? His feelings of inadequacy grew. He did not mind fighting the markets in hope he could win. He thought, "Don't worry, I'm in control of the markets, and I will win!"

Trading was not all about being right and winning all the time, and Fred's willful thinking of fighting the markets could not be more wrong.

What Kind of Animal Is the Market to You?

To end this Pendulum Scenario, I would like to share with you an exercise that I ask my students to do: Pick an animal that describes the market. Some students describe the market with tame or friendly animals, like a rabbit, dog, or monkey; others pick fierce animals, like a leopard, tiger, or snake.

It is interesting to observe how the students who choose to describe the market with friendly animals view the market as friendly. They are not afraid of the market and look to "ride the waves" or learn to be in the rhythm of the market.

On the other hand, the students who see the market as a vicious animal view the market as vicious, untamed, and fearsome. They shouldn't do so. It is my hope for my students, as well as you, to eventually perceive the market as a friendly animal after training to be well-adept traders.

CHAPTER 10

Habit #7: Plan the Trade and Trade the Plan

I heard the following story from a motivational speaker:

When John was young, he had a mentor who guided him on life development, career advancement, and the art of getting rich. One day, the mentor asked him, "I know you are aiming to become rich and successful in life. May I see your plan for this?"

John told him he did not have a plan for the time being. The mentor asked him, "What do you mean by, you don't have a plan now? Did you leave it in your car, your house, your office, or somewhere else?"

John clarified he had not come out with a plan yet. In defense, he said, "When I have more money, I will have a plan."

This was followed by a brief period of awkward silence. The mentor looked straight into John's eyes, and said to him, "Young man, I assure you, when you have a plan, you will have more money."

Some of my students say the same things as John did. Many of them who are beginners tell me they never have any trade plans, and they will define trade plans when they know trading better. But my advice to them is, "When you have a trade plan, you will know trading better."

The Clichéd Wisdom

And many life coaches like to ask their clients the following questions:

"Would you build a house without a blueprint? If not, why would you run your life without a plan?"

I know it sounds clichéd, but the wisdom behind these questions holds true. Transferring it to the trading world, I ask my students this:

"Would you build a house without a blueprint? If not, why would you trade without a plan?"

Winning or losing in trading is usually not a "life or death" situation, but traders are putting their hard-earned cash on the line, so they better know what they are doing! Planning their trades allows them to think through what is supposed to be done when they trade, as well as why, when, and how to do it. Without this pre-trade preparation, few traders will be successful, or should I say, most of them will fail within a short time.

I risk sounding clichéd again when I say that when most coaches, trainers, and motivational speakers talk about planning, they will say, "If you fail to plan, you plan to fail."

The wisdom behind this statement holds true in many aspects in life, in business, in a career as well as in your trading.

Before You Construct Your Trade Plan

You should aim to let your trade plan keep your emotions out of the trading process; therefore, it has to be highly specific, yet easy to follow.

There is no point in establishing a trade plan if you do not plan to follow it strictly. When you trade, make sure you "plan your trade, and trade your plan" and nothing else. Run enough tests on your trading system with your demo account before you trade it live. This will help put you into automatic pilot mode, so you can follow your system with confidence. I suggest running the test with numerous trades in different market cycles until you hit your performance goals; trade it in trend and sideways markets, as well as during volatile times and slow times.

Even after vigorously forward-testing your system in live markets or a demo account, you might still be able to catch its shortcomings. Perhaps you might discover it does not fit your trading personality or preferences as well as you had expected, or you just don't like part of it. No problem because you are free to fine-tune it.

Just as you would not allow a contractor to build your house if he claims, "I have the blueprint in my head," you should not have your trade plan just in your head. When you define each component in your plan, you must write it out.

Write a trade plan for each trade, and write it in conjunction with your checklist. Make sure your checklist conforms to your trading system. For example, if you plan to trade with a trend strategy, your checklist needs to include all the items that have to line up for the strategy as defined in your trading system. The same can be said if you plan to trade with an end-of-trend strategy.

Your checklist also provides you with a basis for review when trading does not go well. You can ask yourself, "Have I forgotten or changed something in my trading strategy? Has something in it gone wrong and needs to be fine-tuned?"

Successful traders have a habit of regularly reviewing their trading performance and trade plans. The review process will be most effective if the traders maintain a trading journal and a trading blotter to track their trading. The trading journal and trading blotter can be in hard copy or in digital format (e.g., a spreadsheet). They typically include elements like the pre-market analysis, trading rules, and confirmations defined in the trading system and the post-mortem analysis.

We will discuss the trading journal and trading blotter in greater length in Chapter 11.

How to Construct a Trade Plan

As described in Chapter 9, a trading system reflects your trading personality and preferences and identifies your profit expectations, money, and trade management rules as well as trading strategies used during different market cycles.

We will begin by confronting a few key concepts around a topic that most traders loathe hearing: losing money.

Money Management Strategy

It might sound counterintuitive, but containing losses is one of the prime concerns of traders followed by picking winning trades.

Typically, traders become more aggressive when they start losing money, not knowing this exacerbates the probability of losing more. When the trader's losses go past a threshold that becomes excessively difficult for him to recover from (financially and psychologically), he is on a one-way downward spiral, and his trading will fail. Because of this dismal effect of excessive losses, one of the first steps in defining a trade plan must be the conservation of trading capital or a money management strategy.

Prior to setting your money management procedures, an important concept to understand is the *drawdown effect*. Basically, a certain point exists where the drawdown (declining balance) on a trading account becomes so dire that it becomes almost impossible to bring the account back to an overall gaining balance.

TABLE 10.1	Down the Rabbit Hole
% Drawdown	% Gain Required to Recoup Losses
0	Starting value
10	11.11
20	25.00
30	42.85
40	66.66
50	100
60	150
70	233
80	400
90	900
100	Busted

From Table 10.1, you can see that once the trading account has been drawn down to about 30 percent of its original value, climbing back to the starting value becomes difficult. Losses are unavoidable in trading. To avoid reaching a level that is close to impossible to recoup from the losses, you must make sure your money management procedures are aggressively limiting your losses.

A money management plan involves setting stop losses at predefined levels. Many traders feel dejected when their stop-losses are hit, but don't be. I teach my students to *look forward* to getting stopped out because not only are losing trades essential to building a "psychological thick skin," but it is also a means to discover mistakes or weaknesses in the trade plan. Furthermore, if your stop losses are hit, that means they work, and you can rely on them to protect your account!

■ About Losing Money

My students often ask me, "How can I avoid losing money?" Well, you can't. If you trade, you will lose. The key is to limit losses.

Do not expect to win much over 60 to 70 percent of your trades. The main focus is to limit the size of the losses and cut losses aggressively. It is common to lose on more than 50 percent of your trades but still make an excellent overall return on your portfolio if you contain your losses well, and the winning trades have much larger gains than the losing trades.

Our society and education have taught us that over 90 percent is "good" and 70 percent is the edge of "bad." As a trader, you must get over this viewpoint and understand that keeping your losses to a minimum and compounding gains is the real name of the trading game. For example, if your success ratio is "only" 50 percent, but you can maintain your losses at an average of 1 to 2 percent and your winning trades at an average gain of 2 to 4 percent, you will be a very happy camper.

Our attention should be turned to how we can "stay in the game" for as long as we can. To be successful over the long run, it becomes a matter of how to limit risks and conserve gains.

Establishing Capital at Risk

A money management strategy requires that *limits per trade* and *limits for multiple trades* be defined to help promote trading longevity. As a general rule, traders will set the following limits:

- Per trade: 1 to 2 percent of account balance

- Multiple trades: 5 to 6 percent of account balance

Establish a reasonable rate-of-return (ROI) target on your investment. What is "reasonable" depends largely on the market being traded. For example, if you are trading stocks, it is best to compare the returns to the benchmark stock index that includes the individual stocks you are trading, such as the S&P 500, DJIA, or foreign markets. Measure your performance against an index, or a combination of indices as in a multi-asset portfolio. The goal is to *beat the index*.

For forex trading, because of leverage, you need a small amount of risk capital to earn a good return. In the United States, the maximum leverage permissible is 50:1. Outside the United States, leverage can be as high as 400:1. We will look at Example 1 below to see how leverage fits into the return equation. Regardless of leverage, most forex asset managers risk no more than 1 to 2 percent on a single trade, to a maximum of about 6 percent of the trading account balance for multiple positions.

Risking a conservative 1 percent on a single trade means a trader can have 100 losing trades in a row before he loses his capital. Ten consecutive losses would erase 10 percent of the capital. At 6 percent risk, a trader will lose his capital after 16 losing trades in a row. This is the worst possible outcome. Examples 1 and 2 below uses 2 percent of capital at risk per trade, which is common in forex and equities trading.

Example 1: Applying 2 Percent Capital at Risk per Trade for Forex Let's say you have a trading account balance of $30,000 and you risk 2 percent of the capital on a forex trade. The amount a trader risks in this example is .02 × $30,000, or $600. Let's assume the stop loss is 20 pips away, which translates into a position size of $300,000. That uses a leverage of 10:1, which is $300,000/$30,000. (Looking at it in terms of 50:1 leverage means a trader would be able to take a position size of $1.5 million, which is 50 × $30,000. If the trader loses the 20 pips, the actual loss would be $3,000 on that position size, which is 10 percent of the equity in the account.)

So, using our $600 at risk example, you could purchase about $300,000 in currency. If the stop loss goes up, this position size goes down, as the position size is a function of the amount of risk taken, which is the size of the stop loss. If the trader manages to make a net profit of 100 pips on 10 trades during the month, meaning five winning trades at 40 pips profit each and five losing trades at 20 pips loss each, the profit would be $3,000. That works out to be a profit of 10 percent on the $30,000 account balance for the month. Annualized, that becomes 120 percent ROI as a result of the leverage.

If, however, you measure the return based on the notional amount traded, the $300,000, the return is 1 percent for the month, or 12 percent annualized. Based on this simple calculation, it is easy to see how returns can be exaggerated or misunderstood when there is leverage involved.

This calculation is simplistic in that it does not include slippage or the overnight funding cost of the currency pair being traded, which is negligible for most pairs in the current low-interest-rate environment. This example, therefore, assumes a net return on capital rather than a gross return. Also, this example assumes a 10-pip move on a $100,000 position size is $100, at $10 a pip. Though this is true for foreign currencies quoted against the USD, such as the EUR/USD or GBP/USD, there are slight differences for pairs quoted with the USD first, such as USD/CAD and USD/CHF.

What happens if we apply the same 2 percent capital at risk per trade for stocks? Example 2 illustrates.

Example 2: Applying 2 Percent Capital at Risk per Trade for Equities The same calculation can be made for buying a $20 stock, assuming a $30,000 account balance. To get an accurate calculation, stock brokerage costs and slippage need to be factored in, but this example excludes those costs. In the United States, you may borrow up to 50 percent of the stock purchase price, which is equivalent to 2:1 leverage (US Securities and Exchange Commission).

1. Calculate the capital at risk: $30,000 × 2 percent = $600 per trade.

2. Calculate the stop loss: The stock is a $20 stock and you decide to place a stop loss at $19.60, so your risk is $0.40 per share.

3. Calculate the number of shares to BUY: $600/$0.40 = 1,500 shares at a cost of 1,500 × $20 = $30,000. (You are now fully invested with your starting capital, but you need only tie up $15,000 at 2:1 leverage.)

4. Decide on the profit target, which is $0.80 at 2:1 risk/reward.

TABLE 10.2	Capital at Risk Summary	
Trader:	$20 Stock	Forex
Account capital	$30,000	$30,000
Capital at risk (2%)	$600	$600
Stop Loss	40 cents	20 pips
Position size	1500 shares	$300,000
Stock Cost at 2:1 leverage	$15,000	
Forex Cost at 50:1 leverage		$6,000
Profit per trade	80 cents	40 pips
Risk/Reward	2:1	2:1
Win/Loss	1:1	1:1
Probability of success	50%	50%
# of trades	10	10
Monthly profit	$2	100 pips
Monthly profit ($)	$3,000	$3,000

In both these examples, the win/loss ratio, which is the number of winning trades over the number of losing trades, is assumed to be 1:1. The success rate, or probability of success is the number of winning trades over the number of total trades, or 50 percent. The risk/reward, which is the expected gain compared to the stop loss, on these positions is 2:1 (40 pips of profit vs. 20 pips of loss in the case of forex, and 80 cents of profit vs. 40 cents of loss in the case of the stock position).

Because the size of the win is twice that of the loss, a 50 percent success rate makes the trade profitable. It is always better to be conservative in goal setting, so setting a 1 percent monthly trading return on the trading account balance is reasonable (10 percent with leverage). Also, 10 trades in a month is reasonable, and the number of trades could easily double or triple. The key is to accept losses, set tight stops, and let profits run to best achieve your goals.

Table 10.2 provides a summary of what we've discussed in Examples 1 and 2.

So, now that we have looked at how the capital at risk and profit and loss parameters for each trade can be established, it's time we look at a sample trade plan.

■ Constructing a Trade Plan Based on a Trading System and Money Management Strategy

Let's say a day trader is using the following trading system.

Chart Setup

Currency Pairs: any major pair

Time Zone: NY market from 8 a.m. until 11 a.m.

Time Frames:

- Daily for larger trend confirmation

- 1-hour and 15-minute for trend confirmation

- 5-minute for trade entry

Indicators:

- 8, 21, and 55 EMAs on 15-minute, 1-hour, and daily

- 5 and 13 EMAs on 5-minute

Oscillators:

- RSI 3 for buy and sell confirmations in a trend

- Awesome Oscillator for divergence

- Pivot points, trend lines, and Fibonacci for support and resistance

Lot Size: 2 lots

General Rules

1. Read these trading rules before every trading session.

2. If you miss the trade, wait for pullback.

3. Plan the trade and trade the plan.

4. Trade with the trend. If the daily and general trends are up, look for buys unless: there is divergence in the oscillator signaling the price action is running out of steam, the market has just made a large move and needs to pause or retrace, or price is way above the moving averages and needs to snap back.

5. Be happy taking profits and losses.

6. Risk no more than 1 or 2 percent on a trade.

Entry Rules

BUY (opposite for a sell)

- Trades taken on the 5-minute chart in the direction of the 1-hour and 15-minute trends.

- Wait for retracement to the 21 EMA on the 15-minute chart.

- Confirm with RSI 3 turning up.

- Confirm with Fibonacci support.

- Confirm with pivot point support.

- Buy above the high of the reversal candle and/or when the 5 crosses above the 13 EMA on the 5-minute chart.

Exit Rules

Stop Loss

- Set stop loss below the reversal candle (opposite for a sell).

Profit Taking

- T/P as candle closes below 5 EMA on 1 lot.

- Use trailing stop 2 to 3 pips below previous candle low.

- Let lot 2 run until market takes you out.

Optional Profit Taking

- T/P as candle closes below 5 EMA on 2 lots.

- Three Profiteers Trade Management (See next section for description).

After analyzing the daily chart, the trader spots a trade opportunity in the EUR/USD market (Figure 10.1). He notes that a correction is beginning after a strong downtrend. He confirms this observation with candlestick analysis and that the market is stretched and the price needs to bounce back to the moving averages with a *rubber band effect*. He, therefore, concludes that the price action will potentially go bullish.

He moves down the time frames to the hourly chart (Figure 10.2) for trend confirmation. The chart shows a sideways market after the initial uptrend, which is usually followed by an additional move up with the same magnitude as the first move. This is called a *move of equality*, where a trader can measure the distance of the first trend leg and project an equidistant move for the second trend leg after the sideways correction.

The trader then goes to the 15-minute chart (Figure 10.3) for further confirmation. He draws trend lines connecting the price highs and lows of the sideways consolidation and anticipates a breakout to the upside to complete the equality pattern.

With the above information, he would set up the trade plan. The analysis method used is a top-down approach, starting with the daily chart.

Finally, the trader executes his trade. He takes the trade on the 5-minute chart (Figure 10.4) in the direction of the 1-hour and 15-minute charts. Based on his exit rules, he takes profits as the candle closes below the 5 EMA.

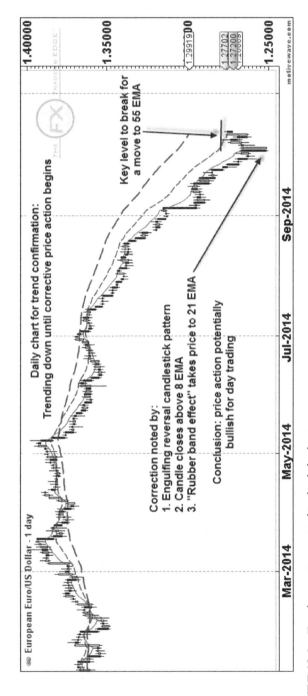

FIGURE 10.1 Trend correction spotted in the daily chart

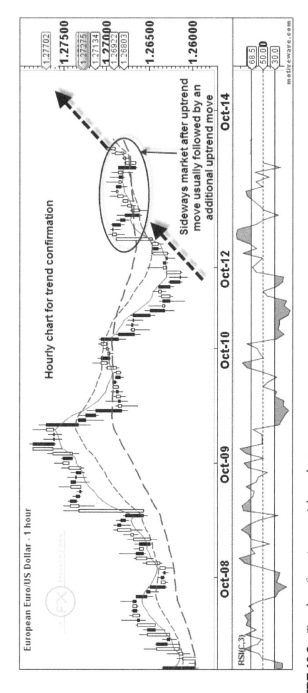

FIGURE 10.2 Trend confirmation on a 1-hour chart

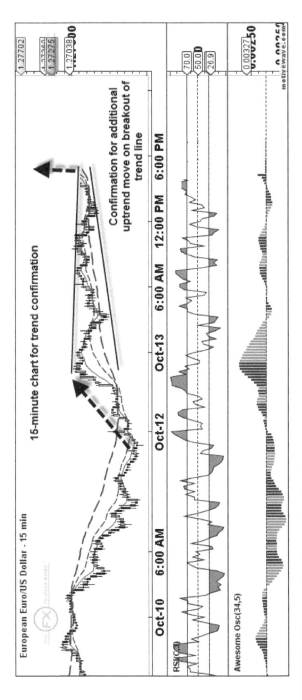

FIGURE 10.3 15-minute chart for trend confirmation

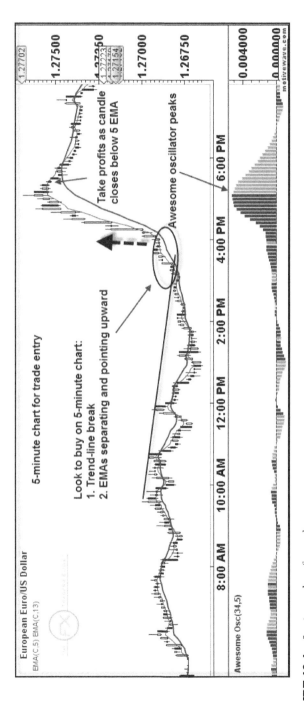

FIGURE 10.4 5-minute chart for trade entry

The Three Profiteers

There is an optional profit-taking strategy listed under the exit rules, which is a trade management methodology called the Three Profiteers. The example that follows applies this methodology to determine the take-profit (TP) levels.

> ### The Three Profiteers: Profit-Taking Methodology
> ### to Reduce Risk and Balance Greed
>
> In Chapter 9, we discussed four trade management strategies:
>
> 1. Getting in and out all at once.
>
> 2. Getting in all at once and taking profits at various levels.
>
> 3. Getting into the position at various levels and getting out all at once.
>
> 4. Getting in and out at various levels.
>
> Most traders enter a trade with the intention of maximizing profit. As a result, they usually enter with a set number of lots or contracts to maximize the anticipated move to the profit target. The simple and least complex choice is to carry the trade and close out all the positions at the same time or get in and out all at once.
>
> There is nothing wrong with this method as it keeps things simple. However, seasoned traders prefer to ladder into and out of trades as this helps reduce risk of loss in case the trade moves against the position. This allows them to stay in the game and let probabilities and small compounded profits do their magic over time.
>
> I use a trade management method I developed called *the Three Profiteers* for getting in all at once and taking profits at various levels. The method was developed for perfectionists who get greedy and annoyed when profits are taken too soon and part of the trend is missed. It also helps with taking profits along the way in case the market turns suddenly so that profits are given back quickly and fear sets in. Scaled Fibonacci profit-taking points are used along the way to the profit target to allow traders to balance the greed and fear elements of trading.
>
> The following example shows you how it works in currencies.
>
> 1. Determine the Potential Profit Area (PPA). For this example, let's assume the PPA is 100 pips.
>
> 2. Use the Fibonacci sequence (8, 13, 21, 34, 55, 89, 144) and pick three profit targets, the third ending at the PPA estimate.

3. Work backward from the 100 pip PPA with the FIBO sequence to determine your profit objectives: 34, 55, and 89 pips. These correspond to take profit targets TP1, TP2, and TP3.

4. Set your stop loss at the first profit target, which is 34 pips in this example, and move your stop to break even once the first profit target is met. Move stop to TP1 once TP2 is met.

5. Calculate Risk/Reward:

   Reward: $(89 + 55 + 34)/3 = 59$ pips

   Risk: 34 pips

   Risk/Reward ratio: $59/34 = 1.74$

To put the Three Profiteers to work, you can enter the trade with the full position size after calculating 1 to 2 percent of capital at risk and break it into thirds for profit taking. When reaching TP1, close out one-third of the position and move the stop to break even. When TP2 is reached, close out one-third of the position and move the stop to TP1. Finally, when TP3 is reached, the final profit target is met, and hopefully the trader has captured a good portion of the move.

You can also use the Three Profiteers when trading stocks or futures. Using stocks as an example, the Fibonacci sequence can be used as cents or dollars. For example, where the PPA is established will determine if the sequence is $.08, $.13, $.21, $.34, $.55, $.89, and $1.44, or whether it is $.80, $1.30, $2.10, $3.40, $5.50, $8.90, and $14.40.

For futures trading, the Fibonacci sequence can be designated as ticks or points, so 8, 13, 21, 34, 55, 89, and 144 ticks or .8, 1.3, 2.1, 3.4, 5.5, 8.9, and 14.4 points.

Let's continue with the forex trade plan example. The trader looks at the 15-minute chart (Figure 10.5). Applying the Three Profiteers strategy, he sets the PPA to be 92 pips, which is the length of the first leg of this move and works backward through the Fibonacci sequence to set three Take Profit levels at 89 pips, 55 pips, and 34 pips.

The trader then determines the exact TP levels: TP1, TP2, and TP3 are 1.2712, 1.2733, and 1.2767 respectively, added to the entry price of 1.2678 (Figure 10.6).

Based on the trading system and money management strategy, the trader formulates the trade plan shown in Table 10.3.

Finally, the trade is triggered from the analysis and managed according to the Three Profiteers strategy.

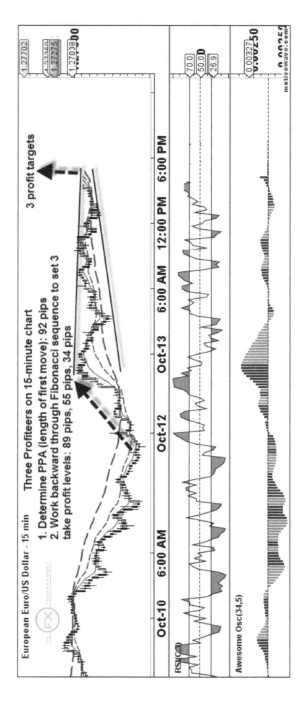

FIGURE 10.5 Three Profiteers on the 15-minute chart: PPA and take-profit levels

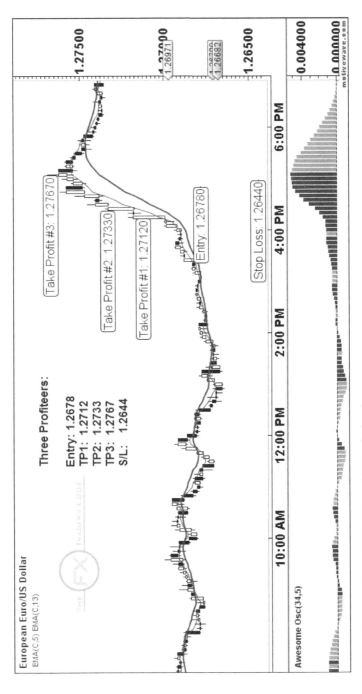

FIGURE 10.6 Three Profiteers: TP1, TP2, and TP3 calculated

TABLE 10.3	A Trade Plan Based on the Three Profiteers			
Trade Plan	**Strategy: Trend-following TT / Reversal ETT**			**Reasons for Entries and Exits**
Entry Strategy	Trade #1	Trade #2	Trade #3	
Long or short	Long			
Position size	3 lots			
Price	1.2678			
Exit Strategy	Trade #1	Trade #2	Trade #3	
Stop loss 1	1.2644			
Stop loss 2				
Profit level 1	1.2712			
Profit level 2	1.2733			
Profit level 3	1.2767			
Profit level 4				
Risk/Reward	1.74			

Take Action!

When creating your trade plan, ask yourself the following questions:

1. What is your maximum allowable drawdown for your trading account?

2. What do you do when you hit max drawdown on an account?

3. Have you been clear about your capital at risk per trade or for multiple trades? How do you establish it?

4. Are you clear about your profit and loss targets? How do you calculate them?

5. Based on your trading system, are you able to formulate a trade plan for each trade?

6. Do you apply a solid money management strategy and trade management methodology (refer to the Three Profiteers strategy) when you set up your trade plan?

■ Pendulum Scenario 10.1: Pragmatic versus Idealistic Trader

> *"Idealism detached from action is just a dream. But idealism allied with pragmatism, rolling up your sleeves and making the world bend a bit, is very exciting."*

> —Bono, Musician

There is some truth in what people say, "Your personality shows up in the way you trade."

Fred always regarded himself as an exceedingly logical and rational guy. Before he entered the trading world, he had heard that to succeed in trading, traders needed to keep their emotions at bay. He thought that would be easy for him because that was how he worked and lived his life.

What he did not know was he was only able to exert rationality on things that were distant from himself: his work, things that he was not directly involved in, and "other people's issues." But for matters close to him, such as his trading business, personality, and money, his rationality was powerless.

Rather surprisingly, Fred found out he was more idealistic than realistic. This showed up in the way he conducted his trading business, his idea of how a trader makes a living trading full-time, and the get-rich-quick mentality of making the first pot of gold by "winning big" in a few trades and living happily ever after. Fred took notice of this and admitted that it could be doing harm to his trading career.

Stacey, on the contrary, chose to be pragmatic out of the fear that wrong decisions would put the financial standing of her family at stake. Unless she was sure about what she did and had enough confidence in the outcomes, she would not plunge into action. Similarly, she would not enter any trade before considering the winning probability and understanding the risks involved. She made sure that due diligence was performed to deal with the risks involved.

Before starting to trade forex on a part-time basis, Stacey was a sales professional. She was aggressive and would do anything fearlessly to hit the sales targets, sometimes even disregarding the outcomes. Little did she expect that when it came to dealing with her trading business, her fearlessness faded. Whenever in doubt, she almost always chose the pragmatic way to go.

Pragmatic Trader versus Idealistic Trader

A pragmatic trader uses his common sense in trading. He has a deep grasp of the psychology of other traders in the market and digs into the reasons why they are making buying or selling decisions at a particular point in time. Although he understands why the crowd is taking a certain position, he is not affected by them. He thinks independently and bases his trading decisions on sound analysis, logical reasoning and a profound understanding of the market.

This is different from how an idealistic trader behaves. An idealistic trader tends to take the easy way out in trading. He hopes to make a quick buck and will follow the herd in making decisions without applying proper steps to verify his moves.

An idealistic trader may also trust his "gut feeling" more than the result of his analysis (if he does analyze at all). When his intuition tells him it is the right time to enter or exit a trade, he will do so. Idealistically, he might think that all he needs is just one out of his many "blind attempts" to hit the bull's eye, and that is when he can be free from money-worries for an extended period of time.

The following scenarios further demonstrate the different ways Fred the idealistic trader and Stacey the pragmatic one deal with their trades.

The Idealistic Herd Follower

Most of the time, Fred was analytical. It is not an overstatement to say he was so obsessed in analyzing the data that he sometimes forgot his main business was making money out of his trades and not studying the market.

That was not the only thing he forgot. Fred also neglected that one of the reasons he was doing all the analyses was to gather confirmations to support his trading decisions. Being an idealistic trader, the "get-rich-quick" mindset sometimes got the better of him. There were times when he observed the crowd was taking positions that he did not expect. Fred would be tempted to check out what they were doing. On some days when his willpower was strong, he would refuse to make any trading decision without properly investigating what the market was going through. But most times, he allowed himself to take chances, even when his analyses did not support his decision, in fear that he would miss the boat when the market changed.

Just four days ago, Fred noticed a sharp dip in the stock market. It seemed to Fred the market had fallen too far and too fast, and he believed it would come back. He found out that other traders' reactions to the market were in line with his thinking, so he should have had a certain level of confidence in it. "So many traders cannot be wrong!" he thought, so he pulled the trigger without substantiating his decision with any analysis.

Sure enough, the trend did not change course because he joined the crowd. Although the market strongly indicated his decision was off the mark, being idealistic, he was still in hope the trend would reverse, and resisted the stop losses, until he almost lost his per-day loss limit. This was when he realized the downward movement showed no sign of slowing down and finally admitted his mistake. He exited the position at a huge loss.

Did Fred learn his lesson? Probably. But we will not know until the next time when he faces a similar situation again.

The Pragmatic, Independent Thinker

Stacey's mind was wired to her trade plan and not anyone else's. It took a lot of courage to behave this way because it meant that sometimes she had to do the opposite when everyone else (the herd) was moving another way. It was easy to waver when she was going against the general direction of the crowd, but from past experience, she always remembered that as long as her decision could be substantiated by her analysis and strategy, she was safe. This was evident from what happened last Thursday afternoon.

Stacey mapped out the EUR/USD trade and was prepared to take the short position because the result of her Elliott Wave analysis showed her that the pair was close to finishing its retracement and was about to reverse direction and join the trend again. It sat nicely at the Fibonacci retracement level that Stacey was looking for, so she was rubbing her hands together in anticipation of the arrival of the trade entry point.

But she hesitated just before she pulled the trigger since everyone else in the market was still buying it. This took away some of her confidence and forced her to repeat the analysis. It came to the same result. To be doubly sure, she used the candlestick patterns to confirm her entry. It pointed to the same thing as well.

It was one of those times that Stacey decided to put on her blinders and trade her plan instead of taking the cue from the crowd. After all, her analysis was substantiating her decision, and she knew the probability of a mistake for this trade was slim.

That was how she treated every one of her trades: in a confident and pragmatic manner. She waited patiently for a market move to set up and once it did, she was in. Other traders might be going along with her decision or against it, but this did not bother her.

If only Fred could follow the same practice, he would become a more successful trader.

■ Pendulum Scenario 10.2: Pulling the Trigger versus Having Regrets

"Inaction breeds doubt and fear. Action breeds confidence and courage."
—Dale Carnegie

Intensive analysis had been performed. Research done. The market indicators properly checked. Almost all the trade entry rules have been fulfilled, and it seemed that the remaining ones would be hit soon, too.

Fred was certain that he was going to make that buy decision. The entry position and stop-loss level were identified, and all he needed was to wait for the setup to come to him.

Moments Before Pulling the Trigger

One minute passed, 5 minutes, 10 minutes, and the last entry rule was finally fulfilled! Fred was about to press the BUY button on his trading platform when a sudden thought froze him.

"Wait, did I check the Bollinger Band support?" He remembered he did. But he quickly rechecked it. And then he thought, "Why was I so positive that the next move would be up?" He remembered he was looking at the 1-hour and 1-day charts, and that was what had told him so.

He should have been left with no doubt with his analysis, but something still felt wrong. "This trade is strange. Is there something I didn't do? Something that I missed out on?" Fred was not sure. His trader's instinct was making him uncomfortable with the buy action that he was proposing.

In fact, the thought of pressing that BUY button made his palms sweat a little. He could not explain it, but he felt uneasy.

So he decided to just give up on this one. One of the general rules he had in his trading system was, "When in doubt, retreat. Move on to the next trade."

He had to think that not pulling the trigger this time was the right decision to make. And he stared at his screen, waiting for the market to prove him right.

Acting Faster than the Skepticism

Stacey did it anyway. When the entry point for the trade was hit, she entered her position and stop-loss level, and in the blink of an eye, pressed the BUY button. All these steps were taken so swiftly that it left her without any room to reconsider her move.

But for this trade, something was trying to hold her back, too. She also experienced unfounded doubt about this trade.

But she had done her analysis, performed the necessary research, checked and double-checked the market indicators, and confirmed that all the entry rules were fulfilled. She had a certain level of confidence with the position she was taking. Her analysis gave her this confidence. She knew she was protected by a reasonable stop loss, so nothing could go wrong. That nagging voice in her head was still trying to make her skeptical about her move.

But she did it anyway. The best plan she could conceive to combat that baseless, nagging skepticism was to act faster than it. So, she pulled the trigger faster than the bad feeling could hold her back.

She did not want to look at what happened in the market next after she executed the order. After a last check to confirm that the stop loss was in place, she walked away from her workstation and started playing with her baby. She was afraid she would not follow through on her trade and change her decision halfway through.

The Need to Feel Right

Fear managed to hold Fred back, and it almost did it to Stacey, too.

Fred was afraid of being wrong in his trade. That was why even when all the due diligence performed should have removed his doubt, he could not make the move. He thought too much about what making a wrong decision in the trade would cost him. He needed to know he had made the right call when he looked back at any of his trades.

It was not the first time this need to feel right had interrupted his trading decisions, and it would not be the last time. To Fred, it was wiser not to enter a trade when he was not *feeling* right about it than to take a trade with lingering doubt. It was better for him to miss a trade entry opportunity than to make any mistakes that he would later feel embarrassed about or regret.

What might sound contradictory however, is if the trade he did not take eventually turned out to be producing the outcome that he originally expected, he would feel regret for not trusting his analysis and for not pulling the trigger at that split second. "If I were brave enough to just 'take the risk' regardless of what my instincts told me … " he always thought. But he had not learned that lesson fully yet.

The Reason for the "Impulsive" Act

What Stacey did to win in the wrestle against her fear might seem to be impulsive. To think she executed the trade when the opportunity struck and walked away from it without even looking back! She had enough proof to verify she was entering a well-planned trade, and only some frivolous self-doubt and fear were talking her out of it.

She trusted her logical thinking but did not want to underestimate the power of her emotions. So, she chose to pull the trigger before the emotions overpowered her. As she walked away from her trade, any nagging voice that was still inside her head became irrelevant. She had shifted her focus to playing with her baby and would not look back once the trade was placed.

How to Temper the Fear

The fear of being wrong is only one of the fears that can tamper with a trader's trading decision. When it is time to pull the trigger, traders can be halted by the fear of loss and fear of losing money.

Here are a few suggestions to temper these fears:

1. *Prepare yourself well before you enter each trade*. Do not skimp on any necessary steps to prove your trading decisions. This will help remove your doubt.

2. *Trust yourself*. As you can see from Fred and Stacey's examples, reasoning with yourself *logically* sometimes still cannot help you win in the wrestle with

self-doubt no matter how much you have convinced yourself you are well-prepared for a trade. You have to trust yourself more to win the fight.

3. *Set a reasonable stop loss.* This will be the safety net for your trading decision. Even if your self-doubt instinct is right and your trade stumbles, you can still have some peace of mind knowing your stop loss is protecting your capital.

4. *Take action.* If everything else fails, you might want to take Nike's advice to "just do it" against all odds. After all, you have done your analysis well, set up the stop loss, and the conditions in the market are meeting your trade entry criteria, so what's stopping you from taking action?

5. *Choose between pulling the trigger now or confronting your regrets.* Remind yourself that your inability to get into the trading position may mean watching the trade playing out as you expected but not profiting from your correct analysis. Ask yourself, would you rather be taking the bold move (which is hopefully backed by your analysis) now or regret later about pulling back at the last moment?

■ Pendulum Scenario 10.3: Conservative versus Impulsive Trader

"Great things are not done by impulse, but by a series of small things brought together."

—Vincent van Gogh

A thousand and one thoughts were spinning inside Stacey's head: Her baby was awake when he should be asleep, she had not picked out the wedding present for her brother-in-law, she had run out of olive oil for tonight's dinner and had to make a trip to the supermarket, and there was a cooking show she had to watch. She even needed to change the light bulb in the kitchen, as her husband was too busy to take care of it.

Her impatience showed up in her trade. She followed her trade plan to identify and confirm a trade entry point, decided on the position size and stop-loss level, and waited for the setup to come to her. Things were moving excruciatingly slowly. She had been monitoring the market, and the setup was not forming yet. "It was close, it was close … ," but it was not there yet. She almost wanted to stand up and start pacing around her workstation to temper her impatience.

The Advantage of a "Timid" Trader

Fred does not trade fearlessly. He has many fears. To name a few: failure, fear of being wrong, and fear of losing money. His fears have sometimes caused him to avoid taking action. These are roadblocks in his progress in trading, but if there is one "advantage" that comes along with them, it must be his conservativeness.

Fred tended to overanalyze his trades, and think too much before he commited to take action. When this habit showed up and had the upper hand, he became conservative in trading.

When he was *excessively* conservative, he would be afraid to enter trades. In this mode, if he had even the slightest doubt in his trading decision, he would rather watch the trades that he expected to be winners play out right before his eyes than to jump into action. Although time and again he wanted to punch himself for losing out on the opportunities to make profits, he somewhat believed that if he was not sure, he should stay away.

But when he was *reasonably* conservative, he was actually a good trader who would patiently wait until all the trade entry rules in his trading strategy were fulfilled and made doubly sure the market indicators clearly aligned with the position he intended to take before he pulled the trigger. In this mode, his success rate was exceptionally high. The only problem was it was not up to him to enter this psychological condition at will.

A Trader Who Acts on Impulse

Stacey could no longer wait. She only had three hours in a day to trade, and she had not taken as many trades as she had planned to yet.

There were only three more entry rules that were not fulfilled on her checklist yet. "It should be close enough now," she reasoned. She thought it was okay to take the risk and enter the position early. She did not have the time and patience to wait.

In addition to that, knowing the market today would be taking its own sweet time to move, Stacey decided to get in a few trades simultaneously. She thought there was no time to carefully analyze each trade before taking positions. She always made it a point to be guided by the trade plan, but the actions she was embarking on now were straying from it. Somehow it crossed her mind that what she was doing now was akin to gambling, but she didn't care.

This was unlike her, as she was usually meticulous. However, today's situation was different. Too many things were hanging over her head, and she lost her calmness and patience with her trading. She wanted to get her trading over with so she could run on the treadmill. Plus, her dedicated trading session for the day was about to end, and she had not made enough progress. She was anxious now.

An Impulsive Trading Decision by a Conservative Trader

Even for Fred, a somewhat conservative trader, sometimes when fear and greed crept in, he could make impulsive decisions, too.

Three weeks ago, the price of the stock that he bought unexpectedly spiked up. Fred instinctively felt that it had gone far enough and thought it was time to sell before the price retraced. But he decided to wait for a while and observe the market before he jumped into action. When he saw the price continually rise sharply, he was convinced it was time to act. It did not seem to him he needed to wait any longer, and he did not bother to run analysis to verify his decision.

So, Fred took the chance and sold all his stock out of impulse as he thought the market would reverse shortly; he thought that if he did not take swift action, he would miss the boat. He was a happy trader when he got out of the trade with considerable profit. But what happened within the next hours took the smile away from his face.

After Fred left the market, the price continued to spike higher, almost uncontrollably. Fred watched the market play out before his eyes in disbelief. It finally peaked and came back somewhat but not even as much as Fred's original take profit price. Fred's face turned red. Although he knew he could be happy over the profits he reaped from the market, he regretted taking the impulsive move of selling his stock too early. The decision was made out of greed as he could not contain his anticipation to take profits and out of fear that he might miss out the profit-taking opportunity if the market suddenly retraced before he sold the stock. He realized later he could have put a trailing stop loss in his trading platform.

Decisions That the Impulsive Trader Regretted

When Stacey reviewed her trades that evening, she realized her mistake. She had allowed her emotions to get in the way of her trading and traded impulsively as she was losing her patience.

She lost money that day, and her losses in trading had caused her major emotional turmoil. She ended up losing her temper with her baby, picking a wedding present for her brother-in-law that made her husband laugh, forgetting she needed to pick up a bottle of olive oil from the supermarket, and missing the cooking show. Worse, she called her husband during office hours and screamed at him for not changing the light bulb in the kitchen.

She regretted all these behaviors and decided to consider staying out of trading if she was not "in the zone" or at least cultivate some patience if she must trade. "No more impulsive trading," she promised herself.

PART IV

The Transformed Trader

CHAPTER 11

Habit #8: Measure Your Performance

Elite performers, such as athletes, chess masters, and concert pianists devote almost all their time to perfecting their crafts. They might be repeatedly practicing their existing skills, fine-tuning them, and learning new ones. They constantly seek improvement and will feel they are not maximizing their potential when they make little or no progress.

How do they know where their skill levels stand? How do they know if they are making progress or moving backward? Professionals set up metrics to objectively measure their performance. For example, a professional golfer's performance can be tracked with his driving distance, fairway hits, green hits, putts, and so on. A chess master's performance is measured with *chessmetrics,* a weighted average of past performance that considers his win percentage against other players' past results.

Measuring the performance with objective metrics reveals where the performer's perceived level of skill is, where the actual level is, and where the expected level is. When the performer and her coach see the gaps among these three, they will work to close the gaps.

Similar to top performers from other fields, successful traders keep track of their trading performance with well-defined performance metrics, too. They track every trade they make and analyze the data every week or month. They monitor the metrics to figure out their strengths and weaknesses, monitor where their current performance stands compared to their past performance, and look for areas of improvement. The habit of regularly measuring performance is one of the keys to their success, and you should adopt the same habit, too.

Successful traders employ certain tools to track their performance. We will look at three of them in this chapter.

■ The Trading Journal

Have you ever wondered what successful traders do after they close out a trade? Do they move on immediately and eagerly dive into the markets again to enter the next trade?

What do successful traders do at the end of the day? Do they quickly wrap up so they can enjoy the rest of the day? Do they leave the failures and successes they have experienced behind, thinking it is a brand new day tomorrow?

No, they don't. Successful traders have made a habit of looking back at their past, in trading at least. They will review their trades at the end of their day and perform post-mortems on their trades to pinpoint what they have done well and what went wrong. Maintaining this daily habit of looking back at their past ensures they learn the good and the bad from their own experience and continue to grow each day.

To track their trades, successful traders keep trading journals. You might imagine it to be a thick physical notebook with almost illegible scribbles and oversized printed charts filling the pages. This might be true for some traders, but in modern, technological days, most traders keep their trading journals using spreadsheet programs.

To keep a trading journal, you need to take two screenshots: One when you enter a trade and another when you close it out. Paste the screenshots on a fresh spreadsheet, note the trade information, your observations, mistakes made or things that went well, missed opportunities, and so on with as much detail as possible. You might want to include a planned against actual running balance of your trading account on a different spreadsheet as you close each trade. See sample trading journal page in Figure 11.1.

Filling a trading journal allows you to take time to analyze your trades and develop new insights.

Also, as you maintain a detailed record of your trades, you can see how well your trading system is serving you. You may continue trading your plan if it goes well, or you may change it if the results do not prove out to be positive over time (test the system on at least 20 trades first). Before modifying your system, make sure the problem is with the plan and not your execution, meaning you are following the plan with discipline.

Do not overlook the importance of the trading journal. Trading is a continual process of learning, and the trading journal is perhaps one of the most valuable tools to help fine-tune your trading and grow your trading account balance.

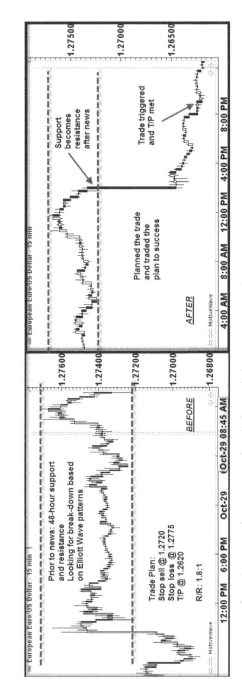

FIGURE 11.1 A sample trading journal page: screenshots before and after entering a trade

The Daily Trading Blotter

The Daily Trading Blotter is a checklist that enables you to review your daily trading performance, specifically, whether you have planned your trade and traded your plan.

It should be used together with the trading journal. The difference between them is the Daily Trading Blotter is filled out before, during, and after a trader enters a trade; the trading journal is a recap at the end of the trading day. In other words, the former covers analysis and trade execution in a live trade setting, and the latter is at the back end with screenshots.

Figure 11.2 shows a screenshot of the Daily Trading Blotter I developed. Besides helping the trader to run through a checklist before writing the trade plan, the trader can use this Trading Blotter for his pre-market analysis and for his post mortem analysis as it prompts the trader to examine his frame of mind during trading, whether he was affected by emotions, how well he had prepared for the trading session, and so on.

You can download the Daily Trading Blotter from the book companion website at www.wiley.com/go/traderspendulum.

Profit and Loss (P&L) Statement

This simple spreadsheet contains only the following columns:

- Trading day
- Initial account balance
- Ending account balance
- Net profit (loss)
- Percentage change

It provides a quick summary of the performance of your trading in terms of the profits you made, the losses you incurred, and the current standing of your trading account. Table 11.1 shows an example of a P&L statement.

Setting Realistic Expectations

You must set realistic expectations. For example, a trader might set an annualized return target of 50 percent of her trading account balance as her growth target. The question is: Is this a realistic goal? It depends on several factors, for instance, how seasoned the trader is.

Daily Trading Blotter

The FX TRADER'S EDGE

Monthly Trend	Up	Down
General Trend		
Monthly Candle		
Weekly Trend	Up	Down
General Trend		
Weekly Candle		
Daily Trend	Up	Down
General Trend		
Daily Candle		

CROSS MARKETS ANALYSIS

Market	Current Price	Yesterday's Close	Change
EQUITIES: US			
Europe			
Asia			
US 10 Yr Note			
Oil			
Gold			

SUPPORT AND RESISTANCE LEVELS

Daily Pivots	FIBO Retracements	FIBO Projections	FIBO Sequence
R3	23.6 %	100 %	0.0013
R2	38.2 %	127.2 %	0.0021
R1	50.0 %	161.8 %	0.0034
Pivot	61.8 %	261.8 %	0.0055
S1	76.4 %	423.6 %	0.0089
S2	100 %	20 day ATR:	0.0144
S3		100 day ATR:	0.0233

CHECKLIST

Trading Rules: Indicators/ Confirmations	Long	Short	Price	Comments
Total the Columns:			Conclusion:	

TRADE PLAN

Strategy: Trend-following / Breakout / Reversal / Range				Reasons for Entries and Exits
Entry Strategy	Trade #1	Trade #2	Trade #3	
Long or Short				
Position Size				
Price				
Exit Strategy	Trade #1	Trade #2	Trade #3	
Stop loss 1				
Stop loss 2				
Profit level 1				
Profit level 2				
Profit level 3				
Profit level 4				
Risk-Reward				

Actual Trade Results	
P1 Target Hit	
P2 Target Hit	
P3 Target Hit	
Stop Hit with Profit	
Manual Exit & Profit	
Stop Hit with a Loss	
Manual Exit & Loss	

POST MORTEM ANALYSIS

Feelings before Trading	Are my Answers Positive	Negative
Was I in a good frame of mind ?		
Had my last couple of trades performed well ?		
Was my personal life running smoothly ?		
Was I "In The Zone" ?		
Did feelings of "perfectionism" creep in ?		
Was I feeling "overconfident" ?		

Actual Trade Planning	Are my Answers Positive	Negative
Did I PLAN MY TRADE based on solid homework preparation ?		
Did I get all confirmations I needed for a high probability trade ?		
Once I entered my trade, did I TRADE MY PLAN ?		
Was my trade impulsive or based on someone else's tips ?		
Was I satisfied with my results or did I show regret ?		
Did EGO take over ?		

FIGURE 11.2 The Daily Trading Blotter

TABLE 11.1	A Sample Profit and Loss Statement			
Trading Day	Initial Account Balance ($)	Ending Account Balance ($)	Net Profit (Loss)($)	Percentage Change (%)
Day 1	102,001	102,083	82	0.08
Day 2	102,083	102,144	61	0.06
Day 3	102,144	102,092	(52)	(0.05)
Day 4	102,092	101,963	(129)	(0.13)
Day 5	101,963	101,383	(580)	(0.57)
Day 6	101,383	101,899	516	0.51
Day 7	101,899	102,326	427	0.42
Day 8	102,326	102,857	531	0.52
Day 9	102,857	102,695	(162)	(0.16)
Day 10	102,695	103,270	575	0.56
Day 11	103,270	103,082	(188)	(0.18)
Day 12	103,082	103,754	672	0.65
Day 13	103,754	103,804	50	0.05
Day 14	103,804	105,152	1348	1.30
Day 15	105,152	105,586	434	0.41
Day 16	105,586	105,090	(496)	(0.47)
Day 17	105,090	104,616	(474)	(0.45)
Day 18	104,616	105,144	528	0.50
Day 19	105,144	105,864	720	0.68
Day 20	105,864	106,407	543	0.51
Day 21	106,407	106,780	373	0.35
Month	106,780	111,559	4,779	4.48

What about a 20 percent return target for a new stock trader? It translates to a consistent monthly goal of fewer than 2 percent growth, and this seems reasonable. If this target goes well, bump it up to 25 percent, then 30 percent, and so forth. By the end of the first trading year, the trader will have a good idea of what her trading system and her trading account can realistically produce. However, don't forget to check out the return of the appropriate stock index and measure your returns against that index. Ideally, you want to beat the index!

Some Important Performance Metrics

The following is a list of performance metrics widely used by traders. They can be downloaded as performance reports from most trading platforms.

1. Number of Trades

The number of trades indicates how active a trader is for a specified period of time. The trader should logically take more trades when the market is more volatile and less when the market is quiet.

What is an "ideal" number of trades? It varies, depending on the market volatility as well as the trader's style. For example, a day trader can likely find two trades in a day, whereas a swing trader might take only two trades a week.

2. Win/Loss Ratio

This is a ratio of the total number of winning trades to the total number of losing trades.

$$\text{Win/loss ratio} = \text{Winning trades} \div \text{Losing trades}$$

For example, if you win on 30 trades out of 50, and lose on 20 trades, your win/loss ratio is 1.5:1 or 60 percent wins.

The amount of money won or lost is not taken into account when the win/loss ratio is calculated. Therefore, it is possible for a trader to have a high win/loss ratio but lose more money on the losing trades than he earns on the winning trades and end up losing money overall.

Similarly, a trader can be profitable with a low win/loss ratio if the size of her wins is greater than the size of her losses. For example, a position taker can have a win/loss ratio of 30 percent but still be successful.

3. Risk/Reward Ratio

The risk/reward ratio is used to compare the expected return of a trade (i.e., how much money it can potentially make) to the amount of risk the trade carries (i.e., how much it can lose given the stop loss). For example, a risk/reward ratio of 3:1 indicates that on average a trade is risking $1 to make $3.

But how is this ratio calculated in the first place? The following example illustrates:

- Let's say a trader purchases 250 shares of a certain company at $20.

- She places a stop-loss order at $18. This will ensure her losses do not exceed $500 (250 × $2).

- She expects that the share price will rise to $26 within 6 months. That gives her an expected gain of $6 ($26 − $20) per share.

In other words, she is risking $2 per share ($20 − $18) to earn $6 per share. Her risk/reward ratio is 3:1. Calculated over a large number of trades, the reward to risk ratio is the expected average size of a winning trade divided by the expected average size of a losing trade.

4. Expectancy

The expectancy is the amount of profit that a trader can expect to win or lose per trade. It is computed by this formula:

$$\text{Expectancy} = (\text{Average gain} \times \text{Probability of gain})$$
$$- (\text{Average loss} \times \text{Probability of loss})$$

For example,

- Let's say a trader wins 30 percent of the time and on average gains $200 per trade. When he loses (70 percent of the time), he loses, on average, $50 per trade (Win/loss ratio is .43:1, Risk/reward is 4:1, and expectancy is a combination of both.)

- His expectancy will be the following:

$$\text{Expectancy} = (\$200 \times 30\%) - (\$50 \times 70\%) = \$25$$

- This means he can expect to win $25 per trade on average.

Sometimes, expectancy is expressed in terms of a ratio:

$$\text{Expectancy ratio} = (\text{Risk/Reward} \times \text{Win \%}) - \text{Loss \%}$$
$$= (4 \times 0.30) - 0.70 = .50$$

This implies that, on average, this trading system will return .50 times the size of the losing trades (0.5 × $50), or $25. This example also demonstrates what we previously discussed: A trader might have a low win/loss ratio, but because the size of his earnings from the winning trades are higher than the size of his losses, he can still be profitable.

5. Total Net Profit

The total net profit represents the total earnings from winning trades minus the losses and expenses. It is usually calculated for a specified trading period, for instance a day, a week, a month, and a year.

This metric tells a trader how much his account size has increased or decreased. It can be found on one of the reports generated by the broker-trading platform used to enter trades.

6. Average Profit per Trade and Average Loss per Trade

The average profit per trade tells a trader the average profit she earns per trade. It is calculated by dividing the total net profit by the total number of winning trades:

Average profit per trade = Total net profit/Total number of winning trades

For example, if a trader makes a total of $1,000 in a week from 20 winning trades, her average profit per trade in that week is $1,000/20 = $50.

Similarly, the average loss per trade reveals the average amount of money a trader loses per trade:

Average loss per trade = Total net loss/Total number of losing trades

For instance, if the trader loses a total of $250 in a week from 10 losing trades, her average loss per trade for that week is $250/10 = $25.

7. Win Percentage and Loss Percentage

The win percentage is simply the total number of winning trades divided by the total number of trades taken, expressed in percentage terms:

Win percentage = (Total number of wins/Total number of trades) × 100%

The loss percentage is the total number of losing trades divided by the total number of trades taken, expressed in percentage terms:

Loss percentage = (Total number of losses/Total number of trades) × 100%

These two percentages tell a trader what percent of the time she is winning on trades taken versus what percent of the time she is losing on trades taken.

8. Profit Factor

Profit factor tells a trader how much he makes for every dollar lost for a specified trading period or trading system.

Profit factor = Gross profit/Gross loss

This metric reveals the efficiency of a system. It provides a reading of the level of gross profit per unit of gross loss from the system as in this example:

- A trader enjoys a gross profit of $50,000 in a year.

- In the same year, his gross loss is $20,000.

- His profit factor is, therefore, 2.5.

Most successful systems have a profit factor between 1.5 to 5: the larger the number, the better. A ratio less than 1 implies a losing trading system.

9. Maximum Drawdown

A drawdown is the decrease in a trader's capital after a series of losing trades. The maximum drawdown represents the worst-case scenario of consecutive losses.

It measures the largest peak-to-trough decline (or the greatest loss) for a specified trading period.

This number can be limited by proper risk management and should be as small as possible. It reveals to a trader the worst-possible scenario she has experienced during the said trading period and the *survivability* of her trading system.

Losses are part of trading, and no traders can avoid drawdowns. However, successful traders carefully plan and execute their money management strategy to make sure their accounts are protected, so they can survive the trading game until the probabilities work in their favor.

10. Compound Annual Return (CAR)

The compound annual return is the average percentage increase in the original amount of capital over the period of one year, assuming the capital grows at the same rate every year.

To illustrate what this means, let's look at the following example:

- Let's say the starting capital of a trader is $10,000.

- The trader claims that he had a CAR of 10 percent over the past five years.

- By the end of the five years, he should have $10,000 \times (110\%)^5 = \$16,105$ in his account.

With the help of these metrics, you can have an objective overview of how well you or your trading business is performing. These metrics can be applied to demo or live trading and can help traders identify which of their trading strategies are performing well or are underperforming. Furthermore, to isolate the strategies and review the performance metrics of each of them independently, you might consider trading different strategies in different accounts. For example, you can take day trades in one account and swing trades in another and compare their results at the end of a certain period.

When you review your performance, do not be afraid to face the facts when the performance metrics tell you that you are underperforming. Do not be emotional about this. Take appropriate action to improve yourself. If it is necessary, pause your live trading and go back to your demo account to troubleshoot and try out fixes to the problems.

On the other hand, when your performance hits your expectations or exceeds it, the metrics will tell you that, too. Reward yourself when you do well. Successful traders have built-in plans to reward themselves as a way to acknowledge and positively reinforce their performance.

Sometimes, even when we have such revealing figures in front of us, we make excuses or turn a blind eye to what our metrics are telling us. This is when having a coach is helpful. Make sure the trading coach you engage is able to interpret the story behind your performance metrics and be frank with you when she evaluates your performance. The hard data from the performance metrics are the key measures with which we judge our performance.

Take Action!

Answer the following questions. They will help you to design your performance tracking system.

1. What information will you be tracking, and how will you record it? For example: daily or weekly profits and losses; weekly or monthly win/loss ratio; weekly or monthly average profitability per trade; and average loss per trade, etc.

2. What will you be looking for with each tracked item? As an example, consider variation from benchmark target.

3. Will you be using a trading journal?

4. If yes, what information will you record and how will you use it?

5. How will you determine when performance is out of acceptable limits?

6. What will you do when performance is out of limits?

7. Will you be using the Daily Trading Blotter?

8. If so, how will you use it in conjunction with the trading journal?

Go to www.wiley.com/go/traderspendulum to download the Daily Trading Blotter. Start using it to track your performance.

Pendulum Scenario 11.1: Organized versus Disorganized Trader

"Out of clutter, find simplicity. From discord, find harmony. In the middle of difficulty lies opportunity."

—Albert Einstein

With a busy life schedule, Stacey realized she could not rely completely on the gray matter between her ears to keep her life in order. So she adapted her habit of writing a to-do list. A big part of the list is filled with the household chores she manages almost single-handedly, and the rest is divided between things she needs to tend to for her newborn and her trading business.

Several Tools to Organize Trading

Completing her to-do list is not the only tool Stacey uses to put some order into her trading business. She uses several other tools.

Before launching her trading business, Stacey put herself through the painstaking process of creating a trader's business plan. That gave her a chance to organize her understanding of this business and the initial ideas of how she should conduct it into a detailed written document. She was grateful she did this because executing the business plan turned out to be a big weight off her shoulders. Along the journey, as she formulated new ideas about the business, she would update the business plan accordingly.

Her trading activities were also planned. She knew exactly which markets she wanted to trade in, what currency pairs to trade, what system or strategy she should use to analyze the market, the specific criteria to enter and exit trades, the stop-loss rules to protect her account, and how much risk she was willing to take. She was committed to trading in an organized way following all the rules in her trading system. The plan was clearly written: This symbolized to her that it was "cast in stone." She had no choice but to strictly follow it.

Stacey was also employing an organized system to check her daily checklist before and after she started trading, by using the Daily Trading Blotter. There was a list of questions in the blotter that she asked herself to find out whether she was trading in the zone. In the same document, she also recorded the technical aspect of her trades: the daily pivots, Fibonacci retracements, and Fibonacci projections. These technical details were useful for her pre-market analysis before she completed the checklist and wrote her trade plan.

Stacey put up a whiteboard on the wall near her workstation. On it, she posted her daily schedule, goals, and general rules for trading. She looked at these lists as part of her daily routine to keep her on track. She double counted it as a vision board, for in the corner of the board she tacked a photo of a beautiful vacation spot that she planned to visit for her second honeymoon. The photo served as her motivation to work hard on her trading business, so that she could afford the trip.

Maintaining a Trading Journal

All the above-mentioned tools helped Stacey a great deal in organizing her trading business, and she owed her success in trading to them. But what she thought was the most indispensable was her trading journal.

Stacey kept her journal as minimal as possible in the form of electronic spreadsheets, where she recorded the following items:

- Screenshots of charts showing trade entry and exit

- Entry date and time

- Position taken and position size

- Exit date and time

- Observations and lessons learned (as detailed as possible)

Every morning before her baby woke up, Stacey reviewed her trading journal to refresh her memory on where she left off from the previous trading session. She wrote every thought she had about the recorded trades. This had become the best self-educational material for her to learn from her past performance, even better than any of the books that taught her about the markets, indicators, trading techniques, and systems.

Stacey kept a record of her daily trading account standing, brief profit & loss statements, and profit targets in the trading journal. She ensured she had these numbers at her fingertips, not only because they helped her see the gap between her goals and her current standing but also because the surprise element was removed.

She maintained a habit of reviewing her trading performance with her coach every two weeks. Her organized trading journal made things easy for them. With this much historical data for her biweekly performance review, her coach could easily identify the patterns in her trading and point out to her what she had done well and what needed improvement. This was one of the keys for Stacey's rapid improvement in trading within a short span of time.

A Disorganized Way to Keep Historical Trading Data

Fred tried to keep a record for his trading, too, but he did not have a dedicated trading journal. Most of his record keeping was done on loose sheets of paper that he pulled out from the drawer of his printer. He did not take screenshots of charts from his trades but roughly sketched the chart out on paper for recording purposes.

Unlike Stacey, Fred thought keeping a record of each trade was pointless because he did not see how a trade from one day to the next could be significantly different. And if they looked similar, why should he bother to record them? The better way, according to Fred, was to record "as and when there is a need", meaning when he spotted something exceptional that produced windfall profits in his account or when he suffered from a major hit on a particular trade. Other "mundane" trades were not worth his time.

Since he was recording his trades on loose paper, did he save them and compile them? Hardly. His records were scattered everywhere in his house: Most were on his trading desk, but you could find some on the living room coffee table, some in his bedroom, and some even in the kitchen in between the pages of the magazines that he read there.

Was it really possible for him to review his trades and learn from his past performance with questionable records like these? Because he did not have an organized way to learn from his trades, he frequently repeated his mistakes and struggled from day to day to survive in trading. He could not pinpoint what he had done right in the past since he had no documented repeatable way to reap the same profits.

Having no trading journal also meant he did not have a way to notate his observations and thoughts in an organized manner. He sometimes wrote them down; well, he scribbled them on a bunch of loose papers. And those loose papers would end up in the same filing cabinet as those handwritten trading records—in the garbage bin. A disorganized trader like Fred missed not only the chance to learn from the market and past performance but also the opportunity to learn from his own ideas and observations.

Pendulum Scenario 11.2: Proactive versus Reactive Trader

"Don't just sit on the runway and hope someone will come along and push the airplane. It simply won't happen."

—Donald John Trump

Stacey was a salesperson before she jumped ship to become a full-time trader. The sales job was a stressful and highly competitive one. It was all about meeting targets: the daily target, the weekly target, the monthly target; the personal target, the team target, and the company target. It was an endless chase after all these cold hard figures.

Her performance was measured by the dollar amount that she brought into the company account and so were her commissions. As a sales professional, she knew she could not wait for prospects to come knocking on her door and enroll themselves onto her customer list. She had to make the move to develop her customer base. She also understood she could not wait forever for them to make a purchasing decision. She had to take the initiative to close the sales.

"No prospects, no business; no sales, no commission," was what her regional manager told her. The eagerness to bring in prospects and close sales had trained her to be a proactive person. She could not stop moving forward. Sitting and waiting were not part of her working style and corporate culture even after she left the sales job to become a trader.

The Differences between a Proactive Trader and a Reactive Trader

Stacey brought the working style of a sales professional into her trading business. She clearly defined her monthly, weekly, and daily targets the same way she set her sales targets. She also strategized her actions to meet the targets as she would for her sales job. During the trade management phase, she did not stand still. She took proactive steps to earn her profits just like when she proactively got prospects into her customer base and closed sales.

Fred took a different approach. He believed his strength was in his analysis, and he was good at reacting to the market moves and changes. So, he spent most of his working hours scrutinizing the market, busy employing his technical analysis skills to take the pulse of the market. He believed he should only take action when the market was moving in the direction of the trend and would stay out of the market when it was not.

Fred reacted to price changes. When he saw price moving in a clear direction, with some analysis to confirm it, he went after it. He was eager to jump into trades because he was afraid of missing out on the opportunities to make money. He kept a watchful eye on the market, and sure enough, when it took a different direction, he changed his position accordingly.

Chasing the price made him tired sometimes, and he would often ask himself, "Is there a better way to trade?" Of course! The answer was in the way Stacey traded.

Stacey did not chase after price. Instead, she let the market come to her. Every day before she began trading, she ran a full market analysis to get an overall market sentiment and focused on the currency pairs she wanted to trade and performed in-depth analysis on them. This way, she could come out with a detailed and specific trade plan and was clear about the position to take, the price targets, and the risks involved well before the price moved to her expected entry point. All she needed to do then was to wait for the right moment to pull the trigger when the setup occurred.

But Stacey did not always wait. For example, while most traders were choosing to wait for the next trend move during sideways consolidations, she chose to learn to make profits from the sideways moves.

Proactive Trader: Trading Not Only the Trends

Stacey understood that the market moves in cycles: Sometimes it is in a trend, but most of the time it is moving sideways. At the beginning of her trading career, she did what most traders do: focus on trading the trend move. But having to stay out of the market most of the time and waiting to take action was not her style. She felt uneasy about the long period of inactivity, so she decided to do some research on whether she could take profitable actions during the sideways movements, too.

She discovered the pros were proficient in capturing and profiting from trend moves and skilled at gaining profits during the sideways consolidation. This excited her. She picked up the strategies to trade trend and sideways markets. When the market was in trend, she executed her high-probability trading setups and took more risk trading it; when it moved sideways, she adopted more conservative strategies.

Unlike trading the market trend, most of the time she could not expect big profits from trading the sideways moves. But Stacey understood that small amounts do add up considerably, and it was better for her to be proactive than to sit there and wait. This suited her personality, which was another reason why she traded all market cycles. When she described the small sums she made out of sideways trading to her peers, she called it her bread and butter business. The money might not be impressive, but it was important.

Passive Trader: Trading Only the Trends

Fred, on the other hand, was not interested in this "small money," but aimed only at making profits by following the trend. He believed that it was smarter to spend the time during the market consolidations analyzing the market and waiting for it to get into trend than to waste time on the insignificant amount of money made during sideways moves. Besides, it was too easy for him to lose money during sideways, whipsaw markets. So, he usually waited until the "best possible entry time" arrived. Sometimes it took hours, sometimes days, but this did not bother him. He believed all the waits were worth his time because he could make huge profits by being more selective in his trades.

Nevertheless, inactivity sometimes made Fred restless, too. When he felt guilty during the window period before the ideal trade entry point showed up, he would peep into what other traders in the market were doing and often followed their moves and took some small positions. This gave him ease of mind: If he could not react to the market move, at least he could react to the crowd's actions. Since so many people were taking these actions, he figured there ought to be some rationale behind them, and the crowd could be right sometimes.

The fact was the opposite almost always happened. His reaction based on the crowd's actions usually cost him his hard-earned money. "Those are insignificant sums of money anyway," he justified to himself, claiming, "At least I learned some lessons from these trades."

Did he? He did not even realize these "insignificant amounts of money" did add up, probably because Stacey's concept of "bread and butter" never rang a bell in him!

Sitting and Doing Nothing during Quiet Times?

During the sideways consolidation phase, the market typically appears to be quiet. It is easy for amateur traders to be lulled into a false sense that there is really nothing much going on when market corrections might be underway. Mature traders will not sit and do nothing, or worse like Fred, do something for the sake of doing it. They will either get themselves prepared for the next onslaught or trade the sideways moves nimbly to make some profits from that.

The actions taken during the quiet times distinguish the proactive traders from the reactive ones. Proactive trading during seemingly inactive times is one of the keys that helps determine the amount of profits a trader can make from the trading business. Take Fred and Stacey's cases, for example. While Fred stayed stagnant most of the time in a week, Stacey did not stop for a moment and had moved miles ahead of him.

Although traders should take proactive steps in trading, they are advised to be mindful and not to overtrade either. There are traders who put themselves on hold during the market consolidation, look and wait for the trend moves, and jump on board to trade aggressively when the trend moves arrive. This rare breed of trader is successful as a result of doing so and can potentially make money in all market cycles. On the surface, they might appear to be passive traders who do nothing during sideways markets. However, during the quiet market period, they are monitoring the market, setting up trade plans, and patiently waiting for the setup to arise. They are traders who let the prices come to them and do not chase the market.

CHAPTER 12

Habit #9: Learn the Secrets of Successful Traders

We naturally learn three ways: by trial and error, by having someone teach us, or by modeling successful people.

First, we learn by trying things out. Give a kid a ball and do not tell him how he should play with it, and you will see that he will get curious about it. He does not know the "right" and "wrong" ways to play and will just do whatever he likes. From there, eventually, he will learn a number of ways he can play with the ball.

Adults do the same thing. We might not realize it, but trial and error is the way we naturally learn. For instance, this is how we discover most of the functions on a smartphone instead of reading the user manual. Traders do the same thing, too. When we want to pick up a new trading skill, we might learn the foundation from a book. But to master it, we try it out on a demo account or a live account and learn from experience.

The second natural way we learn is by getting someone to teach us. Although undergraduate students are encouraged to be independent when they learn, no universities will neglect the importance of having qualified professors or instructors to guide the students in the knowledge mastery process.

The same goes for traders. Traders must be coached and to get a good education. Working with a coach provides a surer and faster path to success than self-learning.

The third way, one that we have not touched upon so far and the central topic for this chapter, is to learn by modeling successful people.

Learning by Modeling Success

Modeling is a process of picking up new skills, behaviors, or mental attitudes by observing and imitating another person who exhibits the qualities to be acquired. For example, a young child might model her parent's walking and standing postures; a student might model his instructor's research methodology; a businessman might model his mentor's business savvy; and a trader might model a highly successful trader to achieve the same results in trading.

In his bestselling book, *Unlimited Power*, Anthony Robbins describes modeling successful people as a pathway to excellence. According to him, if one wants to be a valuable friend, a richer person, a better parent, an athlete with higher performance, or in our case a more successful trader, all she needs to do is to find a person who is there and model him. She has to find out what actions he takes, learn how he uses his mental and physical strengths to produce the results she desires, and duplicate them. Robbins assures us that learning the secrets of successful people and adopting them into our practice can be a huge time saver on the road to success. In other words, the road doesn't always have to be long and winding.

A real-life example is how non-English-speaking students learn English. Some language schools provide video clips and instruct them to watch the clips over and over and observe and model the English-speaking presenter's pronunciation, tonality, and tempo. Some even ask the students to copy the transcript of the speech with handwriting as a way to hardwire the words, sentences, and structure of the script.

These ways have been practiced in many language schools for decades, and the results have been remarkable. Many students faced no major problems with their language when they pursued higher education in English-speaking countries.

So, what can we do to model successful traders? I suggest starting by examining what they do in a typical trading day and modeling their success habits.

A Day in the Life of a Successful Trader

Successful traders plan their activities to maximize their days. They organize their daily life with clearly defined trading times; they keep themselves abreast of the latest developments in the markets and, in general, major events from around the world; they relentlessly analyze the market; and they have plans for trading and trade the plan. See the trader's roadmap in Figure 12.1.

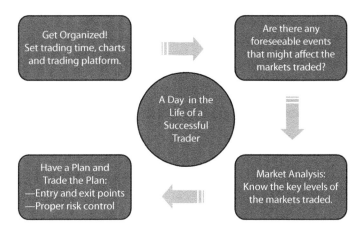

FIGURE 12.1   The roadmap: A Day in the Life of a Successful Trader

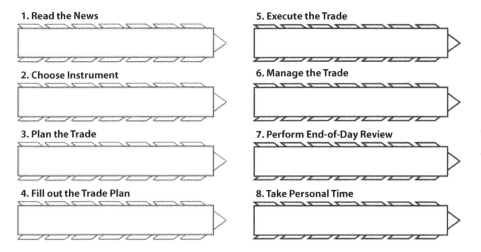

FIGURE 12.2   The routine for "A Day in the Life of a Successful Trader"

There are eight things that most successful traders do every day. This "routine" is presented in Figure 12.2.

1. Read the News to Get the "Flavor" of the Day

Successful traders begin their days by reading news commentary, for example on websites specializing in their traded markets. Many of the investment banks offer professional reports by economists and market strategists. Traders read strategies to get a sense of how the fundamentals from around the world might affect the markets. Every day is a different day for trading, and any news coming out overnight is digested by the markets instantaneously through the price action. Understanding whether or not the news will have a lasting impact, like a change in monetary policy, is key to understanding the medium term trends.

Economic statistics, news announcements, and central bank policy affect the markets and keep traders glued to their screens until they are updated about events affecting the markets. From there, they can determine the market sentiment and the daily direction for their trading.

2. Choose the Currency Pairs/Stocks/Futures to Trade

Once they get the flavor of the day, successful traders will then decide what to trade. During this process, traders typically check out the instruments they are familiar with and take a quick look at cross-market analysis, again to determine the market sentiment in other global markets that might affect their own. Scanning is done to see the best market setups for their strategies. With a strong idea of the fundamentals, they get to work looking for the best trading opportunities for the day or week.

3. Plan the Trade

Now the traders will perform their analysis on the markets they decide to trade. They will determine the trend, choose the direction of the high-probability trades, choose the trade setup to trigger their entries, and evaluate the setups with a list of confirmations.

When trading opportunities arise, the traders will formulate trade plans for the trades. They usually have a number of checklists that they created based on their trading systems, and they will go through these checklists to make sure they abide by all the rules and strategies defined.

4. Fill out the Trade Plan

The traders will determine, based on their trading system, whether to buy, sell, or do nothing against the best trading opportunities they have selected. They will use their trading systems to provide entry and exit points for the trades. For each trade, the entry price, stop loss, and profit targets are clearly defined.

5. Execute the Trade

Pulling the trigger is as important as setting up the trade. When it is time to execute the trades, these traders do not hesitate. They do what their analyses and trade plans dictate. They are aware if their emotions are causing them to hesitate in taking the trades.

6. Manage the Trade

Successful traders manage their trades after they place their entries, stop losses, and profit targets in the trading platform. They have solid trade management strategies that aggressively protect their accounts. As the trades moves in their favor, they move their stops to protect the profits. They constantly check, "Do I need to exit the trades early or move the stop losses?"

7. Perform an End-of-Day Review

At the end of the day, successful traders will perform an end-of-day review. They measure and evaluate their personal performance according to these benchmarks:

- Did I follow my plan?
- Did my emotions get in my way when I traded?
- Were these high or low probability trades based on the confirmations?
- How successful were the trades?

8. Take Personal Time

When all these are done and the trading day is over, the traders will then enjoy the rest of their day. Regularly, they take time out for themselves or to be with their families. Successful traders have their planned trading times in their calendars, and they stick to their plans. They structure their work-life so that they can balance their personal time with work (see Figure 12.3).

Winning Qualities of Successful Traders

Modeling successful traders is not only about modeling what they do but also what they think, how they think, and what their attitudes are.

What can you find in successful traders if you study them closely? Here is a list of qualities and behaviors they exhibit that you can model for success.

- *Ambitious, strong-willed, focused, passionate, and patient*. They also maintain a positive and optimistic attitude toward their lives and trading business.
- *Perseverant*. They hang in there, more determined than ever when others throw in the towel.
- *Not afraid of making mistakes*. They might even feel happy when they make mistakes! They take notes and learn from their mistakes and apply the lessons they learn to increase their winning opportunity the next time around.
- *Uncomfortable when they find themselves staying in their comfort zone*. They take risks, meaning calculated risks. They are effective in dealing with fear of failure,

1. Read the News

Are there any news releases that might impact the market prices during your trading session?

Look at the news announcement calendar and be prepared for announcements that might affect the markets.
Did you check the news today?

2. Choose Instrument

What is the flavor of the day, week, or month?

Read a strategy piece on your traded market that talks about the fundamentals.
Determine daily direction and market sentiment.

3. Plan the Trade

Know in advance whether you are going to buy, sell, or do nothing.

Complete Trading Blotter Checklist.
What is the trend? Do you see a high-probability trade? Choose the trade setup to trigger your entry.
Evaluate your setup and add up your score.

4. Fill out the Trade Plan

Is this a high- or low-probability trade, based on your confirmations or system?

Use your system to provide entry and exit points.
Risk management: entry, stop loss, profit targets.
Is this a high- or low-probability trade, based on your list of confirmations?

5. Execute the Trade

Enter trade in the trading platform.

Pulling the trigger is just as important as setting up the trade! Was there any hesitation in taking the trade?
Did you do what your analysis dictated?

6. Manage the Trade

Manage the trade as price moves in your favor.

Manage the trade after you place the entry, stop loss, and profit target in the platform. As the trade moves in your favor, move your stop to protect profits.
If you have profits, protect them!

7. Perform End-of-Day Review

End the day with a post-mortem analysis.

Measure your personal performance benchmarks. How were your emotions before, during, and after the trade?
How successful was the trade?

8. Take Personal Time

A balanced life is a happy family!

Take time out for yourself or to be with your family.
Enter your trading times in your calender and follow it.
Structure your work life so that you can balance your personal time with work.

FIGURE 12.3   Steps in a day in a successful trader's life

fear of losing money, and fear of making mistakes. They do not allow their egos or emotions to get in the way when they make decisions for their trading business.

■ *Learn not only from their mistakes but also from what they have done right.* They draw conclusions from the successes they achieve and formulate winning formulas they can repeat over and over for further trading success.

■ *Thrive on independence.* Although they do gratefully accept advice and guidance, they do not expect or rely on others to help them in their endeavors. They are take-charge people who can come up with creative and intelligent solutions.

■ *Mentally, psychologically, and physically strong.* Successful traders have that in spades. They know how to maintain this stamina through self-motivation, activities that calm their mind, frequent positive mental stimulation, regular physical workouts, and a balanced life.

- *Masters of time and self-management.* They approach their lives and trading business with discipline.

- *Confident that they are worthy of success.* They know they deserve it, judging from the hard work they put in, their attitude and aptitude, and the skillful practice of their crafts.

- *Keen on training and coaching to help them achieve success.* They do not stop learning and growing throughout their trading life.

- *Masters of their craft.* They have put in thousands of hours to perfect their trading skills. They strive to internalize the skills that are beneficial to their trading.

- *Observant learners.* They are obsessive learners, but they take action, too. They know it is useless to stuff lots of knowledge in their heads without applying it.

If you read the list again, you will find that 60 to 70 percent of the qualities or behaviors listed here have nothing to do with the hard, cold, technical trading skills. Rather, they are mental and psychological attributes. Ask any successful trader and they may tell you that working on the mental game contributes significantly to trading success.

Also, although this list contains the main traits I have observed in successful traders, it is by no means exhaustive. Many other positive qualities have helped the top traders in their shining trading careers, and it is up to you to discover them.

And remember, successful traders practice the 10 habits in this book!

■ Where Do You Find Successful Traders to Model?

There are a few answers to the question, "Where do I find successful traders to model?"

Charlie E. John, a famous author and master of salesmanship, provides a clue. He said, "You will be the same person in five years as you are today except for *the people you meet* and *the books you read*." Let me interpret this in the context of trading.

There are two levels on which you can learn from the people you meet: the conscious level and the unconscious level.

At the *conscious* level, you may seek out successful traders who have attained the level of success you want to achieve, make a conscious effort to uncover their secrets of success, and model them. Where can you find these top traders? Many of them are highly reputed, so finding them is easy. Ask around in the community of traders in your local area, and a few big names will pop up. Otherwise, make good use of today's technology, for example, Google, to locate them.

If you can get to know these traders personally, ask them to coach or mentor you or even go under their apprenticeship; that would be great! This is how you get to observe how they conduct their trading business up-close and personal. But it is fine, too, even if you do not get to work with them. They might be contributing to a blog, producing online videos, publishing a book, or offering courses that you can take.

Study their work like an industrious student, and you will get a glimpse of their working patterns and attitudes. If you want to take it a step further, you can even write to them to ask questions. You might be surprised to find out how many of them are willing to generously share their knowledge simply because they love what they are doing. It is their passion!

A side note to this point of becoming a successful trader is you might not only want to model successful traders. We can learn from top players in other fields that will make huge differences in our trading business too! For example, for the past 30 years, I have benefited from the knowledge shared with me by top life coaches, financial experts, marketers, and educators although they didn't specifically talk about trading with me!

Things get a little tricky when you model the people you meet at the "subconscious" level. Jim Rohn, a great motivational speaker, once said, "You are the average of the five people you spend the most time with." This is true in terms of the income you earn, what you like and dislike, your attitude toward career, family and life, and almost everything.

You might think this is because birds of a feather do flock together, but it is only partly true. The other part of the story is when you hang around with your friends or family members long enough, you tend to mirror the way they speak, act, and think (and they mirror you, too) at a subconscious level.

In other words, you basically model them subconsciously and most likely indiscriminately. If you often hang out with fellow traders, you might find yourself getting interested in the markets they trade in, picking up their attitude toward their trading business as well as trying out and somehow starting to adopt the trading skills they use, no matter whether they are good or bad.

Eventually, like Rohn said, you become the average of these people. You will earn almost the same amount of money, achieve the same level of trading success, and live the same kind of trader's life as them. It will be great if the traders you hang out with are successful traders who reap positive results in trading, but what if they are mediocre at best? Do you believe that they will help bring positive influences into your trading life?

With this lengthy advice, I am trying to stress this: *Choose with deliberation* the fellow traders you mingle with because you will become who you spend your time with.

Learning the Success Secrets by Reading

The second half of John's advice implies you can learn the secrets of successful trading by reading the right books. Successful people have a habit of reading, but they do not read just any books. They read books that enrich them, like education, self-improvement, and career- or business-related books. In particular, they enjoy reading biographies or autobiographies of other successful people to learn from their life stories and perspectives.

Anthony Robbins, in his book *Awakening the Giant Within*, reveals that an effective way to achieve the same results as the rich and successful legends (realistically speaking though, maybe to a different level of success) is by reading and learning from their stories. We should look at how they have overcome unimaginable odds and made differences to their own and other people's lives, be inspired and motivated by them, and mirror their mannerisms, attitudes, and even body language. This is how we can learn the secrets of success of these "giants" even though we might never come into contact with them.

Of more relevance to trading, hundreds, if not thousands, of books are available in the market for our reference. Not all of them are biographies or autobiographies, but many contain notes from expert traders or *trading gurus* on their secrets of success. Being in the trading world for more than 30 years, I have personally witnessed how a whole industry devoted to providing information on trading has grown by leaps and bounds.

These writings of great market success stories are easily accessible nowadays: some are physical books, some are in electronic format. Learn the successful traders' perspective, study their success principles, and model the experts' principles and methodologies of success. Most importantly, put them into practice. In due time, they will become second nature to you, too!

Pendulum Scenario 12.1: I Can versus I Can't

"Whether you think you can, or you think you can't—you're right."
—Henry Ford

Stacey was a changed person after she started her trading business. Her husband, Brad, always knew she was a highly energetic woman with a sense of purpose. This personality had helped her to achieve remarkable results in her previous sales job. She was also brimming with commitment and a "never say no" spirit, always eager to take on challenges, with an almost overpowering sense of fearlessness to advance in her career. These qualities made her stand out in the playing field of the sales job that mainly consisted of men.

After she became a trader, something was noticeably different.

She seemed to be more patient now, probably because she learned that sometimes she had to wait and not rush into taking action. She was still the same results-oriented woman that Brad knew, but now she seemed able to think long-term, and not let short-term gains blind her decisions. Given the choice, she still tended not to fear taking the aggressive path, but she was no longer controlled by her emotions, she could keep her cool, saw the overall picture, and planned things out objectively.

But something *else* was different, not only in her attitude toward her business, but also in the way she dealt with her life and relationships. Brad could not figure out what it was.

The Negative Changes Trading Brought On

Fred became a changed person too after he started trading full-time. But unlike Stacey, he was moving on a downward spiral.

In his previous job, he was also a top performer. His technical expertise was not only recognized by his company but by the local industry at large. When the big players in the industry needed advice on the subject matter of his specialization, he was the go-to person. Eager to show his proficiency, he would always accept any chance to contribute his knowledge. This brought him numerous awards and recognition. The sense of achievement he reaped from his job gave him an air of confidence.

He thought he could bring that confidence to his trading business, but unfortunately, he didn't. Within a few months in business, his successive losses diminished his confidence.

Fred was no longer the confident man that his friends once knew. His friends no longer saw him light up when he talked about his career. Was he still the highly committed Fred? Probably, judging from the number of hours he spent sitting on his office chair but probably not because he spent more time idle than being productive. Although he was still an analytical person, he could no longer guarantee he could keep a clear mind when he had to make logical decisions in trading, especially when his mind was clouded with fear, the fear of failure.

But something *else* was different in Fred. Even his friends noticed it.

The "I Can" Spirit in the Successful Trader

Stacey revealed the change to Brad: The way she thought and the way she spoke had changed thanks to a tip from her trading coach.

Now Stacey consciously chose positive words, avoided making negative statements, and used an uplifting tone when she thought and spoke. She believed these habits would hardwire her mind for optimism and confidence and help her to form a positive mindset. This would give her a psychological winning edge in trading.

In particular, Stacey avoided using "I CAN'T," knowing the harm that this seemingly mundane phrase could cause. She would mindfully change any "I CAN'T" statements into "I CAN" statements. For example, when budgeting for the second honeymoon trip, looking at her account balance, she was tempted to think, "We can't afford it," but she chose to take on a positive angle and changed the statement to: "We can afford it, and we will figure out how." This gave her the motivation to work toward making a few thousand dollars more in trading profits.

When she heard about the profits her peers were making because of the larger amount of capital they were trading, she consciously avoided thinking, "I can't trade like them. I just don't have that kind of money," but thought instead, "Someday, I can do the same, too." Which is a good start. She could power up that statement by setting a deadline for her goal, followed by the question: "How do I do that?"

Once Stacey developed this habit of practicing the "I CAN" mindset, amazing things came into her life. She started to see opportunities everywhere, not only for her trading business, but also for her life, personal development, relationships, and even for the upbringing of her newborn child. For example, she no longer complained to her husband, "I just can't make the baby listen to me" because the "I can teach him to listen to me but how?" thinking kicked in. In the end, she did figure out a proper way to teach her baby!

The "I CAN" attitude became Stacey's second nature. With such a positive mindset, she often felt undefeatable in trading. Even though her trading journey could be rough and even though there was still a long way to go in her trading business, she knew her mindset would carry her forward far and abound.

The Destruction that the "I CAN'T" Attitude Caused

It felt as if it were only yesterday that Fred called all his good friends about his change of career path, threw a party to celebrate his first day in the business, and awaited eagerly for his "trading desk" to arrive at his home. His friends remembered how excited he was when he first got into the trading business and how he was jumping for joy whenever he talked about it.

Now that positive energy had been replaced by a constant feeling of worry and hopelessness. His friends knew Fred was not doing well but did not expect his mediocre performance to bring this level of harm to him.

Moreover, Fred started to speak negatively. Even he noticed how frequently he used "I can't" every day.

"I can't afford the road trip. I need to save my cash."

"I know I should make some changes in my life soon, but I can't figure out what's wrong and what to do."

"I just can't do this yet; it's beyond my control."

And the same pattern was observed in his views about trading.

Even before the end of the month, he thought, "I wish I could hit the earnings target this month, but now it seems that I can't." When he got envious seeing other traders pocketing huge profits in a trade he missed, he lamented, "I just can't make myself take those outrageously brave trades that my trader colleagues take."

In a similar situation Stacey faced, his reaction was, "I can never trade like these big players. They have such huge pools of capital at their disposal. I don't."

The only "I CAN'T" statement that was doing him good was, "I can't give up yet. I did not quit my job to become broke and return to another job." This determination pushed him forward in his trading business.

But he needed to do more than persevere. One of the first things to do was to get that negative thinking out of his head and start growing a positive mindset. How would he do that? Learn from Stacey. Change the choice of words, mindset, and tone of voice when he spoke and thought.

Get rid of "I CAN'T"; think "I CAN!"

■ Pendulum Scenario 12.2: Patient versus Impatient Trader

"He that can have patience can have what he will."

—Benjamin Franklin

If there was something that trading taught Stacey, it was the virtue of patience.

When she was in the salesforce, she was known by her co-workers as an "aggressive go-getter." Patience had little place in her style of execution. If she did not have enough leads to work on, she would not hesitate to buy them or command her assistant to generate leads for her. If a customer did not reply, he could expect to receive a call from her in no more than two days. If the customer took too long to decide, Stacey the go-getter would meet him in the comfort of his own office no more than one week later.

Every action she did not take and every action that ended up in vain would cause her sales results to suffer and make a dent in her earnings. That was why patience had no place in her job. She needed to continuously move things forward, and she needed to do it quickly.

Things were different in the trading world. Stacey did not have any control over the market. When it was time to take action, she would jump on it; but when it was time to wait, she had to be patient because nothing she did would expedite the market moves.

This was frustrating at first for an "aggressive go-getter" like her. For instance, she could get hair-pulling mad when she expected the market to move in a certain way within a certain time frame, but as it turned out, the market was slow-moving. What could she do? Nothing but be patient and "give the market some time."

When she was a novice trader, her impatience would make her rush into taking trades long before the trade entry criteria were fulfilled or take profits too early when her patience wore out. But Stacey was an intelligent trader. Time after time, when she learned that she could earn more, risk less, and avoid losses by being patient, she finally succumbed, and stopped taking reckless actions. In her own words, she was "tamed by the market." There was a certain level of willingness in her doing so, as the dollar amount in her trading account showed her that waiting was always worthwhile.

She eventually understood that being patient in trading was not equivalent to inaction. It was more like "active anticipation" for the right moment to arrive before launching into action.

■ The Wisdom of Taking No Action

Stacey was well aware that markets move in cycles. Over the past few months, she learned to trade not only the trend but also the sideways consolidation. She used different setups to trade sideways markets, but the same principle applied: No matter whether she traded the trend or sideways market, she always followed her trade plan and did not enter and exit the trades unless it allowed so.

She would wait patiently for the price to come to her before she struck. Her husband liked to describe her as a skillful predator who stalked its target closely but kept holding on and sprung into attack only when the opportunity was right. Stacey hated to admit that was true. To her, such a level of patience was fundamental to every successful trader. Impatience was almost a deadly sin.

There were times when some potential trading opportunities arose but didn't exactly follow her trading rules. Stacey learned not to rush into these trades. Instead, she would wait and give them some time to develop. If they did not move into her trade trigger zone, Stacey would just move on. She was seldom affected by this, knowing that many trading opportunities existed in the market. She had to be patient to wait until the next one came up.

The market could also be quiet. During these times, she might choose to do nothing and waited for the "more profitable cycles" to kick into gear. This showed that she detested giving back her profits when the market was pausing. "Why should I risk my hard-earned money when the market hasn't even decided which way it will go?"

She always wisely reminded herself, "Be patient; don't take any premature action that you will later regret."

■ Going from Patience to Impatience, Well-to-Do to Broke

Fred was known to his ex-colleagues as a patient person. They remembered when he worked with them, Fred tirelessly went through every single technical detail during discussions, leaving no stone unturned. Fred knew he could not overlook anything, because every detail could be the key to make or break a project. His attention to detail, perseverance, and patience were highly praised by his ex-colleagues and superiors.

However, he did not seem to have similar patience in his trading business. Although he was mostly conservative in his trading, he was sometimes caught rushing into a trade, rushing out of it, and quickly jumping into another trade. Worse, he often repeated the same process all day long, taking more trades than he should.

This happened when he lost his patience, especially if his trades did not produce the results he was expecting. Fred knew it had some correlation with his attitude toward trading. He was eager to make money, and when emotions kicked in, he would sometimes want to expedite the "enter trade, exit trade, take the money and run" process, without regard to his trade plan.

He did not want to admit it, but deep down inside, this made him feel as if he was treating trading as a get-rich-quick scheme. He knew it was wrong, that he had to be patient with trading, but every time that a trade did not move as quickly as he hoped or for some reason he lost his patience in the middle of trading, he would "enter, exit, take the money and run" again.

Needless to say, he could not make consistent profits trading this way.

■ How to Temper Impatience

With some experimentation, Fred found the best ways to temper his impatience:

1. *Be mindful when he traded.* If he could detect losing his patience and starting to make emotional decisions, he might be able to put a stop to what he was doing.

2. *Adhere to the trade plan, even when he felt the urge to speed the trades up.* This meant even if the price was approaching the target entry point but was not quite there yet, he should resist the temptation to enter early. On the contrary, getting out of the trade before the price target or stop loss was hit, no matter how close it was, should not be allowed.

3. *Cultivate an abundance mindset.* He could do this by reminding himself that opportunities to trade were abundant. Even if he missed a good one, another WOULD appear. So, there was no reason he should rush into trades.

4. *Cultivate the abundance mindset by understanding that there was abundant money out there in the market.* He had to be patient, trade skillfully and meticulously, and keep a winning psychological edge. The money would come to him.

5. *Take a short break or stay out from trading entirely if everything else failed and he still found himself not exercising patience.* This might sound like an extreme action to take, but it worked for him!

CHAPTER 13

Habit #10: Add Balance to Your Life

Just five minutes into the telephone conversation with Danny, one of my coaching clients and an institutional trader, I knew I had to give him immediate attention to salvage his trading career.

Danny was in the beginning years as a trader, and was eager to seek career advancement. He would wake up early in the morning to catch up on events that might affect the market. When he traded, he focused 120 percent of his energy on trading. That was when he rode the emotional roller coaster, fixed his eyes on the computer screen and his body on the office chair for hours, and got the endorphins and adrenaline overdose on a daily basis.

His day never ended with the market close. His team would have a lengthy end-of-day meeting, during which everyone's daily performance was scrutinized by the team lead. This somewhat helped the traders to grow as they were accountable for their trading results, but the pressure was suffocating. In addition to that, the meeting would extend late into the evening. Any form of social life or leisure activities after work were out of the question. And there was his own overzealous daily review, post-mortem, and detailed logging of every trade taken.

Danny would read news on financial sites and do market recaps, study materials prescribed by his team lead, and spend the remaining hours brushing up on trading skills.

By the time all this was completed, it was far into the night. He could get some rest, and the same mad rush would continue on the next day, day after day. He might be exhausted physically and mentally, but he pushed through it with superhuman determination anyway.

Even weekends were lost because he needed to study for certification exams. Family time, social interactions, leisure activities, and even a short break were all luxuries. For many years, this was what he called his life.

■ Symptoms of Trader Burnout

Danny let this carry on without regard to how his body and mind protested against it. His health suffered and he fell into depressive moods easily. Although he took note of the early symptoms of his physical and mental breakdowns, he brushed them away. He thought these were the hardships he needed to endure in the pursuit of a stellar career.

Sure enough, his condition deteriorated, to the extent that he felt lethargic at work the whole day. He could not process the data presented to him with a clear mind and was not making reasonable decisions. He became agitated by his co-workers easily and could lose his patience over the most trivial things, for instance, a small scratch on his coffee mug.

And he started to lose the meaning in life. He would start anticipating the lunch break once he settled in at his workstation early in the morning and would look forward to the end of the day during lunch; he would wait eagerly for weekends and holidays.

Going to work every day was becoming intolerable, and the fights on the trading battlefield were no longer thrilling. He could feel his motivation slipping away.

This was the perfect chance for self-doubt and cynicism to creep in. As Danny's trades no longer went as smoothly as they did before, he started to believe all the initial successes he had were due to beginner's luck. Nothing he tried seemed to work. He couldn't help suspecting, "Perhaps I don't have what it takes to win big. Perhaps I have overestimated my competency. Or perhaps I shouldn't be a trader at all, and there is another career out there that fits me better."

Danny thought it was only a matter of time before he threw in the towel until he came to me for rescue. I recognized the symptoms in no time. They were all too familiar to me as I had seen them on other overworked traders, and I had, for a period of time, experienced them myself. So I pointed out to him that all the disruptions he was having were signs that he was going through trader burnout.

■ Getting out of the Trap

I suggested that Danny follow a four-step method that has helped numerous other traders who were in the same situation.

The first step is to acknowledge the problem. Unless Danny acknowledged his problem, he couldn't confront it head on. This step might sound simple, but it is only when the trader applies it that he will realize how important it is.

Danny had difficulty the first step that he nearly gave up before he started. With my encouragement, he made a list of the troubles that he was going through. That was when he admitted that his life was in poor shape and acknowledged that trader burnout was taking a toll on him. He became determined to counter its attack.

The second step to take is to analyze the causes of the problem. Danny listed the following as the causes:

- Lack of focus at work

- Loss of interest and motivation in trading

- Not feeling happy with his work

- Not getting a sense of achievement and satisfaction from trading

All these looked reasonable on the surface, but when he sent me this list, I returned it to him with a kind note saying, "Danny, this is a good start, but we are not quite there yet." I advised, "Look at your list again. These are the *symptoms* of your problem, not the *cause*. Think about what's causing all these, and you can get to the root of your problem."

Following my advice, he did some soul searching and realized it all boiled down to only one thing: his excessive desire for career advancement had messed up the balance in his life. In other words, he had lost his *work-life balance*. This was the root cause for his trader burnout.

With the root cause identified, the logical next step to take was to formulate a plan to deal with it. Almost immediately Danny knew the solution was to add balance back to his life. In addition, he promised to stop being too hard on himself. To keep himself going, he needed to learn to unwind after work and celebrate the progress he made to ensure constant motivation.

But the question was "How?" Based on our discussion, he arrived at a series of possible strategies.

Finally, the last step was to take action! I provided two useful tips for him for dealing with the trader burnout problem and for tackling most problems in life.

1. *Do not wait until a perfect solution is found before taking action.* Implement what we have in the plan, assess the results along the way, improvise the plan, and implement it again. Repeat these steps a few times, and each time the action we take will be better than before. This is how we move closer to the solution.

2. *Do not accomplish a huge task at one go.* Instead, break it down into small, digestible, and measurable steps, and take one step at a time. That's the famous "How do you eat an elephant? One bite at a time," strategy.

Danny needed several months before he got rid of trader burnout. The four-step method worked and had guided him to walk away from his problem slowly but gracefully. I am sure this will help other traders, too.

To summarize, these are the four steps:

Step 1: Acknowledge the problem.

Step 2: Identify the root cause.

Step 3: Formulate a plan to tackle the cause.

Step 4: Execute the plan, assess the result, improvise it, and repeat this process until the issue is solved.

In the following section, we will discuss some ways to add back balance.

◼ How to Achieve Balance in Trading Life and Maintain Motivation

To get the right answer, we must ask the right question. So, what should you ask yourself to achieve balance in your trading life and stay motivated? Here are a few good questions.

1. How Does Trading Fit into Your Life?

One of the advantages that you as a trader (especially retail traders who are on their own) enjoy is the freedom to fit your trading activities around your life. Admittedly, you might not have more time than office workers; you might need to spend more time than them on your job since you're running your own trading business. However, you do have more freedom in adjusting your schedule.

To do this, you need to decide the market in which you want to trade, your trading hours, and how many days a week to trade. To be successful in your career, you have to make *some* sacrifices, but that doesn't mean you have to sacrifice everything. With proper planning, you can fit other important things into your busy life: family time, a hobby, regular meetups with friends, volunteer work, setting up another business.

2. What Are Your Plans to Simplify Your Life (Personal and Work)?

Prioritization is the key to achieving work-life balance. You need to vigorously check the activities you engage in every day, determine how important they are, and (ruthlessly) cut down on unimportant, meaningless, or unproductive activities so you can focus your energy and time on the important ones. When you keep things simple, you will have more control over your personal life and your work.

3. Do You Have a Life Outside of Trading?

Understand that no matter how passionate you are about trading, how important the income earning potential from trading is, how thrilled you are when you achieve trading success, trading is not and should not be your whole world.

You have to have a life outside of trading too, for at least four reasons:

1. *Over time, if all you do every day is only trading and nothing else, you might lose interest in it.* What follows next will be you giving up on trading. Boredom does kill a trading business.

2. *You want to live your life to the fullest.* A "full" life is not all about work and business.

3. *Putting all your eggs in one basket is a bad idea.* In this case, it is bad practice to pour all your time and energy into one single activity, namely trading. What if your trading business suffers? Do you have something (e.g., your family, friends, and other activities) to fall back on?

4. *You don't want regrets.* When you look back on your life, probably in 20 years, you don't want to regret what you have not done and the opportunities in life that you missed because of the disproportionate weight you allocated to your trading business.

4. How Do You Celebrate When Your Progress Is on Target?

Anyone who has ever been employed knows that a manager's job is to keep employees motivated with the hope that their spirit and, therefore, performance is in top condition. As a trader, you are your own boss. No one is tasked or paid to help maintain your motivation, so you have to be in charge of this.

Here is what you can do. First, define when you should be rewarded, for example, when you master a trading strategy or hit a certain earning milestone, a significant monthly win/loss ratio, or a target account balance. Rewarding yourself when these goals are met not only provides powerful reinforcement but also creates a positive emotional link with the outcome you desire.

Second, find out what rewards you appreciate. Everyone is motivated by different things: Some find joy in overseas trips, some prefer to be pampered by a nice massage or dinner at a five-star restaurant, and some just want a short break so they can do nothing at all.

Third, set milestones in your trader's business plan, promise yourself you will reward yourself when you hit the milestones, and start working toward the reward!

Having your eyes set on the prize heightens your chance of achieving the milestones and gives you jolts of motivation to keep you going.

5. How Are You Planning to Give Back to the Community When You Succeed as a Trader?

Successful people and the rich have a habit of giving back to society. There are a few reasons for this. First, it is one of the ways they put their money into meaningful use: to *do good*, to reach out to help the needy, and to make changes to the society. Second, they understand that when they receive from the society, they should contribute back to the society. Third, giving helps them grow the "abundance" mindset and send a signal of "I am rich" to their mind. Many of them believe this will attract more wealth into their lives.

Last but not least, they do so because they feel happy doing so! This is perhaps the most important reason why they keep giving back.

You don't need to wait until you become "ultra-successful" to start giving back. Start small, and you can reap the benefits of giving, too. Also, your contributions do not necessarily have to be in monetary form. Many successful traders are contributing their time, physical energy, and their expertise as a trader to society.

You might have noticed that the suggestions to plan your trading properly, fit your trading business around your daily activities, add balance to your trading life, and set up your reward system are some of the steps that you can see in the *Trader's Business Plan Workbook* at www.wiley.com/go/traderspendulum. If you plan your trading business well, with some trial-and-error and continuous improvising, you will have no problem achieving a well-balanced life as a trader.

■ Your Life Plan

This chapter ends with another big topic: planning your life and creating your *life plan*.

A trader's business plan is essential for your trading business, and a trade plan should guide your trade execution, just as a life plan is of utmost importance for your life. The same wisdom of "if you don't know where you are going, you are going nowhere in particular" that we discussed in a previous chapter is applicable here, too. The process of creating a life plan allows you time and space to think through what you want to do and achieve in your life, and you will see how this can be linked back to your trading business, and help you succeed in it.

If you haven't taken the time to sit down and draw up your life plan, then you should consider doing so. I will not go into the details of the process to establish it because the same instructions for constructing your business plan can be applied here. Instead, I am providing you a list of questions to ask yourself when you create your life plan.

■ Outline for Developing Your "Life Plan"

- ■ What subjects or activities are you most passionate about?

- ■ Can you integrate things you are passionate about into your profession?

- ■ What are your personal long-term (5–10 years) personal goals?

- ■ How do you plan to achieve them?

- ■ How would you rate yourself on a scale of 1 (lowest) to 10 (highest) as to your current progress toward those goals?

- ■ What are your short-term (1-year) personal goals?

- ■ How do you plan to achieve them?

- ■ How would you rate yourself on a scale of 1 (lowest) to 10 (highest) as to your current progress toward those goals?

- ■ What are your long-term (5–10 years) financial goals?

- ■ How do you plan to achieve them?

- ■ How would you rate yourself on a scale of 1 (lowest) to 10 (highest) as to your current progress toward those goals?

- ■ What are your short-term (1 year) financial goals?

- ■ How would you rate yourself on a scale of 1 (lowest) to 10 (highest) as to your current progress toward those goals?

- ■ What is your personal philosophy?

- ■ Who are your role models in respect to lifestyle? Why?

- ■ Who are your professional role models? Why?

- ■ Who could you solicit to be your mentor? Why?

- ■ What type of education would most help you reach both your personal and professional goals?

- ■ What do you see as your personal weaknesses?

- ■ What do you see as your strengths?

- ■ How can you expand and build on those strengths while managing those weaknesses?

- ■ Ask at least two other people who know you well to provide their appraisal of what they see as your strengths.

Take Action!

1. Create your own life plan by answering the questions listed above.

2. Take the first step to factor work-life balance into your trading business, by asking yourself the following questions:

   a. How does trading fit into your life?

   b. What are your plans to simplify your life (personal life and work)?

   c. Do you have a life outside of trading?

   d. How do you celebrate when your progress is on target?

   e. How are you planning to give back to the community when you succeed as a trader?

   f. What is your plan for maintaining a healthy mind-body condition?

3. Do you think having a trading coach is a good idea? Please support your ideas on this subject.

■ Pendulum Scenario 13.1: Relaxed versus Stressed Trader

"Sometimes when people are under stress, they hate to think, and it's the time when they most need to think."

—William J. Clinton

Because of the long hours he poured into trading almost every day, Fred became easily distracted when he traded. He knew ideally all he needed to focus on were the real-time charts on the computer screen and his trading system, but he could not.

He might have been thinking about his last few trades. The money he won or lost. His current account balance. What kind of setup would come to him, what he should be targeting, and what kind of profit he expected to make on the *next* trade while the *current* trade was occurring.

And he might also have been thinking about his life; most of what came up was not constructive, only complaints: the life that his career switch had brought to him, the kind of money he wanted to make but was not making, and how he had not achieved anything significant in his personal life yet.

Thousands of things went through his mind, most of them negative ones, and he was not in the present. He could not relax when he traded. He could hardly focus for too long, and he was well aware that without concentration, he could not perform.

Stacey, on the other hand, had few problems with her concentration. This was not because she had fewer things to trouble her mind. As a matter of fact, wearing more hats than Fred, Stacey had *more* things to worry about.

Nevertheless, she focused better because she traded only a few hours in a day. Compared to Fred, holding her concentration for a significantly shorter period of time was easier. Also, she was aware that unless she concentrated, she could not maximize the limited amount of time she could spare for trading. This became a good motivation to stay focused.

Another reason why she focused easily is that she practiced meditation on a regular basis. She did not fold her legs and sit on the floor for 6 hours a day like a highly attained ascetic, but she did close her eyes and sit quietly, watching her breath, for several 10-minute sessions during the day.

This increased her concentration and mindfulness and made her a more relaxed person. She traded better when her mind was relaxed.

How a Relaxed Mind Helped in Trading

What happened last month was a good example of how Stacey's relaxed mind had helped her trading and her life.

Stacey's husband went overseas for a business trip, leaving her alone to look after the baby for five days. Not sure what she might be facing when planning her week, Stacey deliberately cut down her time watching the market. She would plan her trades more carefully after spending the limited time she had at night analyzing the markets.

She focused on swing trading that week by reviewing the potential setups every day after the market close. It was particularly stressful for her to trade this way because it was not her usual trading style, and she felt she was not doing enough homework before entering the markets.

But she traded anyway. She tempered her stress by doing the 10-minute "mindfulness on the breath" meditation. She was hoping this would provide her with the much-needed focused and relaxed state of mind.

It helped, and Stacey was able to trade calmly and think with a clear head amidst the change in trading style she experienced with swing trading and the stress that came along with the reduced level of analysis. Her trading outcomes were not excellent, but better than she expected.

Right after her trading session ended, she sat meditatively for another 10 minutes to calm the emotional turmoil from trading. She was ready to put on her "mommy hat" again and did not want to carry the stress from trading over to her personal life.

One week passed in a blink of an eye, and when Stacey looked back at what she went through, she was amazed. "It's so unreal! With less time in the markets,

I was more focused and took only the high-probability swing trades. My consistency improved!" More importantly, she and her baby were still in one piece when her husband returned from his business trip.

Stacey had done well multitasking through the mad rush of the week. Not only did she make profits, but she also tended her home responsibilities without major glitches.

There were many stressful moments, but she weathered them well. If you asked her how she did it, she would tell you it was with a focused and relaxed mind. The regular meditation sittings had certainly played a huge role in this.

The Stressed Trader Who Refused Help

Fred scoffed when Stacey advised him to take up meditation. He refused to make anything "New Age" part of his daily practice. He did not understand how any logical person could believe that a metaphysical practice like this could help in his trading. And he believed he was too cool for sitting like a wooden statue, doing nothing or emptying his mind for even one minute.

He had no outlet for his stress and emotions. Like most men, he mistook talking with his friends or family about his problems as a sign of weakness, so he bottled them up. This did not reduce the stress he was feeling.

How his stress was messing up his trading was revealed in the way he handled his sudden surge of busyness last week. With an unexpected number of tasks at hand, he did not know which ones he should focus on. He was at a loss even where to begin.

The market he traded in was moving, but Fred had other things to tend to. He was so overwhelmed that he could not focus on planning his trades and looking for high-probability setups, so he entered and exited trades almost at will.

When he told Stacey, "I feel like I am in the fast lane and just can't slow down," Stacey recommended him to start the practice of meditation, cultivate better time management, and organize his personal life and trading life.

Fred brushed her off. He thought he was too cool for meditation, sticking to a rigid schedule, and having to live a life too well planned with little element of spontaneity. Stacey stressed this was her best advice for him, but he would not listen.

So, she shrugged, and stopped wasting her energy talking to him about this. She understood why Fred had been unsuccessful in trading and saw no way that Fred could make a breakthrough in trading with such a negative attitude.

She wanted to help but not now, she realized. Perhaps she needed to wait until Fred was ready for her advice before bringing it up again.

■ Pendulum Scenario 13.2: Clear-headed versus Sorrowful Trader

"To do much clear thinking a person must arrange for regular periods of solitude when they can concentrate and indulge the imagination without distraction."

—Thomas A. Edison

As much as we traders want to keep ourselves emotionally neutral in trading, sometimes it is unavoidable to experience periods in life that our emotions are so overwhelming we cannot contain them. In the face of instances like these, shall we suppress our emotions and continue to trade or shall we walk away from trading?

It depends. Let's look at what Stacey and Fred went through in one of their work weeks. There might be a lesson we can learn from them.

Challenges in Traders' Lives

Stacey's husband, Brad, returned home from work late one night before Stacey put the baby to sleep. The baby, upon seeing his daddy home, got into hyper-excitement mode and resisted Stacey's every effort to lie him down in his crib. Daddy was excited, too, because he had not been with the baby for the whole day. Furthermore, it was a long day at work for him. Talking with his baby, playing silly games with him, and laughing together had always been the best way he unwound from stress.

Stacey understood this, and she allowed it. She had no choice anyway because the baby would not let go of his father. But Stacey set a limit. She wanted Brad to stop playing with the baby and let him sleep after 30 minutes because when the baby's bedtime passed, getting him to sleep would be difficult.

Brad agreed. Half an hour later, when Stacey went into the room to check the baby, she saw that Brad was still playing with him. Brad made another promise that he would stop 10 minutes later, but as Stacey had expected, he did not and begged Stacey to give them another 10 minutes.

Several "10 minutes more" later, Stacey finally blew up. She knew what was coming. It was way past the baby's bed time, and now she had to spend extra effort to make him sleep. The stay-at-home mom would have to deal with a tired, grumpy, and restless baby, and she, still awake at this hour, would be tired, grumpy, and restless, too, thanks to daddy's "selfish" decision to let him stay up because he wanted to play with him.

The couple got into a screaming match, both accusing each other of not being considerate: Stacey blamed Brad for the calamity she would have to face the next day, and Brad accused Stacey of not understanding that was the only time for him to bond with the baby after a hard day at work. Neither of them were willing to back down from the fight. For the next few days, there was awkward tension between them.

Things were rough for Fred, too. Around 2:00 a.m. yesterday, he received a phone call from his family informing him that his younger cousin had passed away in an accident.

This came to Fred as a shock. It was 2:00 a.m. and he was about to turn in after watching a happy movie, and in the next moment, a piece of tragic news was forced down his throat.

A few days after the funeral, Fred's denial continued to suffocate him. He could not eat well, rest well, or focus on anything. Every time he closed his eyes, all he could see were the images of his young cousin and the happy memories they shared.

How Life's Turmoils Affected Their Trading

The awkward atmosphere lasted for several days. Stacey felt hurt by how her husband yelled at her, but she remembered herself doing the same, too. She was still annoyed by her husband's inconsiderate behavior that night, but at the same time, she regretted not taking a milder approach to resolve the issue. She blamed herself for not being more diplomatic with her husband.

With mixed feelings of anger, regret, and sorrow, she lost her focus for the next few days. The emotional aftermath of the fight upset her daily life and her dealings with the baby and her trading. Stacey thought she was a highly rational trader and would never be affected by her emotions no matter what. She was wrong.

She could not stay clear-headed when she traded. She repeatedly made careless mistakes in her analysis. She kept losing sight of obvious market indications and missed clear opportunities to enter trades. She took wrong positions, and her position size estimates were inaccurate. She got out of trades without even knowing why she did it.

The same had happened to Fred. Since his cousin's demise, he had been losing on all the trades he entered. He was aware of the losing streak he was in, but he desperately needed something to divert his mind from the tragedy. So, he escaped by trading. Money kept leaking from his account as he sat paralyzed with indecision. He was incapable of doing anything about it.

The Differences Caused by Their Decisions

Stacey decided this could not carry on. Her emotions had caused her trading to suffer, and her weak performance added more emotional stress. After weighing her situation, Stacey decided to take a break from trading. In her current emotional state, she did not see how she could focus on the trades. In addition to that, she needed some space to sort out the strained relationship between her and her husband.

Fred went in the opposite direction. He tried to spend all his waking hours trading because he thought as long as he kept his head busy with the trades, his sorrow would disappear. In this psychological state, he could not think with a clear head. He acted harshly. Like Stacey, his trading mistakes had caused more distress, and the distress had caused greater trading losses. He wanted his trading activities to be an escape but ended up getting pulled even deeper into the vicious cycle of emotions.

As for Stacey, she proved to herself that taking the break was one of the wisest things she could do in light of the situation. With some rest amidst the chaos in her life and trading business, she had a clearer head to reconcile the differences with her husband (although she promised that she would still scream at him the next time he gave her another day of taking care of a tired, grumpy and restless baby). With the emotional distress removed, Stacey knew she was ready to get back to her trading business again.

Moreover, Stacey had regained her normal emotional strength. She even thought she was strong enough to go to Fred and rescue him.

Pendulum Scenario 13.3: Good Mood versus Bad Mood Trading

"The thing with pretending you are in a good mood is that sometimes you are."

—Charles de Lint

Stacey made a strange discovery.

She discovered that the ideal way to start her morning involved waking up early and refreshed, decorating her workstation with a bouquet of her favorite white lilies, lighting the aromatherapy candle and filling her workspace with the refreshing smell of rosemary, and playing soothing music in the background when she traded.

These actions that upgraded the atmosphere of her workspace are what she called the "cheerful morning ritual" because she felt cheerful after doing this, and the change made her cheerful for the rest of the day.

However, she did not always have the luxury to do this and only made the extra effort if she was "in the mood" to do it. It happened if she got a good night's sleep the night before and felt rejuvenated in the morning. But with her busy daily schedule, switching roles between mother, wife, and part-time trader, she was rarely in the good mood to perform the "cheerful morning ritual."

Stacey noticed that the days when she did her ritual were usually her most profitable. This is why this strange coincidence caught her attention.

"Is it feng shui?" she wondered. She might have done something right with the white lilies, aroma of rosemary, and soothing music. She started to wonder whether this combination of her favorite items had some kind of mysterious, magical power that attracted good fortune to her.

But the Going Does Get Tough, and Often

Life was not always smooth sailing for Stacey. Sometimes, she hoped things would improve if she tried harder, but they did not.

She tried to be a better mother, but she could not stop her baby from throwing tantrums, refusing to drink milk, and crying his lungs out because he was feeling unwell.

She tried to be a better wife, but she could do nothing when her husband failed to understand her, asked for too much, or was not helpful in the caretaking of the baby.

She tried to be a better trader, but the market would not obey her, her analysis could be wrong at times, and even her so-called foolproof trading system could be faulty.

Anytime setbacks like these occurred, Stacey's mood would dip to the valley. This affected her relationships with her son and husband and severely hit her trading performance.

The feeling of disappointment from her poor trading results made her mood even worse.

Trading in a Bad Mood

When Stacey was in the wrong mood to trade, she found she entered and exited trades too quickly, too frequently. This was a sign of overtrading. She no longer stuck to the entry and exit rules in the trade plan but traded impulsively and became trigger-happy. "What am I trying to prove?" she might even ask herself in the middle of her trading, but she had no answer to this.

On the "bad mood days," she grew impatient easily and desperately tried to win. She hoped that winning would make her feel better. In her state of desperation, however, she could not expect to operate with a clear mind and strict trading discipline. As a result, most of the trades she desperately tried to win turned out to be losing trades.

Bad moods also caused her judgment and perception to be biased. Trade entry opportunities easily slipped by right before her eyes when her bad mood kicked in and distracted her from her business. Her negative thinking also barred her from holding any hope or desire that the setups would come to her. There were times that she even ignored reliable positive market news as her mood caused her to judge the news negatively or temporarily numbed her desire to win.

Stacey's reflections on what happened during her bad mood days led her to understand how her cheerful morning ritual helped to make her days profitable.

What Really Helped? (It Was Not Only Feng Shui)

Probably the white lilies, rosemary scent, and music did help the feng shui of her workplace, but those were not the main reasons why she could trade more successfully on the days she set them up.

When thinking about how a bad mood affected her trading performance negatively, Stacey realized how a good mood helped her.

The days when she woke up after a full night's rest feeling energetic, and she brightened up her mood by decorating her workstation with the items she loved were the days she enjoyed an uplifting mood. With the nice scent of rosemary essential oil filling her workspace and the music playing, she carried the good energy into her trading.

She was trading "in the zone" with the proper mental energy to maintain her patience, analyze and make decisions with a clear head, and closely follow her trade plan.

Sure enough, her win/loss ratio was higher when she traded in this state, her mood improved more, and her winning probability further improved, and so forth. This positive mood begat a positive mood.

Mood as a Mental Edge in Trading

After establishing how her mood positively or negatively affected her trading performance, Stacey decided to make a permanent change in the way she began her trading session.

She wanted to make sure she always started in a good mood. She wanted to perform her "cheerful morning ritual" as often as possible. Even when she could not, she calmed herself and rid herself of the emotional baggage she was carrying at least 10 minutes before she started trading.

She made sure she treated herself to a cup of herbal tea, too. This calming hot beverage in the morning always lifted her mood in an instant, and with a good mood, she knew she had the mental edge in trading and was prepared to win for the trading session.

CHAPTER 14

The "10 Habits" Checklist

We have come to the concluding chapter of Part IV, The Transformed Trader. In this chapter, I will summarize the "10 Habits" we have examined, and wrap up with additional tips. We will also visit Fred and discuss what he needs to do to transform himself from being in the *Technical Trader's Trap* to becoming an Entrepreneurial Trader.

223

21 Days to Form a Habit?

It has been widely surmised that it takes 21 days to form a new habit. Have you ever wondered where this magic number comes from? Why 21 days (or three weeks), and not more common numbers like 30 days (one month), 50 days, or something else? Is there a scientific basis for this claim?

Researchers generally agree that by repeating a behavior for an extended period of time, a habit can form. It works for everything from quitting smoking, exercising daily and using a shopping list, to habits relevant to trading, like following the trade plan strictly, writing a trading journal, and tracking trading results. However, this mythical magic number 21 creeps up in most of the articles on forming habits or changing your life around.

Apparently, it did not originate from psychologists' consensus or any research. What might surprise you is, based on an article (Gardner 2012) published on the blog site of University College London's (UCL) Health Behavioral Research Centre, this number came from a misinterpretation of a classic self-help book.

We will discuss this further in a while. Let us now review the "10 Habits" of successful traders in this book.

■ The "10 Habits" of Successful Traders

In this book, we discussed in detail 10 common habits of successful traders. The following is a summary of what they are and how they can be applied in your trading business.

Habit #1: Establish a Trading Business for the Right Reasons

Make a list of your reasons for entering the trading business, review them, and make sure they are the *right* reasons. For example, if you launch your trading business to escape from your corporate job, without considering the potential risk of losing your income, your reason for entering this business is not the right one. If your main reason is to make quick bucks, you may as well try your luck at the local casino, buy a lottery ticket, or look into the get-rich-quick schemes you find on the Internet.

Many people are attracted to trading because it appears to promise more money for less work as well as an independent lifestyle. Of course, it can but not without dedication and hard work, and it is also unlikely that success will emerge overnight.

Besides the potential to achieve financial independence from trading, other right reasons successful traders might have include the right to creative freedom, more control over their own time, the freedom to work from anywhere any time, and the privilege to be their own boss and manager.

When the "whys" for trading that are close to the trader's heart are figured out, the "hows" to realize them will surface. It also helps to have a passion and a love for trading and strongly believe the trader's heart and mind are in the right place. Knowing the reasons why he is in the business and what he is fighting for, the trader can see a destination to move toward and prevent himself from giving up prematurely.

Habit #2: Complete a Trader's Business Plan

Is trading a serious business or a "profitable hobby" to you? If you want to make trading a hobby, you can take a leisurely attitude toward it. You probably will not make a lot of money; if you embrace it as a serious business and want to make serious money from it, you will have to treat it seriously and adopt an entrepreneurial manner in running it.

This is true no matter if you trade full-time or part-time. One of the aspects of building a business is to plan it. Define your long- and short-term goals, trading personality and preferences, trading system, daily schedule, performance tracking system, reward and learning plan, money management strategy, work-life balance plan, and infrastructure for your workplace.

Successful traders complete their business planning, write their plans, execute them, track results, review, and fine-tune them periodically. This will be the "success blueprint" for your trading business.

Habit #3: Define Your Goals

How much fun would it be to go to a hockey game where there was no goalie? How interesting would it be to go to a baseball game without a home plate or a basketball game without a net? How far can a game go without goals? What would be the point?

Successful traders have a habit of clearly defining their goals. They will align the direction of their trading business toward the goals and commit to take massive action to achieve the goals.

You should establish a set of goals and let your trading business be guided by them. In defining your goals, answer the following questions:

- Do you plan to trade part-time or full-time?

- What time of day will you set aside for trading on a consistent basis?

- What specific goals do you have about daily, weekly, and monthly profits and returns?

- Do you have certain metrics that you are tracking on a weekly and monthly basis?

- How do you define a successful trader?

Without specifying your goals, you will not get far in your trading business.

Habit #4: Commit to Your Education with a Trading Coach

How do successful players in any field of endeavor, including top-earning traders, structure their learning, maintain their tip-top performance, and keep their motivation high? Most, if not all of them, engage coaches.

Successful traders engage coaches to inspect the performance of their trading business and their performance as traders and provide honest feedback and advice to help them grow. The coaches provide objective insights from a third person's perspective to pinpoint the weaknesses and strengths in the performance.

Coaching is even more valuable for new traders. An experienced trading coach can guide the trader to discover her trading personality and recommend a trading style and system accordingly. He can coach or mentor her to build the foundational skills in trading. When the new trader stumbles or is at a loss in direction, the coach will be there to advise. The coach also provides external accountability and motivation to push the trader forward and keep her going.

A trader might train on her own, without the guidance of a coach, if she knows how to define a comprehensive learning strategy, self-reviewing plan, and self-accountability system. A trader could learn from the *School of Hard Knocks* by trying a lot of things and picking up experience from her errors. However, these are the longer and tougher paths to take. A shortcut, and often a surer path, is to engage a coach to help.

Habit #5: Understand and Exploit Your Unique Trading Personality

There are numerous trading styles out there, each one different from the other. How do you know which one suits you the best? First, explore and exploit your unique trading personality. For example, if you enjoy sitting in front of the screen watching the market action all day long, you may prefer momentum trading or day trading; however, if you like to analyze the markets, establish your trade plan, and let your trade play itself out, you might be better suited to swing or position trades.

After understanding your trading personality, pick a trading style that suits you, such as manual versus automated trading. Remember to take your preferences into consideration, such as what you want to trade, the markets you want to trade in, and how you want to trade.

There is no right or wrong answer in your choice of trading style. The key is to find one you feel comfortable and confident trading with and suits your personality, temperament, and preferences at the same time.

Habit #6: Follow a System

A close look at successful organizations such as McDonald's, Walmart, and Amazon reveals they are doing the same thing the same way every day. These companies have arrived at tested and proven systems for almost every aspect of their business and will execute the systems consistently to get consistent outcomes.

Successful traders do the same, too. They devise winning formulas or systems they apply on every trade to repeat their success in trading.

If you do not have a trading system, establish or find one that matches your personality and requirements for trading. Having a system simplifies your trade execution and heightens your success rate. On the other hand, if you have a system, make sure you follow it consistently. This will help temper your emotions while trading.

You must avoid the *Technical Trader's Trap* of jumping from one system to another, either curiously trying things or aiming to find a "perfect" trading system. Trying a number of systems in the beginning is fine, but you need to settle on one that works reasonably well and follow it consistently.

Habit #7: Plan the Trade and Trade the Plan

A successful trader does not rush into trades. She plans before she trades. She knows what she wants to trade, what she is aiming for, and how to trade. She is clear about when to get into trades and when to stay out of the market. She has a specific strategy to protect her capital and is not afraid to execute it to stay in the game for as long as she can.

The path to greatness lies not only in our performance but also in the systematic practice we put into the performance. A successful trader plans her trades well and trades in strict accordance with her plan. Doing so keeps her emotions away from trading and prevents her from trading impulsively.

Trading mastery is a function of internalizing the market patterns, rehearsing skills for executing trade entries and exits, and learning from continuous market feedback.

Without a trade plan, our emotions get in the way and we run the gamut of fear and greed. Planning the trade and trading the plan is the practice you need to develop.

Habit #8: Measure Your Performance

Elite performers such as chess masters and concert pianists constantly learn new skills and practice their existing ones to improve themselves. But how do they know whether they are making improvements, staying put at the same competitive level, or suffering a decline? They set up objective metrics to measure their performance, and keep notes.

Successful traders do so, too. They look at their ROI, win/loss ratio, profit targets, risk/reward per trade, and other metrics to gauge their performance and act accordingly when the numbers change. Not only are these metrics important for their own performance tracking, but the traders' coaches can also use them to monitor their clients and provide advice.

You should set up your performance tracking system, too. Keeping score helps build the motivation for you to continuously improve. It tells you where you have done well as well as areas in which you need improvement. Track every trade you make and take stock every week or month just as you would take inventory in a business.

Habit #9: Learn the Secrets of Successful Traders

If you study successful traders, you will see that they have ambition, determination, patience, and a positive attitude. They usually hang in there, more determined than ever, when others throw in the towel. They take notes and learn from their mistakes, applying these lessons to succeed the next time around. Successful traders thrive on independence.

They are take-charge people who produce creative and intelligent solutions to problems. Trading needs a lot of stamina, and successful traders have that in spades. And they never doubt they are worthy of success.

The qualities they exhibit are the qualities necessary for trading success and the qualities you want to acquire if you do not have them. Watch successful traders closely (or go under their mentorship), observe what they do, and learn from them. Emulate the attitudes and behaviors responsible for their success, and you can become successful, too.

Habit #10: Add Balance to Your Life

Undeniably, some successful traders sacrifice the quality of life in their pursuit of success in their career. But if you adopt a holistic approach to trading, you will avoid doing the same and understand that trading should not be your whole world. You need to strive for the work-life balance to prevent trader burnout because it can have adverse effects on the well-being of your mind and body and potentially wreak havoc in your trading business.

To add balance to your life, you'll need to ask yourself whether you have a life outside of trading, how trading fits into your life, and how you are planning to simplify your life so that you can have more control over it.

Also, as a way to pat yourself on the back when you have done well in trading or hit some milestones, set up a reward system. This will help you maintain your motivation and encourage you to keep looking forward to achieving successes in trading.

■ "Where Are You Now, and Where Do You Aim to Be?"

Throughout the book, we have looked at the stories of two traders, Stacey and Fred. Both Stacey and Fred were relatively new in trading, but there was a difference: Fred was a typical trader in the *Technical Trader's Trap* struggling to survive in the game, whereas Stacey was a successful Entrepreneurial Trader.

To discuss their current situations more precisely, let's review the Trader's Quadrant in Table 14.1 that you have seen in Chapter 3.

TABLE 14.1	The Trader's Quadrant			
		Trader in the *Technical Trader's Trap*		Transformed Entrepreneurial Trader
New Trader	I	Unsuccessful (developed negative habits)	II	Successful (developed positive habits)
Experienced Trader	III	Unsuccessful (developed negative habits and kept them)	IV	Successful (replaced negative habits with positive habits)

"Technical junkie" Fred often sabotaged his trading results with unproductive practices. He was emotional, did not treat trading as a serious business, relied on "gut feelings" when he traded, made no effort in tracking his performance, and allowed an undisciplined lifestyle to jeopardize his trading business. He was a trader in Quadrant I in the Trader's Quadrant and had developed habits negative for his trading.

Stacey, on the other hand, was in Quadrant II. Although she was still new, since the onset of her trading business, she established a clear vision with goals. She also analyzed and planned thoroughly before entering trades, avoided letting emotions to get in her way when she traded, constantly reviewed her performance and improved herself, and added balance to her work and life. These positive habits were the pillars for her success.

Fred, seeing Stacey reaping the fruits from her trading business, wanted to be a successful trader, too. What should he do?

The Path of Transformation

By practicing the "10 Habits" of Successful Traders, a trader who is in Quadrant I or III of the Trader's Quadrant can move into Quadrant II or IV. The key is to replace habits not supporting the trading business with habits that help.

Take Fred's case, for example. He needed to spend time to do an honest review of his reasons to be in the trading business and examine his expectations (Habit #1). This would help him to understand the business correctly and set realistic expectations. He would no longer treat trading as a "get rich quick" scheme or get out of the business at the first instance of failure, like most amateur traders do.

He needed to treat trading as a serious business. Creating a trader's business plan is the first step he should have taken (Habit #2). He had to plan out his trading system, performance tracking system, money management strategy, and so on. And of utmost importance, he needed to come out with a trading schedule to discipline himself because his unorganized lifestyle and lax attitude toward trading were bringing his business to the brink of failure.

When crafting his trader's business plan, Fred should have taken the opportunity to define his goals (Habit #3), committed to review them on a regular basis, and taken action to fulfill them. Since he was inexperienced in this business, he could have used guidance in establishing the trader's business plan. He might have needed expert feedback on his trading style and skills. In addition, external accountability would have kept him on track towards his goals. All these are good reasons for him to have engaged a coach (Habit #4).

Many times, Fred missed opportunities to make profits or even lost money from trading because his decisions were swayed by emotions. To counter this, Fred should have settled on a tested-and-proven trading system (Habit #6). There is no perfect system in the world, but Fred could have found one that fit his preference and personality the best (Habit #5). And based on this system, he could have planned every one of his trades and traded strictly according to the trade plans (Habit #7). When all trades were executed in an almost unemotional manner, he could have tempered his fear and greed and removed his hesitation. This would have translated to fewer missed opportunities and potentially higher profits!

Trading is a marathon, not a sprint. To excel in this journey, Fred had to stay abreast of the latest developments in the trading world and continuously improve himself. He needed to start a trading journal to keep track of his performance (Habit #8), and through constant review, to learn from his successes and mistakes. Talking with fellow traders and exchanging information with them would have helped him grow, too. So would studying successful traders and modeling their behaviors and attitudes (Habit #9).

Lastly, Fred needed to organize his life! Although almost all his waking hours were spent at his trading desk, most of these hours were unproductive. He had no time for leisure. He stopped having a social life and was not getting enough sleep. He was in desperate need of a plan to add balance back to his life (Habit #10).

◼ More than Theory

This book concludes with two additional chapters, starting with a discussion on an array of analysis tools that are the "building blocks" for constructing trading strategies and trade plans (Chapter 15). At the fundamental level, the trader needs to understand trends and market cycles and how to scrutinize the market using trend indicators to trade the trend. Both the end-of-trend and continuation can be traded to make profit. Several powerful techniques, including 123 reversals, are used to confirm the end of a trend.

Chapter 16 is a bonus as it outlines a sample trading system called the Fibonacci Filter Trading System, and it covers many of the "10 Habits" presented in this book as well. This system details all of the key requirements for setting up a trading system, including the routine to follow, pre- and post-market analysis and the trade plan and checklist.

The synopsis of the "10 Habits" in this concluding chapter and the "action plan" suggested for Fred above are only a summary. Useful tips and action plans are provided in the corresponding chapters to help you put them into practice. In fact, the main reason why these habits are discussed so thoroughly in this book is for you to apply them in your trading business. Don't just read them. Take action and do what successful traders do so you, too, have a chance at succeeding in your trading business.

All of the "10 Habits" come from my observations of the common traits of high performers in the trading world. I am confident that if you show these "10 Habits" to any successful or experienced traders, they will *unanimously* attest to the sentiments behind my recommendation for you to practice them.

Getting back to that magic number 21, you might be surprised to find out that psychologists and writers of self-help articles have never come to a consensus on why it takes *21 days* to form a new habit although this concept is widely advocated.

How the Magic Number Came About

The article published by the UCL busted the "21 days' habit formation" myth, which began as a misinterpretation of Dr. Maxwell Maltz's preface to his classic self-help book, *Psycho-Cybernetics*. The plastic surgeon-turned-psychologist revealed his observation from surgery that it takes *at least* 21 days for an average patient to get used to a change in his face or body (Maltz 1989).

For example, it takes around 21 days for a patient to get used to his "new face" after plastic surgery; similarly, a patient whose limb has been amputated takes about 3 weeks to stop "seeing" his phantom limb. Maltz mentioned "at least" along with "21 days," but most people conveniently drop this qualifier and adopt only the magic number 21 days. Also, Maltz did not attempt to make a clinical statement that 21 days is all it takes to form a habit; he was only stating his observation.

Somehow, readers of his book misinterpreted the fact, and started spreading it decade after decade. This shows how habits are affecting us; when we are so used to hearing a "fact," we stop questioning it.

Why It Does Not Matter

The good news is, although we have been misled for years, whether it takes 21 days to form a new habit or not doesn't matter. What is important to us is we know that when we repeatedly perform a behavior, a habit will be formed.

In Chapter 2, we looked at the old joke, "how to eat an elephant" in relation to forming a habit one *small step* at a time. It is worth revisiting this concept in the concluding chapter, with some new light thrown on it.

1. Don't incorporate all "10 Habits" into your trading life at once. Start from the easier one first or the one you feel comfortable doing. Start from a "sure win" one to get some momentum for your subsequent habit formation.

2. For every habit you form, take one small step at a time, too, and do it systematically. For example, when you establish your trader's business plan, you might not want to complete the whole business plan within one sitting but do it part by part.

3. Record every small step you have taken in writing. This way, you can track your progress and can get a clear picture of the thinking process you have been through and your prior considerations before you reach a decision.

Remember, when you repeat the steps for a long enough period, these habits of successful traders will become second nature to you. Whether it takes 21 days or not doesn't matter. Take the first step and then press on. It is my hope for you that if you cultivate positive habits, coupled with skillful means, you will succeed in your trading business.

Get ready, get set, GO!

PART V

The Trader's Tools

CHAPTER 15

Analysis Toolbox—Your First Mentoring Session

There are certain skills that a trader needs, which I call the *building blocks* for building strategies and trade plans. These building blocks support the skills required to read the charts like a story book. Each chart tells a story about what part of the market cycle we are in and once we understand how to read the various market cycles, we will be better apt to trade what the chart is telling us.

The major building blocks are found in the Analysis Toolbox in Table 15.1.

The tools in the toolbox help traders to stick with their positions during trend moves, to know when the end of the trend is near, and to understand which indicators to use during trend and sideways markets. By understanding a basic approach to the market cycles through Elliott Wave analysis, a trader will be more skillful at navigating the markets, similar to using a GPS when navigating the roads.

Trends and Market Cycles

Let's begin by discussing trends and market cycles, two of the key building blocks in the Analysis Toolbox. A market can only do three things: Go up in an uptrend, go down in a downtrend, or move sideways in consolidation or retracement. A trader

TABLE 15.1	Analysis Toolbox

Analysis Toolbox

Trending vs. Sideways Markets	*Market Cycles (Elliott Wave Analysis)*
Support and Resistance:	*Reversal Chart Patterns:*
Manual Barriers and 00 Prices	Reversal Candlestick Patterns
Pivot Points	Double Tops and Bottoms
Average True Range	Head and Shoulders
Fibonacci Retracements	Rising and Falling Wedge
Trend Lines and Channels	123 Reversal
Trend Indicators:	*Oscillators:*
Moving Averages	MACD and Awesome Oscillator
Bollinger Bands	RSI and Stochastics
Continuation Chart Patterns:	*Fibonacci Projections:*
Triangles, Flags, and Rectangles	Trend Continuation
Internal 123s	Trend Targets

learns how to identify trending versus sideways markets with an understanding of the market cycles across different time frames.

We often hear from the trading world that "the trend is your friend." What does it mean? It means that price may move in one direction and stay there for a long time. If that's the case, trading with the trend will be profitable.

Usually, if the long-term trend is up, you want to be long; if the medium-term and short-term trends are moving in the same direction, that provides added confirmation to go long. The same concept holds true for going short when the markets trend down. Nevertheless, we know that markets move in cycles. Short-term downward movements could occur within the longer-term uptrend. For example, if the daily long-term trend is up, the short-term 15-minute trend might be down on any given day as it works its way through the short-term market cycles. Figure 15.1 illustrates the different time frames working together.

Traders who keep the big picture or big trend in mind are more likely to hold positions longer, take trades in the direction of the trend, and understand how to trade the cycles on the smaller time frames. For example, the smaller time frames will cycle up and down, moving from trending to sideways markets within the context of the bigger time frame trend direction. When the bigger time frame is trending up, the trader's job is to buy the dips on the smaller time frames and keep buying until the end of the trend. When the bigger time frame is in a downtrend, the trader's job will be to continue to sell the rallies.

■ Trend Indicators

A trader can use many trend-following strategies to stick with the trend and trigger buys and sells. These trend strategies involve the use of indicators, which are derived

Trending vs. Sideways Markets

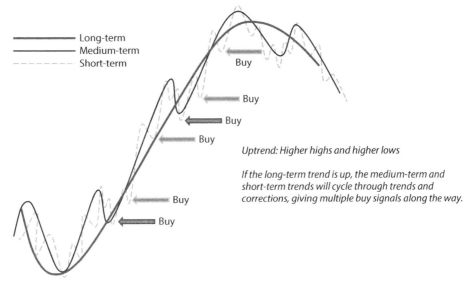

FIGURE 15.1 Looking at different time frames for trending vs. sideways markets

from mathematical formulas using historical price and volume data. They are used to anticipate future price changes to signal trend reversals or continuations. Traders use hundreds of indicators, many of which you can find under the drop-down menu of your trading platform.

Perhaps the most common trend indicators are moving averages. Moving averages can define the trend. For instance, when the trend is up, the moving averages are pointed up and the price action as represented by the candlesticks are tracking above the moving averages. Moving averages are usually described as lagging indicators because they are calculated based on historical price data, and price always leads the way before the moving average catches up. Another way to say it is that moving averages get you into the trend *after* the trend has changed direction. As a result, the moving averages tell you what prices are currently doing, whether rising or falling, but do not warn of any upcoming changes. Notice the moving averages pointed up in Figure 15.2.

A simple moving average crossover strategy involves the crossing of two moving averages such as a 21 period and a 200 period. In theory, when the 21 crosses over the 200, the market is in "Buy" mode; when the 21 crosses below the 200, the market is in "Sell" mode. Figure 15.2 illustrates the change in trend once the shorter moving averages cross over the 200 simple moving average (SMA). However, if you follow this strategy religiously, you will get chopped up during the sideways price consolidation when the averages chop around each other until a clean trend emerges.

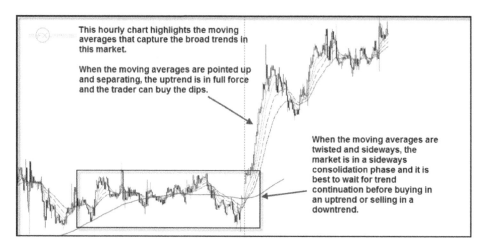

FIGURE 15.2 Using moving averages to define the trend

Trend Lines and Channels

Traders can use other tools to stick with the trend, such as trend lines and channels.

What is a trend line? A trend line is a straight diagonal line that connects the extremes in price movement. It can be an upward- or a downward-sloping line, depending on the trend move.

In a downtrend, successive lower highs are connected. This is called a *downtrend line*. To draw a downtrend line, first identify two lower highs. Next, draw a trend line, starting from left to right, to connect the lower highs. Two well-defined touch points, or where the candles touch the trend line, are usually a good indication the trend will continue in that direction. Identifying three lower highs confirms it. Figure 15.3 illustrates drawing trend lines.

In an uptrend, successive higher lows are connected, and this is called an uptrend line. To draw an uptrend line, first identify two higher lows. Draw a trend line, starting from left to right, to connect the higher lows. Two well-defined touch points are usually a good indication that the trend will continue in that direction. Identifying three higher lows confirms it.

A channel, or a *price channel,* consists of a pair of parallel trend lines. We've established that three hits confirm a trend. To draw a channel, for a downtrend channel, we duplicate the downtrend line and connect the bottoms or the successive lower lows; for an uptrend channel, we duplicate the trend line and connect the tops or the successive higher highs. This is called a *channel line.* The trend line and the channel line create a channel.

Trend Lines

*Learn how to draw trend lines and incorporate trend lines into
your chart setup. Use trend lines to develop trading strategies.*

**Downtrend: Hits 1 and 2 begin the trend
and Hit 3 confirms it!**

**Uptrend: Hits 1 and 2 begin the trend
and Hit 3 confirms it!**

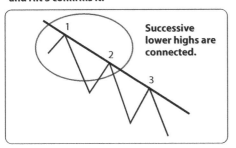
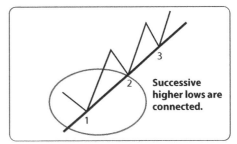

FIGURE 15.3 Drawing trend lines to confirm the trend

Channels

*Draw channels to capture the current trend,
starting with the initial trend line.*

**Downtrend: Duplicate downtrend line and
connect bottoms.**

**Uptrend: Duplicate uptrend line and
connect tops.**

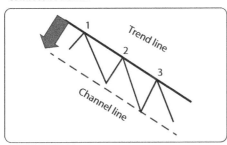
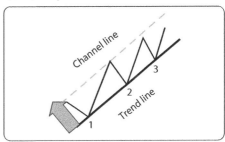

Trends tend to continue in the direction of the momentum.

FIGURE 15.4 Drawing channels to capture the trend

Trend lines and channel lines are completely discretionary, meaning the lines drawn are at the discretion of the trader. Also, there are two camps as to whether to connect the candlestick wicks or the bodies; this is for the trader to decide. See Figure 15.4 for drawing channels.

In an uptrend, place buy orders where the market movement is above the trend line and leave orders to sell at the channel line. Vice versa for a downtrend. As logic follows, when the price follows the trend, it creates opportunities to open new positions in the direction of the trend with the belief the trend line will hold and continue in that direction.

◼ End-of-Trend Market Reversals

Trend lines can also be used to target and confirm where a breakout or reversal could take place. This can be extremely useful and provide great entry and exit points for a trader. Trend lines can be drawn on any time frame but using daily candle charts would be the best starting point for capturing the broad trends.

Channels exist within channels. In the following example in Figure 15.5, we have highlighted the major channel as well as the minor channels within the major channel. When the price breaks the trend line, usually a new channel establishes itself in relatively short order. This signals a trend change, and therefore, a trader may consider trading in the new trend direction once the new trend is established.

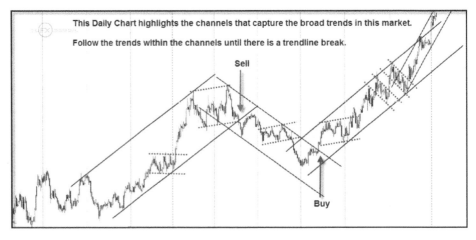

FIGURE 15.5 Major channels to highlight major trends

◼ End-of-Trend Confirmations

There are two types of patterns: reversal and continuation. Reversal patterns occur at the end of a trend, and continuation patterns occur during the trend and are pauses or consolidations in the trend. Several things occur at market reversal points. At market tops, traders and investors are greedy and at market bottoms, they are fearful. Both sentiments lead to market extremes.

There are several end-of-trend confirmations, which include reversal chart patterns, trend-line breaks, reversal candlestick patterns, and divergence using an oscillator. Some common reversal chart patterns include double tops and bottoms, head and shoulders, and rising and falling wedges, which we will not describe here. However, the longer the pattern takes to materialize, and the larger the pattern, the further the prices will travel once the reversal pattern completes.

At either extreme, there is a major trend-line break. In addition, price tends to deviate from the moving averages, so look for price to bounce back to the moving averages at these extremes. Certain candlestick patterns also emerge at the end of the trend, and this is where you tend to see long wicks and reversal patterns such as bullish and bearish engulfing patterns, morning and evening stars, hammers, shooting stars, and tweezer tops and bottoms. Finally, the end of the trend is confirmed by divergence.

123 reversals are powerful end-of-trend confirmations worth highlighting. For a 123 top, the market hits a new high labeled as point 1 and sells off to point 2. It then reverses again and trades higher without taking out point 1. This is labeled as point 3. The trade-entry trigger is when price trades through point 2. The measuring objective is the distance between points 2 and 3 projected below the break-down at point 2.

By contrast, in a 123 bottom, the market hits a new low at point 1 and trades higher to point 2. It then reverses again and trades down without making a new low below point 1 at point 3. The trade entry trigger is when price trades back up through point 2.

A sequence of events takes place to confirm the end of the trend. The first is divergence, where the price makes a new low in a downtrend or a new high in an uptrend but the oscillator does not. The second is the trend-line break, and the third event is the 123 reversal.

Figure 15.6 highlights the end-of-trend confirmations. To sight divergence, almost any oscillator can be used including the RSI, stochastics, MACD, and Awesome

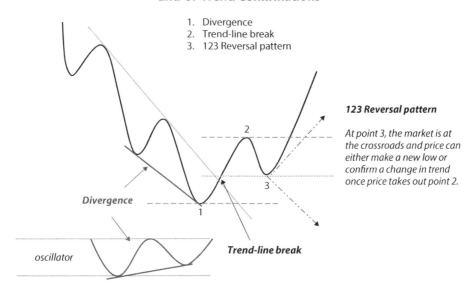

End-of-Trend Confirmations

1. Divergence
2. Trend-line break
3. 123 Reversal pattern

123 Reversal pattern

At point 3, the market is at the crossroads and price can either make a new low or confirm a change in trend once price takes out point 2.

Divergence

Trend-line break

oscillator

FIGURE 15.6 End-of-trend confirmations

Oscillator. My favorite is the Awesome Oscillator, developed by one of my mentors Bill Williams, because the settings (5, 34, 5) approximate the end-of-trend cycle well (Williams 1995).

■ Support and Resistance

Support and resistance are horizontal lines drawn on a chart to show price levels achieved in the past and that contain the current price. We label these price levels R1, R2, and R3 for resistance, and S1, S2, and S3 for support. Resistance is defined as the price level where supply is greater than demand so sellers step in to resist the upward rise in prices. At support, demand is greater than supply, and the buyers step in to support the price from going lower.

Support and resistance can be major or minor: major if a large trend move has already occurred during the trading day and the market needs a breather to recoup some of the losses or gains during the day, and so it reverses; minor if price fluctuates around an area of support and resistance, and finally breaks through to find the next area of support or resistance. Since price action is based on market psychology, one can experience many nuances in the markets to intuitively know if price is going to stall or continue with the trend. Support and resistance is one tool to use, especially since most traders use it to identify market pauses and reversals. Figure 15.7 illustrates how to manually draw support and resistance on the charts.

Support and resistance can be plotted on larger time frames such as the monthly or weekly charts. It can also be kept on the charts when one cycles through the

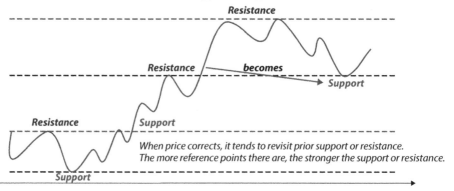

Support and Resistance

Manually draw support and resistance to find price levels that were turning points in the past.

Find "clusters" or "areas" of price support or resistance.
More valid if resistance becomes support or if support becomes resistance.

Resistance

Resistance — becomes

Support

Resistance   Support

When price corrects, it tends to revisit prior support or resistance.
The more reference points there are, the stronger the support or resistance.

Support

FIGURE 15.7   Manual support and resistance

lower time frames. For position and swing traders, these longer-term areas provide a solid approximation for a market turning point. For day traders, these longer-term levels might appear to "stop the market in its tracks" the first time these levels are hit during the trading day. The message is to pay attention to these levels by keeping them on the charts.

Another tool is the average true range (ATR), which tells on average what the day's trading range will be based on historical data. When an instrument is volatile, it will likely be trading at the higher end of the ATR during a defined period such as 100 days. When volatility compresses, so does the ATR, and traders will often comment that the market is slow. But beware, because after quiet times comes volatile times; all it takes is a change in fundamentals or significant news to wake up the market.

Day traders use the ATR to approximate the daily price movement on average. For example, for currency traders trading in the New York market, you must look at the overnight trading range as a way to gauge the move during New York. If the 100-day and 14-day ATR is 100 pips and the market moved 100 pips overnight since the 5 p.m. opening levels the day before, then traders will likely decide that the trading day will be range bound, especially if no major news is being released. If, however, the market was quiet overnight and news is expected in New York, traders can easily expect a volatile trading session and look for price to break out from the narrow overnight range. These are skills that a trader can learn by observing the market moves day in and day out.

Fibonacci retracements and pivot points are additional support and resistance tools to use, but they will not be covered in detail here.

The reason why support and resistance works is because a large number of traders are making trading decisions by looking at the same tools and indicators and plotting them on their charts, either manually or with programs. When enough traders believe that a price should stop at a certain level because of the numerous support points, technical indicators, or the results of their analysis techniques, it usually does, even if only briefly.

The herd mentality that drives the market is the reason why support and resistance can be called a self-fulfilling prophecy and, therefore, has predictive qualities. There have been numerous articles written about this topic, and perhaps this is a good segue into the topic of market cycles and Elliott Wave analysis.

Market Cycles and Elliott Wave Analysis

Ralph Nelson Elliott developed the Elliott Wave Theory in the 1930s by studying various market indices spanning over a 75-year period. He discovered that stock markets, thought to behave in a somewhat chaotic manner, did not. They traded in repetitive, predictable cycles. Elliott discovered the correlation between the markets and the emotions of investors and theorized that the markets were a reflection of the predominant psychology of the masses at the time.

Elliott stated that the upward and downward swings of the mass psychology always showed up in the same repetitive patterns, which were divided into patterns he termed *waves*. Subsequently, many other Elliott Wave theorists have applied his principles to markets other than stocks, such as forex and commodities with great success. This is to say the theory is transferable to nearly all traded markets.

Elliott's work was published in 1938 in a monograph titled *The Wave Principle*, which is now known as the Elliott Wave Principle (A. J. Frost and Robert Prechter Jr. 2005). Elliott's theory ties these patterns of collective human behavior to the Fibonacci sequence, or golden ratio.

Elliott Wave Theory describes how waves will subdivide until a complete market cycle is established. As the market unfolds in repetitive waves, they have predictive value. Waves are patterns of directional movement and once we learn the patterns, we are more apt to recognize trends and corrections as they occur.

One complete cycle consists of eight waves. To start, a movement will unfold in its primary direction in a series of five waves, labeled 1 through 5. This five-wave impulsive sequence is also called a *motive wave*. The five-wave pattern is followed by a three-wave sequence, labeled as A-B-C, which *corrects* the 1-2-3-4-5 sequence by moving against its trend direction. In other words, at any time a price in the market moves in the direction of the larger trend, it will form a five-wave sequence followed by a three-wave sequence that moves in the opposite direction.

In Figure 15.8, the complete eight-wave market cycle subdivides into numbers from the Fibonacci sequence. Five waves subdivide into 21 waves for the motive wave

Complete 8-Wave Market Cycle

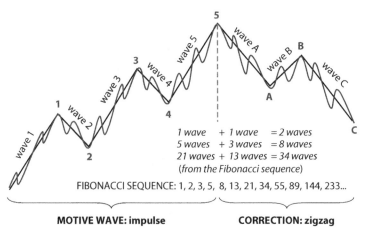

1 wave   + 1 wave   = 2 waves
5 waves + 3 waves   = 8 waves
21 waves + 13 waves = 34 waves
(from the Fibonacci sequence)

FIBONACCI SEQUENCE: 1, 2, 3, 5, 8, 13, 21, 34, 55, 89, 144, 233...

MOTIVE WAVE: impulse   CORRECTION: zigzag

FIGURE 15.8 Complete eight-wave market cycle

and three waves subdivide into 13 waves for the A-B-C zigzag corrective sequence. The beauty of waves subdividing into waves means that the eight-wave cycle repeats itself in all time frames and markets. Once these patterns are internalized, they can be traded over and over again, no matter what market or time frame is traded.

The repetitive pattern implies that it has predictive value. This is why so many traders learn Elliott Wave analysis and profit from it. As an Elliott Wave specialist, I recommend my students learn these patterns to gain market context to increase the likelihood of successful outcomes.

I encourage traders to do a top-down analysis starting from the weekly or daily time frame and move down the time frames for trade entry. Elliott Wave Theory provides that GPS context for navigating the markets.

■ Trend Wave Characteristics

Wave characteristics are a direct reflection of human market behavior. Wave personalities exist at every level of the wave count. We call the start of wave 1 "point 0." Where the five-wave impulsive sequence ends is called "point T" for termination. Figure 15.9 illustrates the wave personalities for waves 1 and 2.

Between point 0 and the end of wave 1, the market is still bearish. Wave 1 is always part of a basing process. There are no momentum clues yet for a change in the trend. The price action is less emotional with little or no volatility, as the crowd is still bearish at this point, so the market participants are still in sell mode since no change in trend is evident.

Wave Personalities: Waves 1 and 2

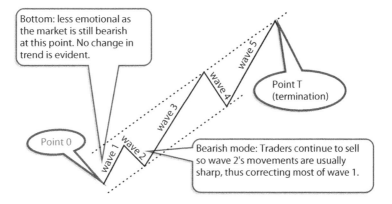

FIGURE 15.9 Waves 1 and 2 personalities

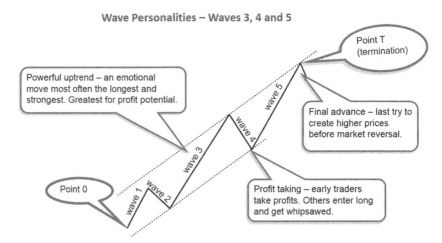

FIGURE 15.10   Waves 3, 4, and 5 personalities

Once the first wave has finished, we anticipate a second wave in the opposite direction. Second waves are created by new selling in an uptrend or buying in a downtrend because traders who are selling in an uptrend do not recognize that this up move is a wave 1 in a new direction. These traders believe wave 1 is another correction in a continuing down move, so they sell at the top of wave 1. Wave 2 moves are usually sharp, correcting most of wave 1.

Wave 3 gives us the greatest profit opportunities, as illustrated in Figure 15.10. One way to recognize a wave 3 is by its steep slope and rocket thrust movement. It is generally steeper than a wave 1. During wave 3, the economic background begins to support the move and fundamental reasons begin to support the technical indicators. Wave 3 is almost always the longest and the strongest with the greatest profit potential. It often extends because volume picks up, the trend move is obvious to traders, and the price action is emotional. Traders must keep buying the dips during wave 3 even if the pullbacks are shallow and do not meet the "expected" 38.2 percent minimum Fibonacci retracement.

Once wave 3 is over, profit taking enters the picture. The most skillful traders, who were into the trend the earliest, are now sitting on profits. The character of wave 4 is different from wave 2 although still corrective in nature. Most trading whiplashes occur during wave 4. Many traders lose money in wave 4. Generally, wave 4 corrections last much longer and do not retrace as much as wave 2.

Wave 5 is the final advance and the last struggle for the market to create higher prices. Typically, momentum divergences occur as price runs out of steam where price makes a new high but the oscillator does not. Blow-offs are common in commodity markets and "wave 5 failures" where wave 5 does not go past the top of wave 3, occurs very often in forex markets. This completes the wave personalities for the 5-wave motive sequence.

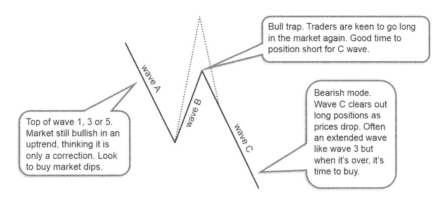

FIGURE 15.11   Waves A, B, and C personalities

Corrective Wave Characteristics

Corrective waves have their own personalities as illustrated in Figure 15.11.

Wave A kicks off the corrective move. Whether it's wave 2, wave 4, or the A-B-C following the larger five-wave sequence, the characteristics are the same. This is the wave where traders are convinced there is a simple pullback before the next leg of the move up in the case of an uptrend. Wave A sets the tone for wave B. If A travels in five waves, the correction is likely to go deep as a zigzag move. If A travels in three waves, then the correction is likely to be a sideways correction like a flat correction or a triangle.

B waves are usually bull traps. After wave A, the market looks to re-buy the uptrend, not recognizing that the correction isn't over yet. The market is keen about the continuation of the trend and the move up after wave A is quite weak and corrective, which is a big disappointment! However, a five-wave move in wave A followed by a three-wave correction in wave B provides a great setup for positioning for the wave C move down.

Wave C is often called the *killer wave* for it can be as strong and long as a wave 3. It clears out the long positions as prices drop in the case of a prior uptrend. Once wave C is done, the trend will continue. Targeting the end of wave C is a good time to go long again. However, a highly profitable trade is to sell the corrective wave B pullback to be able to ride the wave C.

Riding wave C is one of my favorite trade setups. This is also called the equality trade because the conservative measuring objective for wave C is the distance wave A travels.

Understanding the wave personalities of the complete eight-wave market cycle is a start to learning the Elliott Wave patterns that repeat in every time frame and in all market instruments. We call this pattern repetition the *fractal nature* of the markets because the eight-wave structure is similar when scaled in different time frames.

Before we leave Elliott, know the three Elliott rules that cannot be broken, or else the wave count is invalidated:

1. Wave 2 never retraces more than 100 percent of wave 1.

2. Wave 3 is never the shortest wave.

3. Wave 4 does not enter into the same price territory as wave 1.

Elliott Wave strategists attempt to label and count the waves to find market context for the next major move. Understanding how to read analysts wave counts is a skill that can be learned through the study of Elliott Wave analysis. Internalizing the wave personalities is a good place to start.

You have now completed your first mentoring session covering the Analysis Toolbox which is essential for building strategies and trade plans. To learn more about Elliott Wave analysis and receive wave counts, go to elliottwavedesk.com, a premier service powered by FX Trader's EDGE.

CHAPTER 16

Sample Trading System—Your BONUS Mentoring Session

In this chapter, we will look at a detailed trading system that incorporates many of the concepts learned in this book about the "10 Habits." You can use this system in your trading or create your own, using this complete system as a template.

Fibonacci Filter Trading System Overview

This trading system defines the chart setup, trading strategies, trading rules, and trade plan a trader will employ. Traders will plan the pre- and post-market preparations to optimize trading performance. Traders should use a checklist to track their actions and make sure they do not miss anything as planned. Please see *Chapter 15: Analysis Toolbox: Your First Mentoring Session* for a more detailed explanation of some of the concepts discussed in this chapter.

■ A. Chart Setup

In this section, you will define the markets and time frames you will be trading and "dress up" the chart to include any indicators that will be used. The chart can then be saved as a template to be applied to each time frame analyzed in the decision making process to trigger a trade. Finally, make your commitment in this section as to the amount of time you will spend analyzing and trading the markets.

1. What markets I am going to trade:

    a. Position (swing) trades: Stock options only

    b. Day trades: Forex and CFDs

2. Time frames:

    a. Position (swing) trades: These trades will last from 1 day to several weeks. Trades are based on weekly and daily charts. Trades will be taken on daily or 4-hour time frames for position and 4-hour or 1-hour time frames for swing.

    b. Day trades: These trades will be closed out before the end of the day. Daily, 4-hour, and 1-hour charts are used for review, meaning for trade direction only. Trades will be executed on 15-minute or 5-minute time frames.

3. Trading indicators to implement trades:

    a. Stock position (swing) trades: 8, 13, 21, and 34 EMAs, 200 SMA, RSI 3 and Stochastic 14 3 3. Chart patterns, candlestick patterns, trend lines and Fibonacci retracement and projection ratios will be used for further analysis.

    b. Forex day trades: 8, 13, 21, and 34 EMAs, 200 SMA, RSI 3 and Stochastic 14 3 3. Chart patterns, candlestick patterns, trend lines and Fibonacci retracement and projection ratios will be used for further analysis.

Figure 16.1 presents the chart setup for the Fibonacci Filter Trading System. The chart setup is composed of the 8, 13, 21, and 34 exponential moving averages (EMAs), and the 200 simple moving average (SMA). We refer to the four EMAs as the EMA cluster, and moving averages are called trend-following indicators. The oscillators on the chart include the RSI 3 and the Stochastic 14 3 3, and these oscillators are used to stay with the trend. Some traders prefer less on the chart, so using one of the oscillators may suffice because they are similar in how they are used.

4. Time commitment:

    a. I will be committed to trading at least 4-6 hours per day.

    b. Prior to trading, I will do the necessary prep work in researching setups and doing my pre-market analysis as outlined in Section E.

    c. I will be committed to maintaining my trading education by reading technical analysis books, magazines, and professional publications.

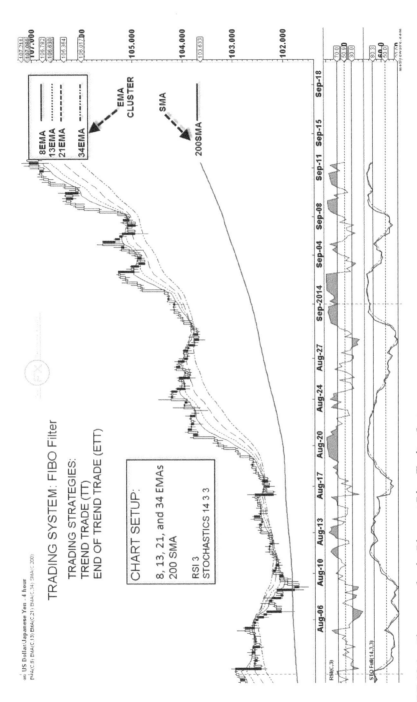

FIGURE 16.1 Chart setup for the Fibonacci Filter Trading System

■ B. Trading Strategies

The market movements unfold into Elliott Wave cycles, which we define as trends and corrections. The eight-wave cycle defined by Ralph Nelson Elliott in the 1930s comprises a five-wave trend phase (labeled 1-2-3-4-5) and a three-wave corrective phase (labeled a-b-c). These patterns are repetitive in all markets and all time frames, which is why we see trends as day, swing, or position trades on the respective time frames. In simple terms, we trade trends and corrections. This is how the trading strategies are mapped out. Trend-following strategies are used for trending markets, reversal strategies are used for finding the end of the trend, and range strategies are used for broad sideways markets where fading the trend is the play.

Trend-following Strategies

The trend trade (TT) is all about getting into the trend when the trend is apparent. It is about buying on pullbacks in an uptrend or selling the rallies in a downtrend. The requirements for an uptrend are as follows (opposite for a downtrend):

1. Prices make higher highs and higher lows.

2. EMA cluster above SMA.

3. Slope of uptrend is between 12 o'clock and 2 o'clock on a clock face.

4. The EMAs expand and contract in an uptrend.

5. The RSI and STOCHASTICS support buying in an uptrend.

6. So, continue to buy in an uptrend until end-of-trend trade (ETT) emerges with divergence, reversal candlestick pattern, trend-line break, and 123 reversal.

Figure 16.2 illustrates the requirements for a trend trade. Notice the EMA cluster coming together or contracting during the corrective phase and moving apart or expanding during the trend phase. Ideally, traders can enter long in an uptrend during the contraction of the moving averages. For an uptrend, the EMA cluster is positioned above the SMA, and as that distance widens, the trend gets stronger.

Figure 16.3 illustrates the areas in which to enter long positions. Notice how the circled buy areas on the price chart line up with circles on the oscillators. In an uptrend, use the oscillators as confirmation to buy on the dip or the sideways correction. When the oscillator dips in line with the price correction, it is a double confirmation. Stated another way, when the oscillator is *oversold* in an uptrend, that is the time to BUY. We don't look for an *overbought* situation in the oscillator to stop us from buying; rather, we look for the oversold situation to get us into the uptrend. The opposite is true for a downtrend move.

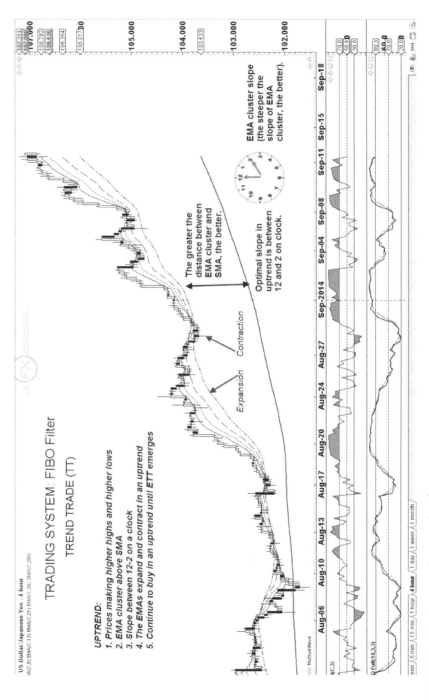

FIGURE 16.2 Requirements for a trend trade

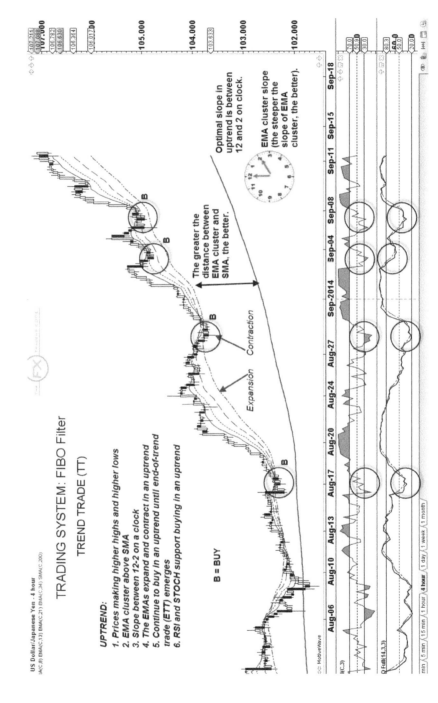

FIGURE 16.3 The areas to enter long positions

Reversal End-of-Trend Strategies

The end-of-trend trade (ETT) is used to find the end of a move to exit a long position in an uptrend and to take a trade in the opposite direction. One word of caution: If the trend is strong, it is better to train the brain to keep thinking BUY on pullback during an uptrend or SELL on strength during a downtrend. The parameters for finding the end of the trend include the following:

1. There is divergence in the Awesome Oscillator. The price makes a new high and the oscillator makes a lower high in an uptrend. The price makes a new low and the oscillator makes a higher low in a downtrend.

2. Trend-line break. Draw a trend line connecting the higher price lows in an uptrend and the lower price highs in a downtrend and wait for a break. That is usually a sign of a change in trend.

3. 123 reversal on the time frame traded or on one lower time frame.

4. Look for a reversal candlestick pattern at the end of a move, such as a shooting star at market tops, an engulfing pattern, or an evening star. At market bottoms, look for a hammer, an engulfing pattern, or a morning star. There are other reversal patterns, but these are the most common.

5. So, continue to BUY in an uptrend or SELL in a downtrend until end-of-trend trade (ETT) emerges with divergence, a trend-line break, a reversal candlestick pattern, and a 123 reversal pattern. Figure 16.4 illustrates this for exiting a trend position for a trend trade (TT). The same analysis is done for an end-of-trend trade (ETT). Figure 16.5 examines the 123 reversal pattern in more detail since it is a reliable end-of-trend confirmation.

Range-Bound Strategies

The range-bound (RB) trade is about finding major support and resistance looking back. If a market is range bound on a higher time frame, such as the weekly or the daily, make note on the chart by drawing thick horizontal lines as a reminder of strong support and resistance. As the price approaches those levels you will want to fade the move rather than look for a breakout of the range. Use the same reversal strategies noted for the ETT for confirmation of a reversal. The trading rules are also the same. See Figure 16.6 for an example of a range-bound market.

■ C. Trading Rules

Once the trading strategies are mapped out for the trend, end-of-trend and range-bound market cycles, we design the trading rules to define the entries and exits

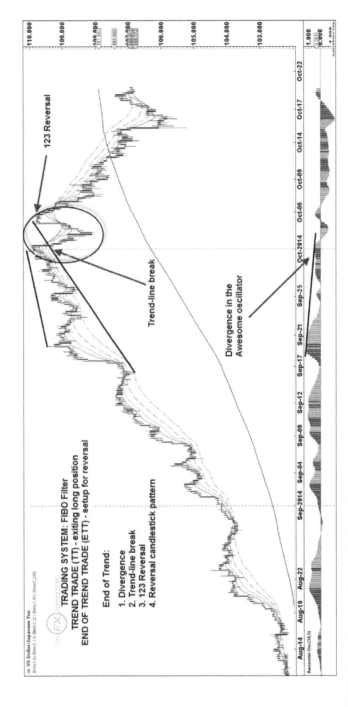

FIGURE 16.4 Fibonacci Filter end-of-trend trade

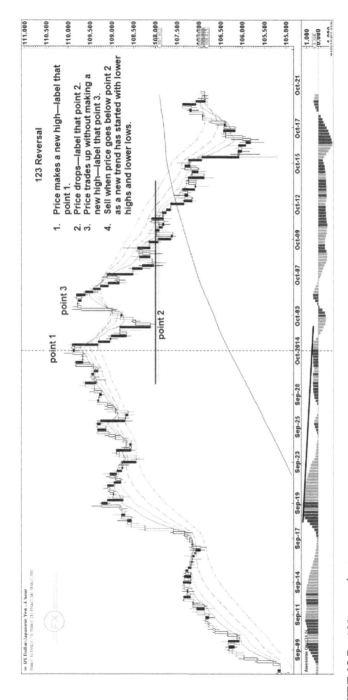

FIGURE 16.5 123 reversal pattern

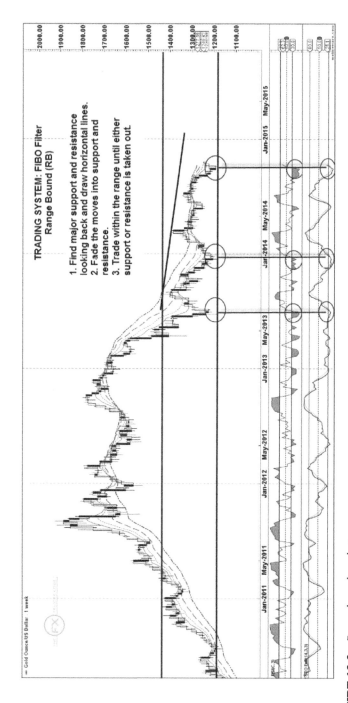

FIGURE 16.6 Range-bound market

for each of the trading strategies. The trading rules form the basis for the trade plans to trigger trades in live markets.

Trend-following Rules

Figure 16.7 illustrates the four components of planning the trade that will then be used for the trade plan: the setup, entry, stop-loss, and take-profit levels. Money management will be discussed separately but is a key component to the trade plan.

1. Setup:

   a. Set up the Fibonacci Filter indicators on the daily, 4-hour, 1-hour, 15-minute, and 5-minute charts for day trading. Set up the Fibonacci Filter indicators on the weekly, daily, 4-hour, and 1-hour charts for swing and position trading.

   b. Scan the charts for buys when the EMA cluster is sloped upward above the 200 SMA.

   c. Scan the charts for sells when the EMA cluster is sloped downward below the 200 SMA.

   d. For further confirmation, set trend lines, Fibonacci retracements and extensions, support and resistance lines, and pivot points.

2. Entry (trigger the trade):

   a. Wait for the candle to close above the EMA cluster for a buy (or below for a sell) after the EMA cluster contracts and price corrects. (Refer to Figure 16.7.)

   b. Look for a reversal candlestick pattern for clues of resumption of the trend.

3. Stop-loss levels (exit):

   a. Place the stop below the lowest candle low in the EMA cluster for a buy (highest candle high for a sell).

4. Profit taking levels (exit):

   a. Exit on a 123 reversal or with divergence and a trend-line break. A 123 reversal is a chart pattern where a new trend in the opposite direction is established. Divergence is when price makes a new high (or low) from the previous swing high and the oscillator makes a lower high. My favorite oscillator to use for divergence is the Awesome Oscillator, developed by Bill Williams.

See Figure 16.4 for an illustration of these exit methods. Figure 16.4 presents the profit-taking exit strategy with a 123 reversal and divergence. Figure 16.5 explains a 123 reversal for establishing a new trend.

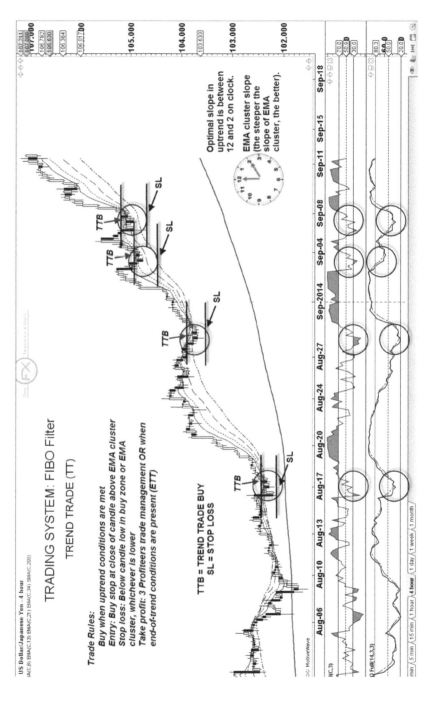

FIGURE 16.7 Four components for planning the trade

5. Three Profiteers trade management methodology (see Chapter 10 for details):

   a. Enter with three positions.

   b. Determine the Potential Profit Area (PPA) by looking at a higher time frame chart.

   c. Set three profit targets using the Fibonacci sequence: 13, 21, 34, 55, 89, and 144.

   d. Move stops when stacked profits are reached.

6. Money management:

   a. Losses are not to exceed 1 to 2 percent of account balance, so determine position size accordingly.

   b. Set daily and weekly goals for returns and profits.

Reversal End-of-Trend Trade (ETT) Rules

Figure 16.8 illustrates the chart setup and the analysis for planning the trade, which will be used for the trade plan.

1. Setup:

   a. Set up the Fibonacci Filter indicators on the daily, 4-hour, 1-hour, 15-minute, and 5-minute charts for day trading. Set up the Fibonacci Filter indicators on the weekly, daily, 4-hour, and 1-hour charts for swing and position trading.

   b. Scan the charts for end-of-trend moves by looking for divergence in the Awesome Oscillator as a starting point.

   c. For further confirmation, draw trend lines and pivot points, identify divergence, look for reversal candlestick patterns, and label the 123 reversal chart pattern.

2. Entry (trigger the trade):

   a. When there is divergence at a market top or bottom, SELL (BUY) on the candle close below (or above) the trend-line break. (Refer to Figure 16.9.)

   b. For confirmation, look for a reversal candlestick pattern at the market top or bottom, previous resistance or support, or a 123 reversal pattern.

3. Stop-loss levels (exit):

   a. Place the stop above (below) the candle high (low).

4. Profit-taking levels (exit):

   a. Exit on a 123 reversal or with divergence and a trend-line break.

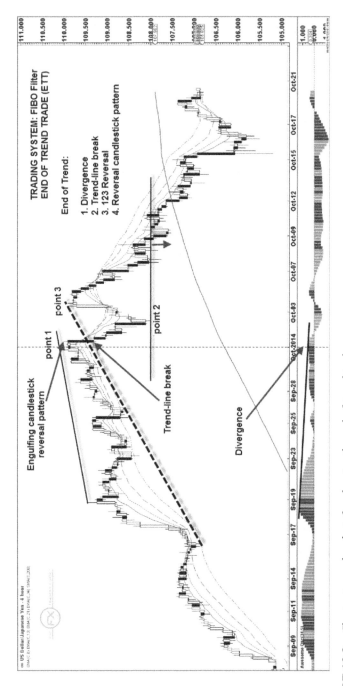

FIGURE 16.8 Chart setup and analysis for planning the end-of-trend trade

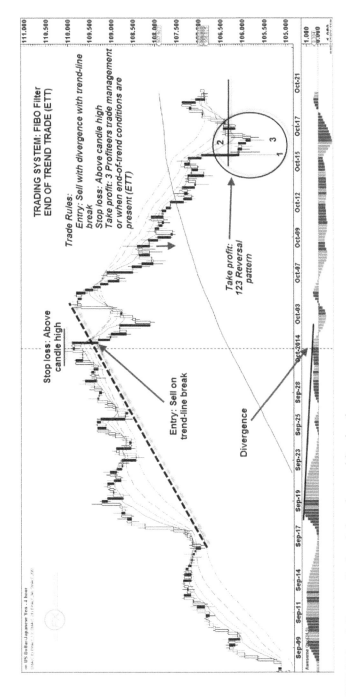

FIGURE 16.9 Sell on candle close below the trend-line break

5. Three Profiteers trade management methodology

   a. Enter with three positions.

   b. Determine the PPA by looking at a higher time frame chart.

   c. Set three profit targets using the Fibonacci sequence: 13, 21, 34, 55, 89, and 144.

   d. Move stops when stacked profits are reached.

6. Money management:

   a. Losses are not to exceed 1 to 2 percent of account balance, so determine position size accordingly.

   b. Set daily and weekly goals for returns and profits.

■ D. Trade Plan

Once the trading rules are established, print them and scan for trades at the beginning of each trading session. With high probability setups detected, it is time to plan the trade and trade the plan.

Trade Execution

The trade plan in Table 16.1 is taken from the Daily Trading Blotter (see Chapter 11 for details). Some traders will choose to write it out on the blotter, others in

TABLE 16.1	Trade Plan			
Trade Plan	**Strategy: TT / ETT / RB**			**Reasons for Entries and Exits**
Entry Strategy	Trade #1	Trade #2	Trade #3	
Long or short				
Position size				
Price				
Exit Strategy	Trade #1	Trade #2	Trade #3	
Stop loss 1				
Stop loss 2				
Profit level 1				
Profit level 2				
Profit level 3				
Profit level 4				
Risk/Reward				

a trading journal, and still others on the chart itself. It is a matter of personal preference as long as it gets done. The trade plan allows for the Three Profiteers trade management methodology to be used with three profit levels.

Monitor Trading Results

1. Maintain a daily journal:

   a. At the end of the day, prepare an entry in the daily journal about your trading day. The daily journal can be a hard or soft copy. If it is a hard copy, use a notebook or a three-ring binder. If soft, create a daily journal folder on the computer and record the journal in Word, Excel, or OneNote.

   b. Describe the trades taken in detail.

   c. Take screen shots of the before and after charts and post them in the hard or soft journal.

   d. Describe in detail the trades not taken and the reasons why not.

2. During the trading day, take notes about setups and possible trades.

   a. Describe how you are feeling during the day.

   b. If you do not feel well or are not in an up mood, do not trade.

Record Trade Performance

1. At the end of the day, enter your trade results in your journal (using Word, Excel, or OneNote) with the documented charts.

2. Complete a post-mortem from your trading blotter or use it as a guide for your trading journal.

3. Monitor the daily and weekly performance directly from the trading platform reports.

4. If you reach your weekly goal, stop trading.

E. Daily and Weekly Preparation

The daily preparation that you will do for your trading business is summarized in three different routines: the daily pre-market routine, the end-of-day routine and the general routine. The more you can structure your trading life, the better organized you will be and that will lead to being able to focus and embrace your trading day with a clear head.

1. Daily pre-market routine:

   a. Meditate in the morning for 30 minutes using a meditation to your liking. Picture yourself as a disciplined trader riding the market cycles and cashing in on profits and taking losses quickly.

   b. Read the 10 General Trading Rules (see Chapter 9 for details). Keep a hard copy handy in a binder on the desk or a soft copy readily available in a folder on the computer.

   c. Read the Positive Trading Beliefs and Affirmations (see Chapter 9 for details). Keep a hard copy handy in a binder on the desk or a soft copy readily available in a folder on the computer.

   d. Read two to three analysis reports on some of your favorite websites to get the fundamental flavor of the day or week.

   e. Review the calendar of events to be prepared for economic releases during trading times.

   f. Review your trading strategies.

   g. Scan the markets you trade for trade setups alongside the checklist.

   h. Plan the trade(s) and trade the plan(s): Document trades on the Daily Trading Blotter or on live charts.

2. End-of-day routine:

   a. See Monitor Trading Results section above.

   b. Post-mortem on day's trading activities on the Daily Trading Blotter or the journal or the Excel spreadsheet.

   c. Post-mortem on week's trading activities on the Daily Trading Blotter or the journal or the Excel spreadsheet.

3. General Routine:

   a. Walk or exercise daily.

   b. When daily and weekly goals are met, quit trading, relax, and do an activity you enjoy!

■ F. Checklist

Table 16.2 is a checklist to make sure you are following the trading rules.

I stress repeatedly that once you have developed your trading system, you must adhere to it when you trade. Remember that the benchmark for an acceptable

TABLE 16.2   **Trading Rules Checklist**

Trading Rules:

Indicators/ Confirmations	✓	Long	Short	Price	Comments
Read two to three analyst reports	✓				*Is there a bias?*
Check calendar of events	✓				*Important news out?*
Weekly and daily trends	✓				*Up, down, or sideways?*
Evaluate trend (higher highs and lows)	✓				*Up 12–2 (on clock); down 4–6*
Clear steep trend or sideways market?	✓				*Up, down, or sideways?*
Is EMA cluster above/below 200 SMA?	✓				*Bullish above/bearish below*
Bullish or bearish candlestick patterns?	✓				*Within trend or end of trend?*
Reversal candlestick patterns?	✓				*Combine with divergence for ETT*
Divergence signaling end of trend?	✓				*Scan markets for divergence*
Note support and resistance: previous swing high or low, pivot points, Fibonacci retracements or projections	✓				*Is there confirmed support in an uptrend?*
Draw trend lines and channels	✓				*Often, a channel captures trends*
Note chart patterns: triangles, flags, boxes	✓				*Look for continuation patterns*

day-trading system should be at least 65 percent wins over time (at least 50 trades) because the risk/reward for a day-trading system is often 1:1, which means the number of wins have to be greater than the number of losses to have positive results over time.

A swing and position trading system will have an entirely different set of benchmarks; a swing or position trader can be successful with 30 to 50 percent wins, as long as the size of the win is greater than the size of the loss. Keep in mind that you may test your system with a demo account, but it only gives you a close approximation of the actual performance of the system and not its actual performance.

As you begin to trade with your trading system in the market, you might discover some weaknesses in it. You might need to fine-tune your system, but do not do it on-the-fly while you are trading. Go back to your demo account, modify it, and test it over and over until you feel confident with your changes before you trade it in live markets again. You have now completed your bonus mentoring session covering a Sample Trading System which you may use as an outline when preparing your own trading system!

The FX Trader's EDGE Scorecard and Your FREE Coaching Session

Now that you have finished reading the book and implemented some new trading habits, it's time for you to complete the Trader's Scorecard again. This short assessment will help you to understand how close you are from becoming an Entrepreneurial Trader, and whether your current habits and mentality supports the success of your trading business.

Go to www.wiley.com/go/traderspendulum (see About the Companion website page for more information), click on the link for the Trader's Scorecard, and answer the following questions directly on the interactive webpage. The results with a complete report will be e-mailed back to you. Go directly to the interactive site here: http://fxtradersedge.com/scorecard/.

Completing the Trader's Scorecard is the first part of the process. As the next step, I would like to invite you to set up a brief personal discussion with me to review your results.

I do not have a clear vision of my future.	1	2	3	4	5	6	7	8	9	10	I have a clear, well-defined vision of my future.
I do not have clear goals for my trading business.	1	2	3	4	5	6	7	8	9	10	I have clear goals for my trading business.
I am not operating my trading as a business.	1	2	3	4	5	6	7	8	9	10	I am operating my trading as a business.
I do not have a business plan to achieve my trading objectives.	1	2	3	4	5	6	7	8	9	10	I have a business plan to achieve my trading objectives.
I do not have well-defined trading strategies.	1	2	3	4	5	6	7	8	9	10	I have well-defined trading strategies.
I am not making as much money as I would like as a trader.	1	2	3	4	5	6	7	8	9	10	I am making a lot of money as a trader.
I am doing everything myself.	1	2	3	4	5	6	7	8	9	10	I have a coach and a support group helping me achieve my goals.
I react emotionally to the markets.	1	2	3	4	5	6	7	8	9	10	I have a disciplined and committed approach to trading.
I tie my self-esteem to the success and failure of my trades.	1	2	3	4	5	6	7	8	9	10	I am detached from my wins and losses in the markets.
I do not feel I am achieving my full potential as a trader.	1	2	3	4	5	6	7	8	9	10	I feel I am achieving my full potential as a trader.
ADD COLUMN TOTALS											YOUR SCORE _____

■ What's Covered in the Free Coaching Session?

As I have discussed in various parts in this book, the best way to accelerate your trading business success is for you to be guided by an experienced coach.

I would like to offer you a *free* 30-minute coaching consultation. During this time, we will discuss the following question: *Over the next year, what has to happen in your trading career for you to feel you are achieving your full potential as a trader?* We will end the session with an action plan for the three most important action steps you can take right away.

■ FX Trader's EDGE Coaching Process

An ideal coaching program is tailored for you and is not a one-size-fits-all program. Coaching, the FX Trader's EDGE way, is the proprietary coaching process we use when coaching traders. This will give you a guideline on what to look for in a coaching program. You are most welcome to contact me if you are interested in furthering your trading career through the FX Trader's EDGE Coaching Program.

The trader's ultimate goal is to become an Entrepreneurial Trader based on the "10 Habits" described in this book. The FX Trader's EDGE Coaching Process includes the Assessment, the Roadmap, and the Implementation as outlined below.

FX TRADER'S EDGE COACHING PROCESS

A. THE ASSESSMENT

1. The Starter Kit: Helps you assess your current strengths and weaknesses as a trader

2. The Starter Session: Helps you assess your current situation and clarify your goals as a trader

B. THE ROADMAP

3. The Planning Session: Helps you develop a step-by-step plan to achieve your goals as a trader

4. The Blueprint: Outlines the strategies, tools, and timelines required to achieve your goals as a trader

C. IMPLEMENTATION

5. The Toolbox: Professional resources and capabilities to help you implement your blueprint

6. The Progress Coaching Sessions: Coaching sessions to keep you on track toward your goals

During the Assessment phase, either I or one of the FX Trader's EDGE coaches will ask you a series of questions to better understand your vision, trading strengths, current routine, and roadblocks. You will end the session with a clear vision of your trading business with an initial set of goals.

The Roadmap is the planning phase to develop a step-by-step action plan to work through during the coaching program. The final product for this phase is a blueprint, outlining the strategies, tools, and timelines required to achieve your trading goals.

The Implementation phase includes skill-building modules as well as regular progress coaching sessions to keep you on track toward your goals.

Your accelerated trading success starts with a short conversation with me. To schedule your session, please go to the following page: http://vcita.com/v/jody.fxtradersedge or e-mail jody@fxtradersedge.com. Please quote "10HABITS" during your booking.

■ Other Valuable Resources

Charting software:

The charts posted in the book were created using a sophisticated charting software called MotiveWave. As a reader of this book, you will be eligible for a 14-day free trial to test drive the software by going to the following page: www.software.fxtradersedge.com.

Elliott Wave Counts:

"The Analysis Toolbox—Your First Mentoring Session" (Chapter 15) and some of the Pendulum Scenarios throughout this book discuss Elliott Wave analysis as a way to navigate the market cycles for the big picture roadmap. This context helps traders to see the trades as they unfold in patterns, which are called waves, in the market. To receive wave counts on forex, indices and commodities, go to: www.elliottwavedesk.com, a service offered by FX Trader's EDGE.

Jody Samuels
CEO, FX Trader's EDGE
jody@fxtradersedge.com
www.fxtradersedge.com
Connect with me!
skype: jodyfxedge
facebook.com/fxtradersedge
@FXTradersEDGE_
Youtube.com/TheFXtradersedge
Linkedin.com/in/jodysamuels

BIBLIOGRAPHY

About.com. "Social Learning Theory: How People Learn by Observation." http:// psychology.about.com/od/developmentalpsychology/a/sociallearning.htm (accessed August 17, 2014).

Bridgeland, John M. "The Silent Epidemic: Perspectives of High School Dropouts." https://docs.gatesfoundation.org/Documents/thesilentepidemic3-06FINAL.pdf (accessed September 6, 2014).

Chessmetrics. "Formulas." http://chessmetrics.com/cm/CM2/Formulas.asp (accessed September 8, 2014).

Drucker, Peter. *The Practice of Management*. New York: Harper Business, 2006.

Duhigg, Charles. *The Power of Habit*. New York: Random House Inc., 2012.

Frost, A.J., and Robert Prechter, Jr., *Elliott Wave Principle: Key to Market Behavior*. Gainesville, GA: New Classics Library, 2005.

Gardner, Ben D. "Bursting the 21 days habit formation myth." *The Health Behaviour Research Centre Blog of University College London*, 2012.

Goyal, Nikhil. *One Size Does Not Fit All*. New York: Bavura Books, 2012.

Hill, Napoleon. *Think and Grow Rich: The Original 1937 Unedited Edition*. Wise, VA: Napoleon Hill Foundation, 2012.

Maltz, Maxwell. *Psycho-Cybernetics, A New Way to Get More Living Out of Life*. New York: Pocket Books, 1989.

Matthew, Gail. "Goals Research Summary." http://www.dominican.edu/academics/ahss /undergraduate-programs-1/psych/faculty/fulltime/gailmatthews/researchsummary 2.pdf (accessed September 4, 2014).

Merriam Webster Dictionary. "Definition of Habit." http://www.merriam-webster.com /dictionary/habit (accessed September 2, 2014).

Monrad, Maggie. "High School Dropout: A Quick Stats Fact Sheet." http://www .betterhighschools.org/docs/nhsc_dropoutfactsheet.pdf (accessed August 6, 2014).

PGA Tour. "Stats Report." http://www.pgatour.com/statsreport.html (accessed September 8, 2014).

Robbins, Anthony. *Awaken the Giant Within: How to Take Immediate Control of Your Mental, Emotional, Physical and Financial Destiny!* New York: Free Press, 1992.

Robbins, Anthony. *Unlimited Power: The New Science of Personal Achievement.* New York: Free Press, 1997.

Söderlund, Göran B. W. et al. *"The Effects of Background White Noise on Memory Performance in Inattentive School Children."* Behavioral and Brain Functions, 6: 55, September 29, 2010, http://www.behavioralandbrainfunctions.com/content/6/1/55 (accessed September 23, 2014).

US Securities and Exchange Commission. "Margin: Borrowing Money to Pay for Stocks." http://www.sec.gov/investor/pubs/margin.htm (accessed September 9, 2014).

Williams, Bill. *Trading Chaos: Applying Expert Techniques to Maximize Your Profits.* New York: John Wiley & Sons, Inc., 1995.

*T*he *Trader's Pendulum* comes with a companion website at www.wiley.com/go/traderspendulum (password wiley 15).

On the website, you'll find a series of tools to use on your journey to becoming a better trader:

Trader's Scorecard: *Introduction*

Are you an Entrepreneurial Trader or a "technical junkie"? Are you in danger of falling into the *Technical Trader's Trap*—or are you in it already? Do your habits and mentality support your trading success? In general, how well have you advanced as a trader, and how can you progress further?

Complete the 10 questions in the Trader's Scorecard to find out your current standing as a trader. Use this interactive tool and get your results immediately! http://fxtradersedge.com/scorecard/

Trader's Business Plan Workbook: *Chapter* 5

One of the first steps in transforming yourself into an Entrepreneurial Trader is to plan your trading business. The Trader's Business Plan Workbook walks you through the nine steps in setting up your business plan. Find the detailed explanations and tips to get the most out of each step in the workbook.

Simple Trading System Template: *Chapter* 10

A number of well-thought-out rules are all you need to construct a no-frills trading system you can rely on for your everyday trades. Download this simplified trading system template to help you get started in designing your trading system.

Daily Trading Blotter: *Chapter* 11

The Daily Trading Blotter contains pre-market analysis, checklist and trade plan, and post-market analysis to provide self-accountability and keep track of your progress. The technical and nontechnical sides of trading are covered.

■ Bonus Videos

A short review of the "10 Habits" and their application is presented in this series of 10 video clips. Each "10 Habits" video is fewer than three minutes long. The videos provide a quick review of what these "10 Habits" of successful traders are and how you can implement them in your daily trading activities.

Printed and bound by CPI Group (UK) Ltd, Croydon, CR0 4YY

16/04/2025

14658469-0001